D1570151

ONCE A MARINE

is the exciting combat story of the man who led the Marines to victory at Guadalcanal and served as the Commandant of the Corps in World War II.

"General Vandegrift, perhaps more than any other Marine, added luster and glory to our elite Corps that has already won enviable battle honors during its long history of military achievement. His long and successful struggle to hold Guadalcanal against seemingly overwhelming odds will live long in military history. Many veterans of the Marine Corps and of the sister services who participated or were associated in the Guadalcanal episode of World War II will relive their experiences in reading *Once a Marine*. And this includes yours truly who, perforce, had to witness this struggle from afar."

Chester W. Nimitz,
Fleet Admiral, U.S.N.

Other MCA Heritage Library Books You Can Enjoy

ONCE A MARINE

The Memoirs
of
General A.A. Vandegrift
United States Marine Corps

As told to

Robert B. Asprey

BALLANTINE BOOKS   •   NEW YORK

*This book is dedicated to my wife, Kathryn,
without whose insistence, encouragement
and patience this tribute to Marines
would not have been written.*

_____

_____

*The opinions expressed in this book are those of the author and
do not reflect the views of the Navy Department or the Marine
Corps.*

Reprinted by
The Marine Corps Association
Quantico, Virginia
August 1982

Library of Congress Catalog Card Number 64-10576
ISBN: 0-940328-03-8

This edition published by arrangement with
W. W. Norton & Company, Inc.

First printing: October, 1966

BALLANTINE BOOKS, INC.
101 Fifth Avenue, New York, New York 10003

Contents

Illustrations

Author's Note

A SCHOLAR once told me that autobiographies properly belong only to great men, biographies only to great *dead* men, and memoirs to those who claim a fleeting prominence by accident of time and place. This left me little choice when I was persuaded to write the story of my life.

But for an accident of time and place someone else would have written this book. It happened to be my lot to command the 1st Marine Division of the first United States offensive of World War II, the battle for Guadalcanal, subsequently to command the landing at Bougainville, and finally to serve as commandant for the remainder of the war and during those acrimonious postwar years in which the pressure for service unification threatened to abolish the Marine Corps.

General Joffre once said he did not know who had won the battle of the Marne, "but if it had been lost I know who would have lost it." Such is the price of command, but since we took Guadalcanal and Bougainville as we did all of our Pacific objectives and since we won the unification battle I can write of my part in these campaigns without shame.

Because my earlier years prepared me to take this part I have touched on them in this book. I have not included my retirement years. The reader would scarcely benefit from learning of my work on various advisory committees or from my speeches to various civic groups. My personal friends realize what the loss of my first wife meant to me, and they realize the happiness that I have gained from the love of my second wife. They know, too, about the infirmities of old age—arthritis and failing eyesight are tedious and uncomfortable, but not interesting.

So I have confined my story to the active years, which makes it in part the story of the United States Marine Corps from 1909 to 1949. I have tried to be careful to describe events as I saw them, not as historians later analyzed them.

For this reason I have doubtless neglected many heroic deeds by many heroic men and I fear that except by indirection have nowhere paid heartfelt homage to those hundreds of thousands of Marines who wrote a classic chapter in the history of warfare.

In telling this story I have tried not to hurt anyone unnecessarily. Many of the principals are dead and thus cannot fight back. Where I disagreed with certain of them, as with certain of those still living, the dispute rarely if ever flowed into personal hard-feelings, at least not from my standpoint. Considering our individual habits, backgrounds and tasks, some command conflicts had to result; considering the majesty of events we helped to mold, I do not find the conflicts in excess.

In recording these events I have relied on memory buttressed by several thousand letters and documents which eventually will pass into the public domain. Where memory and documents chronologically failed I have used the many available official histories. I have also relied on Colonel Robert Heinl's excellent history, *Soldiers of the Sea* (Naval Institute, 1962), and Brigadier General Samuel Griffith's exciting new history of the Guadalcanal campaign (Lippincott, 1963), which he generously placed at my disposal in manuscript form.

To cull the richness of the past I have shamelessly used the time and energy of old friends and shipmates and here wish to thank General Thomas Holcomb, USMC (ret), General Holland M. Smith, USMC (ret), General Gerald C. Thomas, USMC (ret), General Lemuel C. Shepherd, USMC (ret), General Allen H. Turnage, USMC (ret), Lieutenant General Robert Luckey, USMC (ret), Lieutenant General Fred Wieseman, USMC, Lieutenant General James P. Berkeley, USMC, Major General Richard Mangrum, USMC, Brigadier General Lewis Walt, USMC, Brigadier General John H. Masters, USMC, Brigadier General Robert Kilmartin, Jr., USMC (ret), and Colonel Ray Schwenke, USMC. I am also indebted to Mr. Hanson Baldwin for his careful recollection of certain events on Guadalcanal, not to mention his outstanding fairness in covering many of the events in this book for *The New York Times*.

I wish also to thank the present Commandant, General David M. Shoup, USMC, for his co-operation and interest.

My wife, Kathryn, General Thomas, General Griffith and Mr. Shaw and Mr. O'Quinlivan of the Marine Corps Historical Branch, have read the manuscript critically and their help is greatly appreciated. Finally my editor, Mr. Eric Swenson, is to be thanked for his encouragement, patience and professional advice.

A. A. VANDEGRIFT

Delray Beach
Florida

Collaborator's Note

I met General Vandegrift when he was seventy-six years old, blind as a bat and badly crippled with arthritis - which is why he had asked me to help him with his memoirs. He had warned me from his Florida home of fading memory so I had done some homework in Washington, working in Marine Corps records, interviewing a host of his career associates (an arduous but delightful task since most of them had become outstanding commanders in their own right). CMC cooperated by providing a truckload of reference books and an excellent secretary who awaited my arrival in Delray Beach one Sunday night in late 1963.

The General and I started work at ten the next morning in my apartment. He agreed to tape the sessions. He was nervous and hesitant until I got him talking about his Virginia boyhood. From ante-bellum Charlottesville it wasn't far to the Old Corps, to the School of Application at Parris Island (and a general courtmartial), to Haiti with Smedley Butler, to China, Quantico, Washington, World War II — Guadalcanal, Bougainville, Tarawa, the Marshalls, Saipan, Tinian, Peleliu, Iwo Jima, Okinawa, to all of his years as Commandant and his last supreme battle where he won survival of the Marine Corps as we know it today.

I interviewed the General every morning. Our secretary transcribed the tapes in the afternoon and in the evening I worked these words into new pages of a rough manuscript. We revised this work the next morning, then pushed on to new fields. As we worked into our daily routine the General's memory cells took on new life and so did he. He started coming at nine-thirty, then nine. Transcriptions grew longer, we worked six mornings a week — I can see him now, sitting erect, gnarled hands with swollen knuckles resting on a cane, his face lighted by pleasant memory as slowly the story of an outstanding forty-year Corps career emerged. We finished the job in December and I returned to Bermuda to put it in final form.

That was the technical side. There was a personal side. I had been warned that General Vandegrift was an aloof man who kept his own counsel. He was and he did – at least for a while. But as we worked, as we bridged the years, we grew to know and trust each other. The barriers started to bend early, and in time a few even disappeared.

We had our differences. As the General mellowed he began coming up with anecdotes that would have livened the narrative, then drawling, "But a 'course, Rahbut, we couldn't use that." "Why not, sir?" " 'Twouldn't be propuh, Rahbut." I tried to change his mind on one story that can now harmlessly be told. One day we were talking about General Holcomb, former Commandant and a wonderful man. "Tommy Holcomb was one of my oldest friends," the General said, "and was largely responsible for me becomin' Commandant. But, Rahbut, once I was Commandant there was no way gettin' him out of my hair so I could get on with the job." "What did you do, sir?" "Well, Rahbut, I finally went direct to President Roosevelt with my problem and he shipped Tommy off to Africa as some kind of diplomat." One day the General showed me a trunk full of letters that he had written to his first wife, Mildred. Since stacks of them had come from Guadalcanal I began licking my historical chops: "I'll start on these tonight," I said. "No, Rahbut, I just wanted your advice as to where they should go once I die. No one can read 'em while Ah'm alive." Our only serious argument concerned his courtmartial which he originally agreed should be in the book. We were just about to go to press when he changed his mind – "it just wouldn't be propuh, Rahbut," he told me on the telephone. I thought it would be very proper and gave him a list of reasons why. He held his ground, but this time I held mine. "No courtmartial, no book," I told him. He yielded at the last minute (and later told me he was glad he had done so).

He was delighted with ONCE A MARINE, with its good reviews, the publicity and the paperback edition that followed. I am sure that he would be pleased with this new edition. I know that I am. General Vandegrift was one of the finest leaders of World War II, and his career should continue to inspire tomorrow's Marine commanders.

Robert B. Asprey
Malaga, Spain

June 1982

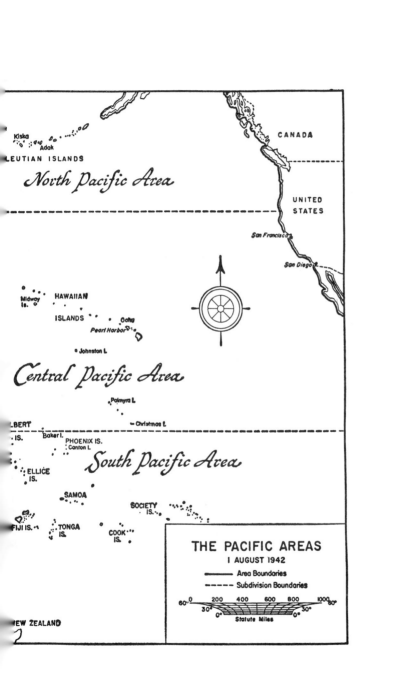

Kiska
Adak
LEUTIAN ISLANDS
North Pacific Area

CANADA

UNITED
STATES

San Francisco

San Diego

Midway
Is.
HAWAIIAN
ISLANDS   Oahu
Pearl Harbor

Johnston I.

Central Pacific Area

Palmyra I.

LBERT   — Christmas I.
IS.   Baker I.
PHOENIX IS.
Canton I.
South Pacific Area
ELLICE
IS.

SAMOA

SOCIETY
IS.
FIJI IS.   TONGA
IS.   COOK
IS.

THE PACIFIC AREAS
I AUGUST 1942
———— Area Boundaries
------- Subdivision Boundaries

60° 0   200   400   600   800   1000 80°
30°   30°
0°
Statute Miles

NEW ZEALAND
2

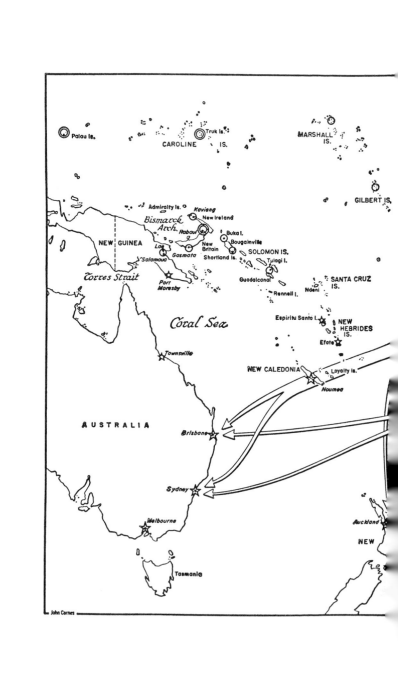

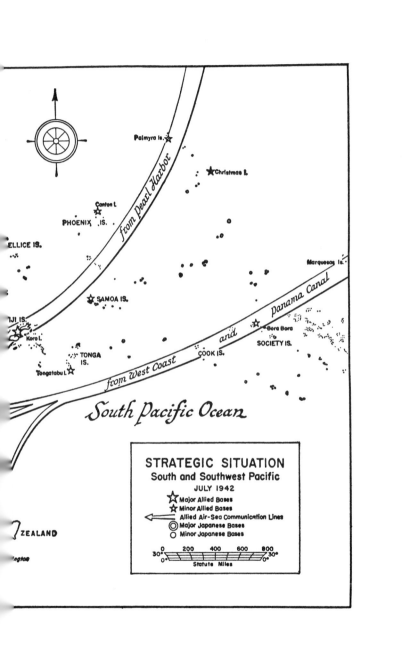

Palmyra Is. ☆

★ Christmas I.

from Pearl Harbor

Canton I. ☆
PHOENIX IS.

ELLICE IS.

Marquesas Is.

☆ SAMOA IS.

FIJI IS. ☆
Koro I.

Panama Canal

and

☆ Bora Bora
SOCIETY IS.

TONGA
IS.

from West Coast

COOK IS.

Tongatabu I. ☆

South Pacific Ocean

STRATEGIC SITUATION
South and Southwest Pacific
JULY 1942
☆ Major Allied Bases
☆ Minor Allied Bases
← Allied Air-Sea Communication Lines
◎ Major Japanese Bases
○ Minor Japanese Bases

300°   200   400   600   800   300°
0°   0°
Statute Miles

ZEALAND

ington

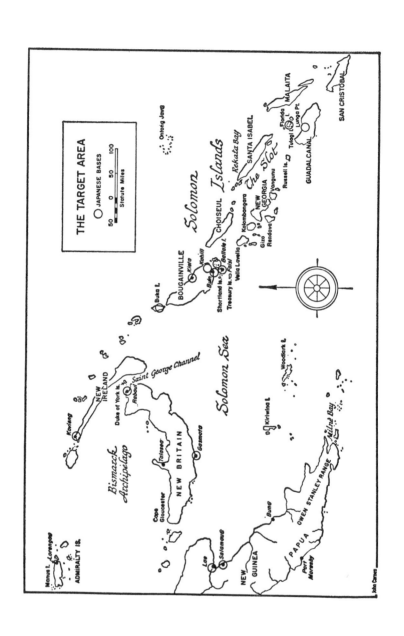

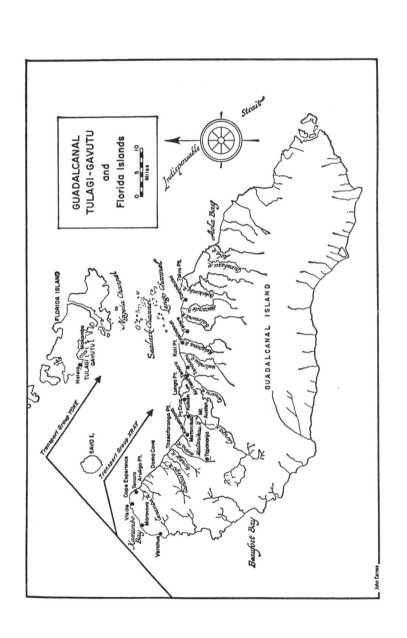

GUADALCANAL
TULAGI - GAVUTU
and
Florida Islands

0   5   10
Miles

Strait

Indispensable

FLORIDA ISLAND

Nggela Channel

Haleta
TULAGI I.   Makambo
GAVUTU

Sealark Channel

Savo Channel

Lengo Channel

Transport Group YOKE

SAVO I.

Transport Group XRAY

Koli Pt.
Taivu Pt.
Tenaru R.
Lunga Pt.
Ilu R.
Pt. Cruz
Kukum
Tenavatu

Aola Bay

Bokokimbo R.
Berande R.
Balesuna R.
Malimbiu R.
Matanikau R.
Poha R.

Tassafaronga Pt.
Matanikau
Mt.
Austen
Tapananja

Vitale
Cape Esperance
Tenaro
Aruligo Pt.
Marovovo
Doma Cove
Kamimbo Bay
Verahue

GUADALCANAL ISLAND

Beaufort Bay

John Carnes

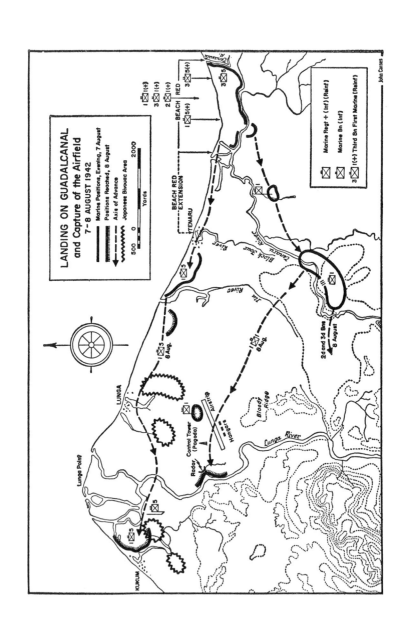

LANDING ON GUADALCANAL
and Capture of the Airfield
7–8 AUGUST 1942

Marine Positions, Evening, 7 August
Positions Reached, 8 August
Axis of Advance
Japanese Bivouac Area

Yards
500   0   2000

John Carnes

Marine Regt + (Inf) (Reinf)

Marine Bn (Inf)

3 ⊠ I(+) Third Bn First Marine (Reinf)

BEACH RED

1 ⊠ I(+)
3 ⊠ I(+)
2 ⊠ I(+)

3 ⊠ 5

1 ⊠ 5(+)

BEACH RED
EXTENSION

ILU R.

ITENARU

Block Stout River

Tenaru River

Ilu River

I ⊠ 5

2d and 3d Bns
8 August

1 ⊠ 5
8 Aug.

1 ⊠ 5
8 Aug.

LUNGA

⊠ I

Airfield

Control Tower
(Pagoda)

Radar

Hangars

Bloody
Ridge

Lunga River

⊠ 5

⊠ 5

KUKUM

Lunga Point

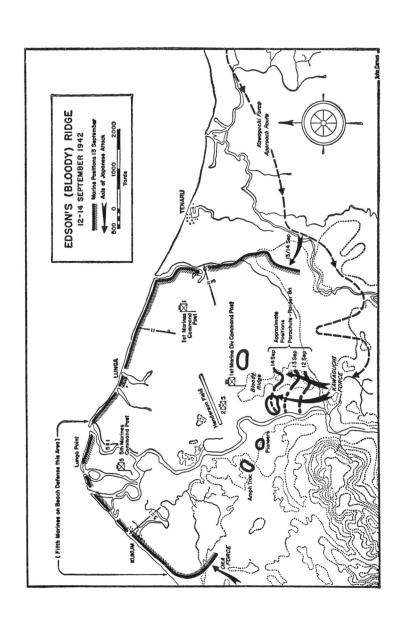

EDSON'S (BLOODY) RIDGE
12-14 SEPTEMBER 1942

Marine Positions 13 September
Axis of Japanese Attack

500 0   1000   2000
Yards

(Fifth Marines on Beach Defense this Area)

Lunga Point

KUKUM

OKA
FORCE

Henderson Field

Amph Troc

Pioneers

5th Marines
Command Post

5 ┼┼ 1

5 ┼┼ 5

1 ┼┼ 1

LUNGA

TENARU

1st Marines
Command Post

1st Marine Div Command Post

5 ┼┼ 2

Bloody
Ridge

14 Sep

13 Sep

12 Sep

Approximate
Positions
Parachute — Raider Bn

13/14 Sep

KAWAGUCHI
FORCE

Kawaguchi Force
Approach Route

John Dames

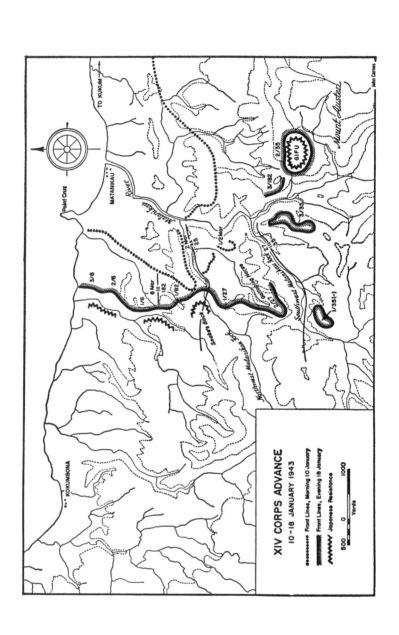

TO KUKUM

MATANIKAU

Point Cruz

Matanikau River

GIFU
2/35
3/182
3/35
2/35
1/2 Mar
25
6 Mar
182
I/82
3/6
2/6
1/6
Sea's Beach
1/27
Southwest Matanikau
Northwest Matanikau
1/35(-)

Mount Austen

KOKUMBONA

XIV CORPS ADVANCE
10–18 JANUARY 1943

•••••••• Front Lines, Morning 10 January
▬▬▬▬ Front Lines, Evening 18 January
⌁⌁⌁⌁ Japanese Resistance

500   0   1000
        Yards

John Carnes

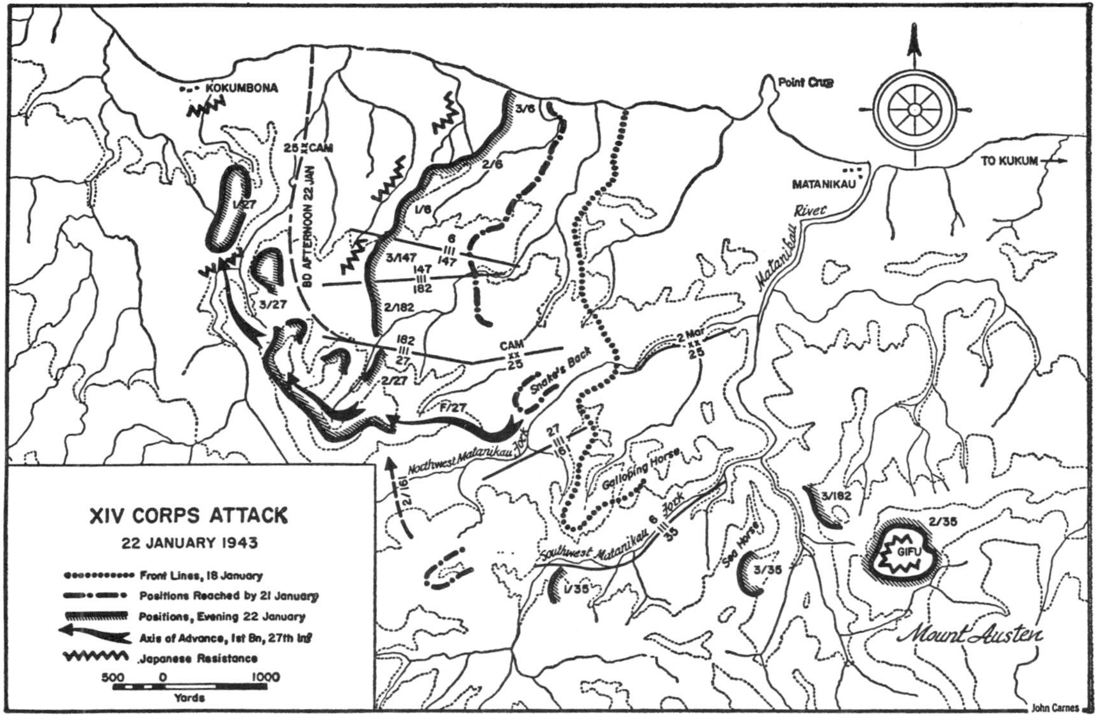

XIV CORPS ATTACK
22 JANUARY 1943
Front Lines, 18 January
Positions Reached by 21 January
Positions, Evening 22 January
Axis of Advance, 1st Bn, 27th Inf
Japanese Resistance
500
0
1000
Yards
KOKUMBONA
Point Cruz
MATANIKAU
TO KUKUM
Matanikau
River
BD AFTERNOON 22 JAN
25
CAM
1/27
3/27
3/6
2/6
1/6
3/147
2/182
2/27
F/27
6
147
182
27
25
2 Mar
Snake's Back
Northwest Matanikau Fork
2/161
161
Galloping Horse
Southwest Matanikau Fork
35
1/35
Sea Horse
3/35
3/182
2/35
GIFU
Mount Austen
John Carnes

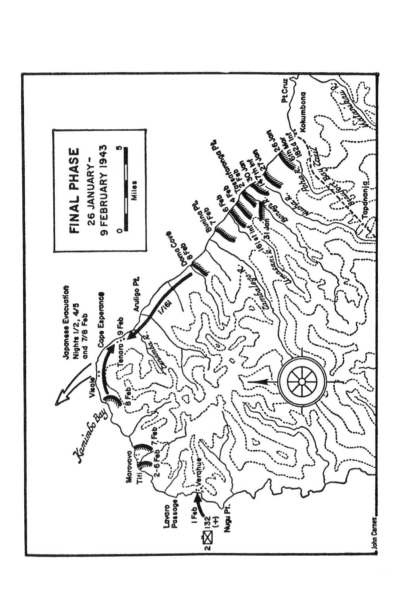

FINAL PHASE
26 JANUARY –
9 FEBRUARY 1943

Miles
0   5

Japanese Evacuation
Nights 1/2, 4/5
and 7/8 Feb

Cape Esperance

Visale

Kamimbo Bay

Tenaro 9 Feb

8 Feb

Aruligo Pt.

1/161

Doma Cove
8 Feb

Marovovo
Titi
2–6 Feb 7 Feb

Verahue
1 Feb

Lavoro Passage

Nugu Pt.

2 ⊠ 132
(+)

Bunia Pt.
7 Feb

Tassafaronga Pt.
6 Feb

Tassafaronga Pt.
7 Feb

2 Feb

30 Jan
27 Jan
1/7 Inf

26 Jan
6th Mar
182d Inf

Pt. Cruz

Kokumbona

61st Inf

Umasani R.

Bonegi R.

31 Jan

Poha R.

Hill Trail

Tambalego R.

Rifle Trail
Tapohanja

John Carnes

PROLOGUE

Evening of August 6, 1942

I WAS standing by the rail of the *McCawley*, the steel core of an amphibious task force steaming at 12 knots through the treacherous waters of the Solomon Sea.

A group of cruisers and destroyers covered the transports and miles beyond another task force built around America's three remaining major aircraft carriers covered them. For several days leaden skies had hidden all of us from an enemy vastly superior in ships and planes. Now it was too late for the enemy to stop us from unleashing our first offensive ground action of World War II. In twelve hours Marines were going to land on two enemy-held islands, Guadalcanal and Tulagi.

A few weeks earlier most of us had never heard of Guadalcanal or Tulagi. We now knew where they were, roughly their size and terrain characteristics, and we knew they held enemy troops. We had no proper maps, we did not know if the beaches were defended nor how many enemy to expect.

Even had we known, we still would not have been ready. Less than a month before, I had brought two thirds of the 1st Marine Division to New Zealand, where, according to orders, we would have a minimum six months to complete training begun at New River, North Carolina. Many of the units were ragged, many of the Marines but boys only a few months out of boot camp. A third regiment, which had joined us a few days ago in the Fijis, was an unknown entity. A great deal of our heavy equipment was sitting back in New Zealand because we did not have ships enough to carry it. For the same reason we were packing only ten days' supply of ammunition, sixty days' of bulk rations. Some of the ships were combat-loaded, some were not.

Our mission was to land, seize and defend the two islands— in short, that amphibious mission which I and my senior officers had spent two decades in developing and learning how

17

to execute. Any one of us could have listed a hundred reasons why this operation would fail. In my case I had soldiered since 1909 and knew the rigors of jungle warfare from campaigns in Nicaragua, Mexico and Haiti. I had seen the amphibious doctrine grow from General John A. Lejeune's first thoughts in the early twenties to General John Russell's Fleet Marine Force exercises in the early thirties. I had served as military secretary and later as assistant to the Commandant, General Thomas Holcomb, who continued to iron out the wrinkles in this demanding type of warfare. I knew only too well that if someone at Marine Corps Schools had answered a problem of this nature with the forces now at my disposal he would have failed the course.

Bleak as was the picture, I did not think it hopeless. I realized and so did the other senior officers that it was going to be difficult, what Wellington after the battle of Waterloo called "a near-run thing." We didn't have much of anything, we didn't know what we were going to hit, but we did know enough, in my opinion, to justify what military writers like to call "a calculated risk."

We knew that America needed a shot in the national arm. Since December 7, 1941, our national heritage had yielded to a prideless humiliation. Half of our fleet still sat on the bottom of Pearl Harbor. The Philippines were gone, Guam and Wake had fallen, the Japanese were approaching Australia. What Admiral King saw, and what he jammed down the throats of the Joint Chiefs of Staff, was that just possibly the mighty Japanese had overextended. He saw that just possibly a strike by us could halt their eastward parade. The only weapon he held, the only weapon America held, was a woefully understrength fleet and one woefully ill-equipped and partially trained Marine division.

This division, no matter its equipment and training, was my secret weapon because the division was a part of the Marine Corps, both in fact and by the tradition which made the fact. For six days I had prowled the decks of the *Mc-Cawley*. I had watched younger officers with rough sketches of the landing area explaining matter-of-factly to the troops what we were going to do. I had watched veteran sergeants checking the fit of individual rounds in machine gun belts. I had seen boys who should have been enjoying other pursuits sharpening knives to a keenness that in a swipe would have cut from their faces the whiskers some of them did not yet possess. I knew enough about fighting men to know that these were fighting men.

Standing there by the rail thinking these things I could not help but take stock of myself and my life. A major general in rank, I was fifty-five years old with thirty-three years of active duty behind me. Excepting a bad knee, the result of early football days, and bad night vision, I was in good health. Despite the ominous burden of facts, I was also in good spirits because I knew that if the job could be done we somehow were going to do it.

I stayed by that rail too long. It was dark now and I did not know which way to go. I was cursing myself heartily when I heard the voice of my aide, Ray Schwenke. "General, what in the world are you standing out here for?"

"Ray," I told him, "I am just egotistical enough to believe that the Landing Force would be better off with than without me. Would you be kind enough to show me to my quarters?"

Back in the small, hot cabin where I could again see I turned to some unfinished business. Marines below decks were also writing letters home and now I finished one begun earlier that day:

Tomorrow morning at dawn we land in the first major offensive of this war. Our plans have been made and God grant that our judgment has been sound. We have rehearsed the plans. The officers and men are keen and ready to go. Way before you read this you will have heard of it. Whatever happens you'll know that I did my best. Let us hope that best will be enough. . . .

I

I Join the Old Corps

THE VIRGINIA town of Charlottesville is a good place to remember. I was born there on March 13, 1887, and lived there until 1909 when I left for a new home, the Marine Corps. Forty years later I returned, then moved to Florida, my present home. Charlottesville is still a good place to remember.

To me Charlottesville will always be a little town sitting quiet at the foothills of the Blue Ridge Mountains, the home of some 8,000 people, dirt streets lighted by gas lamps, a yellow glow that on a winter evening peeped comfortably through the drawn drapery of the red-brick houses on East High Street—my route when I was hurrying to explain to my parents why I was late for supper.

The Vandegrift family lived at 112 East High Street, a two-story red-brick house with green shutters. Set in a comfortable garden, our home consisted of a big front porch, an old-fashioned parlor, a dining room, kitchen and pantry, and upstairs four bedrooms and a bathroom. At that time a bathroom was a curiosity—people still relied on outdoor Chic Sales.

The Vandegrift family was my heritage, and because I think heritage is important I want to tell a little about them. My father's people, two brothers, sailed to America from Holland in the 1770's. After a spell in Amsterdam, New York, they came down to Virginia and developed a farm outside of Charlottesville. This farm stayed in the family until my Grandfather Carson returned from fighting in the Civil War. A soldier in the Monticello Guards, Grandfather Carson was wounded at Antietam and in Pickett's Charge at Gettysburg. Still a young man he sold the farm and moved to town and started a contracting business. My father, William T. Vandegrift, studied architecture, then went into Grandfather Car-

21

son's business. In 1883 the firm set up a display booth at the Richmond State Fair where my father met Sarah Agnes Archer. They married two years later.

My mother's people, a Mr. John Archer and brother, came to this country from England in 1668. John won a land grant around Amelia Courthouse, near Richmond, and his brother a grant in Henrico County, near Hanover Courthouse. They developed a long line of magistrates and judges and people of that yoke. My grandmother, Anne Franklin, married Mr. Alexander Dubois Archer, a member of the famous Richmond Blues. He was the last of these male Archers to marry and was killed in the early fighting of the Civil War.

My own mother, Sarah Agnes Archer Vandegrift, was a perfectly beautiful lady, a gentle and artistic person who painted very well. She was interested more in her home and children than in civic and social activities and devoted much of her time to me and to my sister Constance, four years my junior. We were very close to her and experienced a terrible loss when at forty-eight years of age she died—only two weeks before I left home for the Marines.

My early life did not visibly differ from those of my contemporaries, most of whom are now gone. My neighborhood chums included James Lewis Bibb, who later became a well-known internist in Tennessee; Alphonso Carver, who died of tuberculosis in 1911; Nelson Leitch, who became a successful chemist with Dupont; Littleton Wood, later Charlottesville's prosecuting attorney; his cousin, Will Wood; Charley Moran, who served as court clerk until his death a few years ago; Taylor Twyman, who was killed in an automobile accident in the twenties; and Emmett Gleason, still a successful businessman.

There were others of course and a few of them went with me to school at the Randolph Kindergarten, on to Jones Boys School, then to Grammar School, and finally to Charlottesville High School. At first I suffered rather than enjoyed school. A letter to my aunt, written when I was eleven, informed her that "I have the meanest teacher in the school building . . . she is all time fusing [sic] and gives such long lessons."

Fortunately Miss Carrie Burnley and Miss Katie Lapopp later made me appreciate real elementary teaching and I went on with the others to sweat over Latin verbs taught by Miss Serepta Moran and learned the mysteries of geometry from the very patient Mr. Dinwiddie. As young boys, though, I'm afraid we infinitely preferred games of "Chase the Wicket" and "Home Sheep Home" and sandlot football and baseball and the weekends and vacations that allowed us to learn our physical heritage.

In those years we lived rather close to the Civil War, an atmosphere that molded our likes and dislikes almost into one. We were so soundly Democratic that our parents always pointed out Charlottesville's only Republican to any visitor. The first time politics meant anything to me was during Grover Cleveland's second campaign. My mother took me to the balcony of the Monticello Hotel to watch a torchlight political parade which to me meant my father handsomely dressed in a gray alpaca coat, a gray beaver hat and a rooster on his shoulder.

Such state occasions rarely occurred. Most of the time we entertained ourselves. In spring, when Virginia smells sweeter than any place I have since visited in the world, we went blackberrying to bring back loaded pails which Henrietta, my mother's cook of long years, baked into fragrant and delicious pies. Summers we swam in the Rivanna River, a muddy little stream about two miles from town; sometimes we fished it from an old flat-bottomed boat and occasionally pulled out a perch or catfish.

When the leaves turned brown we took schoolbags and hiked to the nearby Ragged Mountains to garner bushels of chestnuts and later to cook them over red coals and enjoy their odor as much as their meat. After Christmas the little ponds sometimes froze over, which meant digging out skates from the hall closet and trying our luck on ice never more than an inch and a half thick—and many were the duckings that we took.

Compared with today's juvenile pursuits our amusements seem rather simple. Motion pictures, radio and television all lay years ahead. The town dentist, Dr. Morse, owned the town's only automobile—if we went anywhere we went by shanks' mare, horseback or, on rare occasions, by buggy. For a special treat we were allowed a Saturday afternoon in the peanut gallery of the Opera House where for 10 cents each a traveling stock company enthralled us with the villain (duly hissed) strapping the heroine to a sawmill and then in the nick of time the hero (duly cheered) saving her life. Sometimes a dog and pony show came to town and almost every year Primrose and Dockstader's Minstrel Show turned up, a lively and gaudy performance thrilling young and old alike.

As I grew older some of these activities gave way to others. Ringling Brothers and Barnum and Bailey circuses began to visit Charlottesville, a treat my sister and I never missed because we received free tickets in return for sawdust from Grandfather Carson's planing mill. Still later, the town's mule-drawn streetcar gave way to an electric car line, a big event in our lives. The manager's son, a friend of mine, got us free rides to Fry Springs, an old-fashioned summer resort about three miles outside of town. We rode out in a summer car or trolley similar to that featured in the film *Meet Me in St. Louis*. Once at Fry Springs, we watched the first Mack Sennett comedies or danced at the pavilion, then rode back in the open, swaying trolley of which we never tired.

When I was ten my father gave me a .22 rifle and a few years later a single-barreled shotgun. I was now considered old enough to go off on my own a little and with my English terrier, Mike, made long explorations of the countryside.

Sometimes in the summer a group of us spent a couple of weeks in a large camping area called Sugar Hollow. Swimming and fishing ruled but we also learned woodlore from Dr. Hal Hedges, at the time quite a famous woodsman. Other summers we went to the Barracks, a farm run by a widow lady who in return for a small sum fed us and let us work farm machinery, care for the animals, and generally do as we pleased. The Barracks historically was important as the place where Hessian prisoners were billeted after the battle of Trenton in the Revolutionary War. From here they were allotted to the farmers of Albemarle, Nelson and Fluvanna counties. Some were obviously skillful workmen—a beautiful mantel carved by one of them still stands in my wife Kathryn's family home at Winton.

My interest in history was growing in those years. Monticello, Thomas Jefferson's home, stood a stone's throw away; every surrounding hamlet and terrain feature had played a part in either the Revolutionary or the Civil War. But mostly I learned from reading. I was a keen G. A. Henty fan—Henty wrote dozens of books about a young British subaltern and I read them all. I fought with this fellow in India and in Canada and in the Boer War and on the Peninsula and in the Orange wars—every place a British soldier ever fired a shot. I was also fond of Lever's stories about Charles O'Malley, an orderly to an Irish Fusilier captain in the Peninsular War. Much to my disgust, for every one of these my father forced me to read a standard classic, usually Scott, Thackeray or Dickens. But I was and am incorrigible and still prefer Lever's books to Mr. Dickens' best.

This being only thirty years after the Civil War, Charlottesville abounded in military experiences. From as long as I can remember Grandfather Carson told me stories about his campaigns. He was a very impressive man and I listened carefully to his tales. He was also very devout. A Baptist deacon, he said prayers before breakfast; if you missed these, you missed breakfast. He held few men in awe, but those few he treated mighty respectfully—he always prayed to "the God of Abraham, Isaac, Jacob, Robert E. Lee and Stonewall Jackson."

Thanks to reading and to Grandfather Carson a military career early claimed my ambition. This was cemented at about sixteen when I went to work after school for my cousin, Colonel Charles C. Wertenbaker. Cousin Charles had fought as a captain in the Civil War and a colonel in the Spanish-American War and now ran a prosperous cigar factory. My job was packing hand-rolled Havana cigars according to grade and of course putting the best ones on top. In summer I earned a princely sum of $5 a day doing this. But best of all through this job I came to know better our family physician, Dr. Wilson Randolph, the grandson of Thomas Jefferson, and his boon companion, Major Mickey. Both were Confederate veterans and close friends of Cousin Charles. Each noon the trio met to drink a pint of claret punch and spin yarns about the Civil War. After a year or so I could have told any one of the stories better than the teller, but it was these gentlemen who really interested me in going into the service and tried to arrange it.

It was not so easy. Dr. Randolph secured me an appointment to West Point, and by dint of very hard studying I passed the mental examination. But up at Fort McHenry in Baltimore I failed the physical. The Army informed my father that I could still go to summer camp at West Point and, if I then passed another physical, enter a fall class. But my mother, who didn't want me to go to West Point or any other military school, persuaded him to send me to the University of Virginia. I did not know about this parental skulduggery until years later. At the time I saw my mission as surviving the English, mathematics, German and geology curriculum until I was twenty-one and could take an examination for an Army commission.

I spent two years at the university before Cousin Charles took me to see our family friend, Senator Martin. The senator was sorry but no Army examination was scheduled—on the other hand, the Secretary of the Navy had just asked him to nominate two persons to take the Marine Corps examination. Having never heard of the Marine Corps, I asked him what it was. The old gentleman told me, then leaned back in his swivel chair and said, "Son, if you go into the Marine Corps you will spend a large portion of your life fighting small wars in the southern American hemisphere." How right he was.

To prepare for the examination "prescribed by the President of the United States" and rumored to be difficult—only 57 out of 500 would be selected, a number that later earned for this particular class the nickname "the 57 Varieties"—I entered Swaveley, a Washington cram school designed to help such ignoramuses as myself. It was a fortunate move because there I learned to answer such questions as, "If you started at Chicago and traveled to Manila via the Suez Canal, name all the waters, all the countries, all the capes and all the bays that you would pass on your course."

Came November and the examination at the Washington Marine Barracks. To be more precise, the Marine Barracks Band Hall, an old drafty building complete with musicians practicing in the balcony. To the accompaniment of horns, sousaphones, tubas and fifes we hopefuls began a spelling test which for some reason centered on medical terms such as psoriasis, physiognomy, tonsillectomy and other horrors.

In three of the most ghastly days of my life, algebra followed spelling, then plane and solid geometry, trigonometry, English grammar, history and geography. By the end of the week the drums had taken over to help us through the geography exam. The final question was: "If you started at Chicago and traveled to Manila via the Suez Canal, name all the waters, all the countries, all the capes and all the bays that you would pass on your course."

I returned to Charlottesville to "sweat out" the examination results. Despite the vigorous schedule in Washington I had seen enough guard mounts and parades at the Marine Barracks to know I would never be satisfied with any other career. People in later years have asked what I regarded as the highlight of my life. Certainly one highlight occurred on December 20, 1908, when I learned that I had passed and would be commissioned in the Marine Corps. No matter that I wasn't too high in the class. I wasn't at the bottom and the important fact was to have passed.

On January 21, 1909, our prosecuting attorney, Mr. Gilmer, swore me in. The day after the ceremony I received a letter from the Secretary of War inviting me to take an examination for an Army commission—I replied to this rather smugly.

My new uniform was a beauty. At that time Marine officers, or anyway second lieutenants, wore a dark-blue tunic frogged across the front, light-blue trousers with a bright red stripe down each leg, shiny black shoes and a dark-blue hat with a little gold cord across the visor. Anxious to impress Grandfather Carson I topped this with a long blue boat cloak, one side of which I casually threw over my shoulder to expose the red lining.

Piece by piece Grandfather Carson took it in. He sat in his Morris chair stroking his white beard and peering over the top of his steel-rimmed glasses and finally said, "Well, Archer, I guess you look all right, but I never thought I would see the day when a grandson of mine would be wearing a *blue* uniform."

That was only my first comeuppance and it wasn't very serious. The School of Application was the second one: it nearly ended my career before it had begun.

In 1909 the School of Application—which that year was renamed the Marine Officer's School and is today's Basic School —was located at Parris Island, a short distance by boat from Port Royal, South Carolina. From the deck of an ancient mail boat, *Summer Girl*, the island appeared about as inviting as the Arctic and a first look ashore did not change matters.

To save money, Headquarters Marine Corps used the buildings of a defunct Navy Yard for its school. Our quarters occupied the upper floor of a machine shop roughly converted to a dormitory partitioned on both sides. Potbellied coal stoves, spaced to provide the minimum of heat, lined the center hall. Three of us lived in each room and the entire class shared a lavatory and shower. We messed in a nearby establishment run by a civilian, Mr. Burrows, to whom we paid $30 a month for our food plus a boy who cleaned the rooms once a week.

These physical arrangements provided only the first shock. We had no more than settled in when formation sounded. Standing at attention we then received what is still known in the Marine Corps as "the word." All of us being college men, we had expected to be treated as commissioned officers. Instead we learned we were to resemble inmates of some sort of penal institution.

Organized into a company of sections, we began a routine that did not greatly vary in the next eleven months. Reveille sounded at six. We fell out to setting-up exercises followed by a doubletime run around the station. We then washed, made up bunks, breakfasted and marched to class. Class lasted for forty-five minutes, then a short break followed by another class, and so on all day.

Lieutenant Colonel Eli K. Cole commanded the school. A small staff of Marine officer instructors treated us to a bewildering curriculum that included drill regulations, guard duty, small-arms firing regulations, the rifle in war, signals, security and information, organization and tactics, military law, administration, engineering, hygiene and naval gunnery.

Such courses sometimes produced amusing situations. I never could draw well, a failing that Captain Pickering, the instructor in naval gunnery, soon observed. One day he sent me to the board: "Mr. Vandegrift, draw a cross section of a Sweets Fuze." Fortunately I had studied this object the night before and with confidence drew the diagram. Captain Pickering studied it a moment. "Mr. Vandegrift, is that a picture of a Sweets Fuze or George Washington?"

Captain Cutts of tactics proved most entertaining. A veteran of Philippine campaigns, he told us so many stories of his adventures that we named him Behuka Dick. His favorite sea story concerned one of his Philippine patrols which came to a river deeper than he had estimated. But so disciplined were his men, who were marching at attention, that they proceeded right through that river with only the muzzles of their rifles emerging, and they came out still in perfect formation and continued the march, to the everlasting glory of the Corps.

Captain Cutts meant well, as did all the instructors. But, as I said, we were used to more intelligent education and soon grew rebellious. We grew so rebellious that, as the adjutant told me years later, Colonel Cole grew determined to make an example of the first miscreant he could identify.

Unfortunately I became that miscreant. Owing to a complete misunderstanding, I returned late from a liberty at Port Royal. To my amazement Colonel Cole charged me with absence overleave and with making a dishonest statement. I was awarded a general court-martial, which found me guilty on the first count only but nonetheless reduced me five numbers in grade (at the time this ensured my being a junior second lieutenant for some years).

As an anticlimax, Colonel Cole in my spring fitness report graded me unsatisfactory in everything but health which he judged "excellent." To my no great surprise I learned that he did not wish to have me under his "immediate command in peace or in war" nor did he consider me "fit to be intrusted with hazardous and important independent duties."

I received the report for written reply and answered, "Sir, I have the honor to state that I have no satisfactory explanation to make." That was not entirely true, but rather than point out what I felt and still feel was injustice, I swore I would eventually show Colonel Cole that he was wrong.

As the reader will learn, I succeeded in this before the old man died in 1929. Later I occasionally reflected on such youthful incidents. Two of the service chiefs of World War II —Admiral Ernest King and I—not to mention Admiral Chester Nimitz, commander of the largest naval effort in history, had courts-martial on our records. I hope this fact encourages young officers who have fallen into scrapes (and who has not?), and I hope it may influence those senior officers charged with promotion to select an officer for what he is and what he is likely to be without undue weight on early recorded errors.

To return to 1909. In the next few months—a summer somewhat enlivened by a stay at Sea Girt, New Jersey, where we learned to fire the Springfield .03 rifle and the Colt .45 revolver—I improved enough for Captain Cutts in his final report to grade me "very good" in "attention to duty." He held no objection to my being under his "immediate command"—but, alas, he noted that I lacked "force."

Compensations existed, as they generally do anywhere. The school proved interesting in a number of ways and I certainly learned a considerable amount, including discipline. I also began friendships that later ripened, one with Bill Upshur, a young instructor, another with Roy Geiger, a fellow student. But I cannot say I regretted graduation day.

Orders scattered our small class to the winds, with Lester Wass and me going to the Marine Barracks, Portsmouth Navy Yard, New Hampshire. After ten days' leave I traveled north.

The Marine Corps of 1910 numbered about 350 officers and less than 10,000 men. The bulk of these served either aboard ship or in Marine Barracks on various naval stations from where they were garnered to make up provisional battalions for various expeditionary duties.

The Portsmouth Navy Yard, which operated in conjunction with the Navy Prison, was the home port of the Atlantic Cruiser Squadron—"the harmless cruiser squadron" from the Navy ditty of the day. The Marine Barracks, with a mission of providing security for the Navy Yard, was a relatively simple institution commanded by a 48-year-old crustacean, Lieutenant Colonel Theodore Porter Kane.

Lester Wass and I quartered in the Barracks, an old-fashioned New England building also housing the commanding officer's quarters and office, the guardhouse, the mess hall and the galley. We held down two bedrooms, a sitting room, dining room and kitchen below. An Irish girl cooked and cleaned for us—in all a comfortable arrangement that lasted until Wass shipped out to the Philippines a few months later.

We worked very hard because we pulled day on-day off duty as officer of the day or OD. Even on Wednesdays, when the quartermaster took the duty while we hiked, whoever held the duty upon return from the hike put on his proper uniform and relieved the quartermaster in time to make the midnight inspection.

As OD I inspected sentries three times in the 24-hour tour, usually once before noon, once in the afternoon, and once between midnight and reveille. I had to be present at all meal formations and report on the quality and preparation of the food. Each morning I stood a formal or informal guard mount (unless there was too much ice on the parade ground), then I inspected the parade and guardhouse and reported to Colonel Kane for office hours where I met my relief. The colonel read through the logbook, asked any questions he desired, awarded punishment to reported miscreants, and relieved me. This did not end my day because I had to hold close order drill several times a week and also noncommissioned officer school. I also held additional duties, such as post exchange officer and legal officer.

This formed one side of the duty. The other occurred under Major Henry Leonard who, besides commanding the Navy Prison, was in charge of all garrison training including both Marine and Navy detachments from various ships. Besides running formal schools he conducted all joint drills, hikes and field exercises.

Major Leonard was something of a character as were the majority of our senior officers who numbered only one major general, eight colonels, eight lieutenant colonels, and 26 majors. Major Leonard had made his name in the Boxer Rebellion in China where, in rescuing a young officer named Smedley Butler during the Tientsin fighting, he lost an arm. He was still an impressive figure of a man and was a fine Marine.

Major Leonard insisted that his officers know military theory as well as practice. Under his tutelage I read twenty-three standard military texts including Clausewitz *On War* and Stonewall Jackson's *Life and Campaigns*. I not only read them but wrote an essay on each which he corrected in discussion periods. His instruction proved a wonderful extension of my childhood interest in military writing; under him I gained and retained a strong interest in military history.

Major Leonard did not limit himself to the academic. He kept in splendid physical condition and held no compunction about hiking us to York Beach and back, 15-20 miles under full pack. If toward the end of a hike men began straggling he marched them at attention. The troops always said, "Of course the old—can hike out. He don't have to carry a knap-sack and he ain't got but one arm to pack."

One day Leonard took a young lieutenant, a good friend of mine named Joe Fegan, on a 15-mile hike. When Joe was soaking his tired bones in a hot bath Leonard's orderly appeared: "Compliments of Major Leonard and would Mr. Fegan like to play some tennis?" Joe wanted to play tennis about as much as he wanted a court-martial but he duly reported. After two sets Leonard said, "Well, I think we have exercised sufficiently today."

Colonel Kane also enjoyed little jokes. A large man with a luxurious mustache, he at first resembled God. It took us some time to realize he was very genial and human. I was still new on station when about three o'clock one morning he telephoned the OD's office: "Mr. Vandegrift, I have reason to believe there is trouble in the town of Kittery. You will please take a detail, patrol the town, eliminate any disturbance and report back to me."

In ten degrees below zero weather I turned out my detail and marched it to the neighboring town of Kittery, which of course was slightly more dead than Arlington Cemetery. Several hours later and half frozen I reported my findings to the colonel, sitting by a cozy fire in his drawing room. He nodded pleasantly. "Thank you, Mr. Vandegrift. That is very good indeed."

Later when I got to know Mrs. Kane, a lovely person who was an invalid, I told her about this and other jokes. She smiled. "Just remember, Mr. Vandegrift, he never plays jokes on persons he doesn't like."

Noncommissioned officers provided another healthy influence on my education. My chief tutor was First Sergeant Barney Sullivan, a 62-year-old veteran campaigner and a Marine from his close-cropped gray hair and clipped gray mustache to the mirror shine on his shoes. Having learned that I enjoyed good music he often asked me to his quarters where an early model Victrola with a big horn played a splendid variety of classical Red Seal records. He told wonderful stories about what he called the "old" Marine Corps. While serving in the Army early in life he was a member of the detail that captured Chief Sitting Bull, and I guess there wasn't much of anything he missed in his career. I certainly was flattered to have him as a friend, and I learned an enormous amount from him.

Quartermaster Sergeant John Edwards was another fine instructor and friend and so was Gunnery Sergeant Lattimer. Lattimer had fought in the Philippine Insurrection, a campaign etched on his face by the broad scar of a bolo. I met

him on my second tour of OD duty when, investigating a
racket out by the guardhouse, I found him confronting a
drunken Marine. To my question of what was going on he
replied, "If the lieutenant pleases, the sergeant of the guard
will handle this." Fortunately I had sense enough to please,
and the racket soon ceased. Next morning Lattimer hauled
a very subdued private before Colonel Kane, who awarded
him five days' bread and water. The experience taught me
that many activities in the Marine Corps must be handled by
noncommissioned officers.

Both noncoms and men were an interesting lot. Generally
uneducated in the formal sense, they were powerfully
wise in the ways of the world. For the most part the noncoms were older because at the time you often served a four-
year cruise before making corporal and such was discipline
that stripes vanished easier than they came. Most of them
wore mustaches, a few beards, and all but the most recent
recruits featured lurid tattoos with the same aplomb that
many of us today wear campaign ribbons. The majority of
men drank, and since a private's pay amounted to $14.80 a
month he was usually broke long before pay call. Because
he didn't have much money he depended on his own merits
for entertainment which is why I suppose the ranks bred such
incredible characters. The things they said and did were
normally funny as the devil even though on occasion they
misbehaved badly. But outstanding in their character, I believe, was an intense loyalty and I shall never forget how
much they wanted to help and did help a new lieutenant.

All of us were thrown rather much on our own devices. Talk
wasn't a sin in those days and neither was group singing nor
amateur dramatics. We younger officers were frequently invited to the older officers' homes and of course we chummed
around together on our own. Our mainstay was the Brown-
tail Moth Club, named after a current pest then ravaging New
England. We behaved more mildly, limiting our informal
meetings to Hamms Restaurant in Kittery where for 85 cents
you got a tremendous lobster, hash-brown potatoes and a stein
of good beer. Sometimes after pay call we would go up to
Portsmouth for a bust-loose or as much as you could bust
loose in that good city.

I was pretty careful of the pennies because during my soph-
omore year at the University of Virginia I had fallen in love

with a visiting schoolteacher from Lynchburg, Miss Mildred Strode. Immediate marriage as a second lieutenant was out of the question. I had gone into considerable debt for uniforms; besides, the Commandant, Major General George Elliott, had made himself clear on the subject before we left for the School of Application. "I wish to emphasize one point," he told us. "You are now Marine officers. As you are drawing $141.67 a month and thus have more money to spend than you have ever had before don't think you have enough money to get married. You do not have enough money to get married, you will not have enough money for several years, and I don't want any of you to get married."

Despite this admonition I kept in touch with Mildred, who in the spring of 1910 accepted my proposal of marriage. Unlike a classmate who sent the Commandant a wedding invitation and for his courtesy was immediately ordered to sea, I neglected to invite General Elliott to our wedding.

We returned to Portsmouth and easily fitted into the married social life of the Barracks and Navy yard, making lasting friendships with the young John Marstons and others. I now worked harder than ever coaching at the rifle range in addition to other duties. This was a time-consuming task but worth every minute since that year our team placed second in the New England matches.

Portsmouth was good to me and I look back fondly on this first tour even thought I would not recommend garrison duty for newly commissioned officers. But despite the many kindnesses of the Marines and the New England townspeople and despite my marriage and the birth of my son, Archer, I was very pleased to be ordered to Philadelphia to join an expedition mounting out to Cuba. The sea stories told by Major Leonard and First Sergeant Sullivan had fired my imagination beyond belief. Now, suddenly, I was to become a Marine of those stories.

II

Action with Smedley Butler

OTHER than organized units in Panama and the Philippines, we relied on makeshift provisional battalions and regiments to answer the demands of expeditionary duty, particularly revolts in Cuba or the Caribbean countries.

On the east coast these provisional units, composed of detachments levied from posts and stations along the eastern seaboard, mounted out of Philadelphia or Brooklyn. It spoke well for our training that we could take these diversified groups and in short order have a first-class battalion or regiment on our hands.

I had been ordered to Panama from Portsmouth but while on leave my orders were changed to Philadelphia, there to pick up 100 Marine recruits and with no noncoms deliver them aboard ships in New York. Making the largest Marines acting lance corporals, I stationed them at the door of each railroad car and through this precaution delivered the entire complement to the ships standing in Tompkinsville Roads. To my delight when I reported aboard *Michigan* I found numerous men from Portsmouth commanded by my old skipper, Captain Manwaring.

An uneventful cruise took us to Guantánamo Bay, Cuba, from where we shipped to El Cuero in the now famous Oriente Province. Unloading ships was rather primitive at that time and included such hazards as a Buzycott, a pig iron stove, dropping from a winch to plunge through the bottom of a whaleboat.

At El Cuero we protected a valuable American-owned manganese mine, a mission since familiar as guarding "the lives and property of American citizens." During the few weeks of this duty I commanded a platoon in Captain Manwaring's company. Except for one night when we were fired upon, the mission proved somewhat boring. We returned the

35

fire and on the next day sent out patrols under Sergeant Dan Daly who reported negatively.

Upon recall to Guantánamo Bay I met Lieutenant Colonel John A. Lejeune for the first time. He looked very much as he later appeared in life and pictures, the same lock of dark hair draped over his forehead to give him a striking resemblance to Napoleon.

Under separate orders I now shipped to Panama to join Major Smedley D. Butler's battalion. Everyone in the Marine Corps at this time had heard of Smedley Butler just as nearly everyone in America was to hear of him before his career ended prematurely. To officers and men he formed an almost legendary figure, the hero of the Boxer Rebellion and famous throughout the Corps for his drive, determination and intelligence.

I reported to Bas Obispo or Camp Elliott, his headquarters, with considerable trepidation. I found him dressed in spotless khaki. He was under medium height, weighed probably about 130 pounds, and inclined toward a round-shouldered posture that defied a correct fit of uniform. He was most courteous but there was no missing the scrutiny of his searching deep-set eyes, his most prominent facial feature other than his beak nose. He assigned me to Company D, commanded by Captain John ("Johnny the Hard") Hughes.

Captain Hughes also received me courteously, gave me the afternoon off to get settled, and ordered me to report at 7:00 A.M. for drill. The next morning I observed Captain Hughes drill the company for some time. He then ordered me to take over. I explained that I had not seen the new Navy manual which he was obviously using and he said, "Very well, this is Friday. On Monday morning you will be prepared to drill this company." On Monday morning I drilled the company to his satisfaction.

A few weeks later Captain Hughes called me to his office. "Vandegrift, the end of the month is coming up. I want you to prepare the company payroll and muster roll. When you have finished bring them to me for signature."

In those days the muster roll and payroll were made out in long hand with no erasures allowed on any page—in all, a tedious but exacting task for even an experienced person. Fortunately, one such, First Sergeant Slingloff, took me aside. "If the lieutenant pleases, the captain is never in the office in the afternoons. I would suggest we work on this job in the afternoons."

We started the next day with the muster roll. First Sergeant Slingloff said, "Arnold, John J.," and I wrote, "Arnold, John J." When in doubt I asked him how to spell a name. For days this routine continued until finally I took the completed reports to Captain Hughes. He glanced at them and signed them. "Well done, Vandegrift. You will never have to make them out again."

Johnny the Hard came by his name rightfully. A tall chap, over six feet, he was hard as nails both with us and with himself. But next to General Harry Lee, he was the best drillmaster I ever served with and he taught me a great deal.

As was common in most garrisons, learning and teaching formed our major activities. In addition to company duty, Major Butler also put me in charge of teaching field engineering. Mostly practical, this consisted of building single- and double-span field bridges across creeks, using only felled trees and line.

The entire battalion trained constantly, as anyone familiar with Major Butler would expect. His breadth and imagination were as deserving as they were famous. For example, while I was teaching engineering, which later stood us in very good stead in Nicaragua, another group rode the local railroad, learning how to run engines; still another group served in the railroad dispatcher's office, learning how to control the trains.

Major Butler put us to anything that enhanced our all-round combat capability. Indefatigable himself, he saw no reason for anyone else to need rest. Once I spent an entire morning conducting close order drill and an afternoon in the field building bridges. That evening I had showered and was walking to the tennis court when I met Major Butler. He asked me where I was going and I told him. He scratched his head: "Well, damn it all. If you have enough energy to play tennis in the evening, then something is wrong with my training schedule."

Nothing was wrong with his schedule. Not only was the battalion superbly trained but it stood ready to go anywhere, any time. One afternoon I came back from the field to learn that we were shipping out to Nicaragua to put down another revolt. In just over forty-eight hours we loaded our equiva-

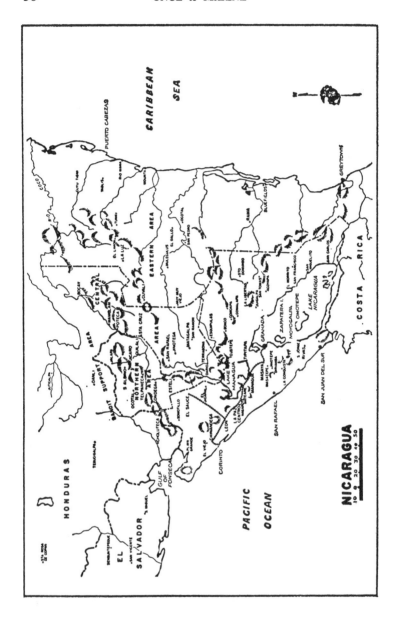

lent of today's reinforced battalion into railroad cars and, at Balboa, aboard ship.

Butler called these Nicaraguan revolts "the Punic Wars." Basically the trouble centered on a backward country emerging into daylight of civilization. For some years one of two political parties called the Nicaraguan play. In 1910 Liberal party excesses under the leadership of one Zelaya, originally backed by President Taft's "dollar diplomacy," touched off revolt by Juan Estrada's Conservative party—a revolt that brought Butler's battalion to this Central American country.

With Estrada's Conservative government in control, Butler returned to Panama. But severe financial problems soon dogged Estrada and led to a break in his government. By this time both American private capital and the American government were inextricably involved in Nicaraguan affairs, which gave rise to a form of anti-Americanism so familiar today. The issues finally forced Estrada from office in favor of one Adolfo Díaz. In 1912 the Liberal party, this time under Benjamin Zeledon, revolted. Díaz meanwhile had fired his principal general, Mena, who fled to Masaya where his son, commanding an Army barracks at Granada, together with a good many dissident Liberals joined him in a second revolt.

The situation upon our arrival was this: Díaz, the Conservative president representing the legitimate government of Nicaragua, requested U.S. intervention to protect American lives and property. In August a small party of sailors from *Annapolis* landed at Managua; another party of Marines and sailors from *Tacoma* landed at Bluefields. In mid-August our battalion landed at Corinto and boarded trains for the 90-mile ride to Managua and there joined the small landing party from *Annapolis*.

A rebel force now took León, which put them between us and Corinto. We heard also that Admiral Southerland was coming down from Corinto with a contingent of Marines. The naval officer from *Annapolis*, a commander senior to Butler, decided to clear the way for them. Taking a group of Marines and sailors he started out. Upon meeting a group of rebels his courage vanished—he turned his train over to them and walked the troops back to Managua, an act that earned him the title of General Walkemback.

A furious Smedley Butler now organized an expedition in which I took temporary command of Company D. Going was slow because the rebels had pulled up some rails but presumably from laziness left them alongside the track for us to put back. They also smashed some culverts which we were able to crib over—all the training and cross-training of Panama days was obviously paying off.

Outside of León we met a force of rebels who demanded our return to Managua. Butler said he would like to comply but unfortunately would have to contact Admiral Southerland in Corinto for instructions—a simple matter since we had a radio with us.

The Marines were quite up to the farce that followed. With a fat rebel general looking on, two husky Marines cranked up a generator of a spark-gap radio that possibly would carry ten miles. Standing with feet apart and hands on hips, Butler dictated to an operator who sent out a great shower of sparks and odd noises. After thirty minutes Butler nodded imperceptibly to the men, who repeated the performance with the operator taking down Southerland's "message." Frowning in concentration Butler read this and then told the general he was sorry but orders were to carry on. So impressed was the poor man that he took his force and disappeared. I tell the story as an example of the flair for showmanship and desire for fun that were so characteristic of Smedley Butler.

We weren't yet out of the woods. A mile or two farther on we encountered the main rebel force, a screaming mob headed by another fat general who confronted Butler. This time Butler did not indulge in play-acting—he simply disarmed the man. Having lost face the general permitted us to proceed through León.

A native next informed us of mines planted along the roadbed to Corinto. Butler looked at me and casually ordered, "Vandegrift, take a corporal, get up on the front end of this train and look for mines." Upon leaving León the corporal asked, "Mr. Vandegrift, what should we do if we see a mine?" I told him, "You see a mine, you yell *mine* as loud as you can and jump as far as you can." Although we saw no mines, this experience accounts for my nickname of "Sunny Jim" which Butler later called me. Asked why, he replied, "Because I put him up there on the engine to look for mines and when we got through he had a kind of grin on his face. It wasn't much of a grin but it was still a grin so I named him Sunny Jim." Later, when I was promoted to captain, Butler came to me and said, "Now that you have the exalted rank of captain, Sunny Jim is not dignified enough so I will call you James." He did for the rest of his life and so did some of my friends.

The trip into Corinto proved a busy spell for me because we repaired sixteen breaks in the track plus several bridges. My temper was not improved at Corinto, where for protection the naval force had pulled up the tracks across the bridge outside of town and mounted a six-pounder at the following end. The next day they relaid the tracks and we proceeded into town, picked them up and returned to Managua, stopping along the way to repair track and build bridges.

The building of one of these bridges demanded an S-curve approach on either side. Having no transits we relied on guesswork, I having been detailed one side and a Lieutenant Commander Steele the other. When we finished I looked at his job and told him that the engine was not going to get around his curve. Hotly defending his work he bet me a case of beer on the outcome. He dutifully paid off once we got the engine back on the track.

Dropping most of our force at León, Butler took a few of us on to Managua. By the time we reached the southern city it was dark. Thinking we were rebels, government sentries opened up on us but fortunately our brakes failed and we rode into town so fast that no one was hit.

Our next mission was to proceed to Granada in the interior from Managua. Our route included the town of Masaya some 15 miles from Managua. Here General Zeledon commanded a large rebel force which, while not openly attacking us, did nothing to help our journey. On the sharp railroad grades rebels covered the tracks with milkweed which forced us to dismount frequently to push the train over the hills. After a difficult trip we reached Masaya that night, immediately engaged in a sharp fire fight, and later counted five of our men wounded and three missing. An envoy soon approached Butler with an apology. In his usual vigorous style Butler told him to produce our three men or he would attack immediately. The men returned to us unharmed within the hour.

We spent another several days traveling the short distance to Granada where General Mena commanded the bulk of rebel forces. After considerable palaver with Mena's emissaries, Butler put us into attack formation to march on the city. We were approaching the outskirts when another emissary met us with Mena's surrender.

While we were cleaning up Granada, Colonel "Uncle Joe" Pendleton arrived in Managua where he attempted to persuade Zeledon to surrender. Zeledon refused, and Pendleton ordered his battalion of Marines and our force to attack. In what would be known as the battle of Coyotepe I commanded a group of eight Benet-Mercies, a 30-caliber, air-cooled light machine gun similar to the British Hotchkiss. Along with our artillery we commenced fire at dawn to cover the advance of the troops up the hill. Shortly after daylight we stormed the rebel positions, killed a number of the enemy, the rest fleeing. With that the Nicaraguan revolution ended.

The battle of Coyotepe proved a personal defeat for me. We were paid in $10 gold pieces. At the beginning of the battle my trousers held two such—at the end these were missing. I scoured the hillside but did not find the money, a considerable sum to a young lieutenant.

I learned a great many things in Nicaragua. Most important was the value of leadership as demonstrated by Smedley Butler. He impressed not by words but by action. He was a fighter in the fullest sense of the word—at one point in the campaign he was terribly ill of malaria and yet with a 104-degree temperature he not only held on but carried on.

Tactically the importance of fire distribution impressed me the most. Men are very prone to fire on a pronounced portion of the enemy, that is, most of them will fire on one main target leaving the other portions of the enemy line free. I learned beyond doubt the necessity for distributing your fire, not just grouping it.

The need for water discipline became obvious when almost an entire platoon went down with dysentery. Along with this the necessity for proper physical conditioning stood out, particularly in jungle campaigns where mobility is all-important. My tours in Panama and Nicaragua and later Haiti explained why henceforth I took walks that tired more than one aide. I also discovered, completely to my astonishment, how long one can go without sleep and yet perform very rigorous duties—in a fitness report Major Butler noted that I worked without sleep for four days and nights repairing the railroad.

After a brief but pleasant occupation of Nicaragua we returned to Camp Elliott just before Thanksgiving, shook down the battalion, and commenced a regular training schedule. During a tour at rifle range I came down with bad malaria. Current treatment was the devil's own: it consisted of doses of liquid quinine. Since I could not hold it I had to take muscular injections. I went down to 98 pounds, suffering as much from abscesses in my buttocks caused by the injections as from the malaria. Once out of danger I was sent home for a month's recuperative leave. Oddly enough I never suffered a recurrence of this debilitating disease.

In the winter of 1913 first water flowed into the Panama Canal, which meant the eventual abandonment of Camp Elliott. Before we had time to regret it the Mexican crisis blew up. In January we shipped out to Vera Cruz, transshipped there, and steamed up to Tampico. Returning to Vera Cruz we again transshipped, this time to *Chester,* commanded by Commander Moffett, one of the ablest and finest naval officers I have ever known. Learning that Tampico was under shell fire, we returned to evacuate the American residents to a battleship, then steamed back up the Pánuco River to remain on station for several sweltering days.

When Moffett received news of our landing at Vera Cruz he ordered full steam south, an effort that strained about every seam in *Chester*. We reached the port that night. Without lights Moffett conned *Chester* into the inner harbor, a piece of seamanship that drew praise from even Admiral Cradock, commanding the British fleet there.

In darkness, we disembarked and went into position for the morning assault, my platoon taking the company's right. We jumped off early, hit some heavy street fighting but pushed on until some of our own naval five-inch shells took us under fire. We secured the town that day, my platoon suffering no casualties. With the battle over we moved to the railroad depot, the men sleeping in the roundhouse and the officers in boxcars.

Shortly after we were settled I was ordered to establish an outpost line of standing trenches on the sand dunes west of the city. This is not the easiest task but it was vastly simplified when an alert gunnery sergeant indicated a deserted house off to our right. We were tearing it down when an irate Mexican approached and through an interpreter complained that we were dismantling his house. To get him off my neck I scribbled a note stating the circumstances, signed it and gave it to him.

Some months later I received a letter from the Claims Commission demanding an explanation of why I destroyed a Mexican house claimed at 5,000 pesos. My explanation was returned disapproved as were a second and a third. In a desperate attempt to save 5,000 pesos I asked to see Colonel Lejeune, who commanded the regiment.

To my halting story he responded, "What are you worried about?"

"About paying five thousand pesos which I don't have."

"Who told you to build those standing trenches?"

"You did, sir."

"It is therefore my responsibility and I shall take care of it." Noting my relief he added, "Let this be a lesson to you. Never sign your name to a foolish paper when you don't have to."

Garrison duty quickly settled down to routine with only a few incidents to break the boredom. Once when I was commanding an outpost line at Vegara with orders to prevent anyone from crossing to the Mexican side I noticed a gentleman in civilian clothes proceeding toward the line. I sent a corporal to inform him of the regulations. The corporal reported that this man claimed to be Admiral Cradock, commanding the British fleet at Vera Cruz—according to the admiral, no American soldier could tell him where he could or could not go. I sent the corporal back with my compliments—if the admiral stepped beyond that line I would arrest him. The corporal returned the admiral's compliments—I was on report to Colonel Lejeune. I immediately got Colonel Lejeune on the field phone, explained the situation—and heard no more about it. A short time later, with the opening of World War I, the admiral went down with his ship in the battle of Coronel off the coast of Chile.

Most of my days went to studying for the promotion examination, my number finally having come up in Panama. Because of my poor record at the School of Application I knew a good showing was imperative despite my having been cited by Major Butler for the Nicaraguan campaign, by Commander Moffett for the Tampico action, and by Lieutenant Colonel Neville for the Vera Cruz landing. I guess I became a terrible pest because I kept asking the other officers to hear my lessons. One day Butler asked if I was prepared on drill regulations. I told him I could start at the beginning of the manual and recite it verbatim.

"Five dollars says you can't."

I took the bet and welcomed the money.

In the event, the examination proved similar to the final held at the School of Application. This time I handled both oral and written questions with considerably more ease and dispatch—undoubtedly the influence of Major Butler's teachings. The examination board included Colonel Lejeune, Major Dunlap and Captain Hooker. When coming to drill regulations they posed several questions on the duties of the guard. I answered one or two when Major Dunlap, who was not from the South, asked what in the world I was talking about. Colonel Lejeune, who *was* from the South, said, "He is talking about *gahd* duty which he spells g-u-a-r-d but correctly pronounces *gahd*." That took care of that.

Of course I had no idea of the board's opinion—at least not until my wife wrote me from Philadelphia where she met a senior officer on leave from the brigade. "He wore out the board," the officer told her. "Once he started quoting the book they couldn't stop him talking."

"But did he pass?" my wife demanded.

"Did he pass? Of course he passed."

This intelligence brightened the future, but not for long. One could not be promoted unless there was a vacancy to be promoted into. The captain who was taking *his* examination for major failed the physical, which meant that the first lieutenant who was going to fill his shoes could not advance—which left Second Lieutenant Vandegrift where he had always been. Not until a few months after I reached Philadelphia did a vacancy occur, and then only because some poor devil committed suicide.

In late 1914 we received our long-awaited orders home. Early the next year Major Butler arranged for me to join his regiment and begin studies in the Advance Base School. This lasted until autumn, when trouble again flared in the Caribbean. This time it was Haiti. We sailed at once.

III

Haiti: A Challenge

NAMED Hispaniola by Columbus, the land mass formed by the present countries of Haiti and the Dominican Republic for years had been festering in the heat of the Caribbean sun. Since 1803, when Jean Jacques Dessalines led Haiti to freedom from French domination, dictators one after the other ran the affairs of this impoverished country.

The political routine did not greatly vary. A Haitian desirous of rule went north to recruit a following of bandits known as Cacos, a name allegedly derived from a bird of prey whose cry resembled ca-co. With their help the aspirant seized power, floated internal bond issues, borrowed whatever money he could from France, Germany and America, and lived splendidly during his tenure. Soon someone else went north, recruited some Cacos and drove out the incumbent, who fled with the treasury.

Between 1908 and 1915 when we landed no less than seven presidents had come and gone. The last one, Vilbrun Guillaume Sam, in a moment of pique had ordered some two hundred political prisoners executed, a hideous act that plunged Port-au-Prince into vengeful frenzy. Shortly before our arrival Sam fled to the French Legation but a mob found him, dragged him into the street, and hacked him to bits.

With Haitian government thus neutralized, two contenders began fighting for the presidency. One was Dr. Rosalvo Bobo, the other Senator Philippe Sudre Dartiguenave.

Foreseeing the situation in July, 1915, Admiral Caperton who commanded our fleet in those waters requested assistance. President Wilson responded by giving him a Marine provisional brigade commanded by the colorful Littleton Waller Tazewell Waller—"Tony" to his intimates. Colonel Kane brought in the 2d Marine Regiment from Cuba while Colonel Cole, my nemesis from the School of Application,

46

scraped together the 1st Marine Regiment which followed hard on from Philadelphia. Smedley Butler commanded a battalion in Cole's regiment; I served as Butler's adjutant.

Waller together with Kane's regiment landed at Port-au-Prince, policed up the area and arranged an election which installed Dartiguenave as president. Our regiment landed at Cap Haitien to the north and pushed outposts into the countryside. Our major mission was to protect villages and farms from the depredations of the Cacos, once again in rebellion under Dr. Bobo. We also were to accept and pay for rifles turned in by disillusioned rebels. These were the old French 45-caliber Gras rifles. Lacking proper ammunition, the rebels used to wrap smaller caliber bullets with goatskin to hold them in the Gras chamber, a field expedient which helped to explain the general ineffectiveness of their fire.

This was a busy time for me. As adjutant I was the battalion personnel, intelligence and operations officer all in one. Soon after our arrival in Cap Haitien, Captain Beaumont, commanding a company of Gonaïves, informed us that he was beseiged by a force of Cacos. Major Butler and I hurried to this small coastal town by boat. Butler organized a rush that successfully drove the rebels out of town. That evening we learned they were burning the railroad. Butler led all of us, some clad only in underclothes, to the danger area where we routed the Cacos in a brisk fire fight. We immediately pursued and the next day captured their leader, General Rameau, who was sent south under arrest.

To accomplish our mission we fanned out companies to Fort Liberté, Grand Rivière and Ouanaminthe. From these bases patrols pushed out to seek Caco strongholds. One of them, Fort Capois, was located by a reconnaissance that nearly cost Butler, "Deacon" Upshur and First Sergeant Dan Daly their lives—an action in which I did not participate, having been directed to move battalion headquarters from Cap Haitien to Fort Liberté. I did get in on the minor action that captured the rebel camp and for a time greatly reduced Caco activity in our area.

Once we established a fair semblance of peace and order throughout Haiti, Washington decided to organize and train a native Gendarmerie to preserve the peace. In recruiting Marine officers and noncoms for this duty Butler proved his usual eloquent self. That man could talk the stripes off a

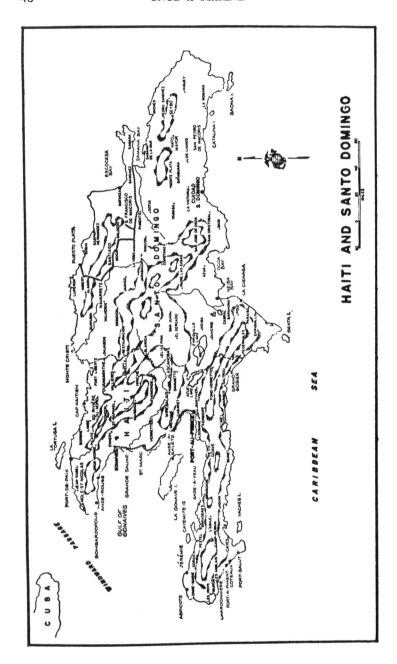

HAITI AND SANTO DOMINGO

zebra. Hal Turnage, another young lieutenant in the battalion, and I sat open-mouthed while Butler fired his staccato arguments: he had it on good authority (after all, his father was a congressman) that America would never enter World War I; as Marine lieutenants we would be majors in the Gendarmerie which meant $150 a month extra pay; he, himself, would shortly assume command of the Gendarmerie as a Haitian major general; finally—and here he nearly reduced us to tears—we faced an obvious challenge, a country that needed our help.

On the last point he was right. Haiti was not a poor country but corruption made it so. Poverty embraced its 10,000 square miles. Illiteracy and disease claimed over 90 per cent of its 3,000,000 population. The natives knew nothing of sanitation. They were constantly subject to corruption whether in the form of politicians emptying the treasury or Cacos forcing farmers to pay a tribute to get their wares to market. With the customhouses now in American hands, a steady income would put many matters right. With the Cacos suppressed— and we seemed well on the way to accomplishing this—a Gendarmerie, if properly organized and trained, could not fail to help the country.

My first task was to recruit, organize, equip and train two companies of 100 natives each at Cap Haitien, a job I could not have performed but for Marine Sergeant Degalle who spoke fluent French. I was studying French and together we were able to organize and give our first Haitians rudimentary training. We were immensely aided by an early enlistee, a fine-looking man named Jules André who spoke excellent English and whose intelligence was such that I got him commissioned a second lieutenant, the first Haitian officer in the Gendarmerie. (Years later he became chef de gendarmerie).

We had trained only a short time before I was ordered to post units into various subdistricts. I took the first company out myself. We had not marched very far when I noticed the men were barefooted. Having issued them new Marine Corps shoes, I instructed the first sergeant to have them replace their shoes. The march visibly slowed. Upon coming to a river the men asked the first sergeant if they could remove their shoes. This time I let them remain barefooted. The march again quickened. Whenever we came to a town we stopped, the men put on their shoes, we marched through the town smartly, then outside off came the shoes. This became a standard operating procedure in Haiti for years.

Despite the enthusiasm of the gendarmes I did not know how they would behave in combat. On this same trip I found out when a group of Cacos took us under fire. Considering their short training my men behaved splendidly, driving off the attackers in a brief fire fight.

These natives were not always the most intelligent in the world but they generally proved loyal. One of them who participated in the above action later gained distinction in a fight up north. To save his company commander from a rebel machete blow he threw his arm over the officer's head. The machete took the arm off at the elbow. He was later transferred to Port-au-Prince and retained as an orderly at brigade headquarters.

When Major Butler captured the rebel stronghold, Fort Rivière, in November the Caco movement pretty well subsided except for local forays. By now I had outposted two companies of gendarmes to the field which meant almost continual inspection trips either on horseback or by mule.

I heartily enjoyed this duty. After a healthy breakfast I normally hit the trail about 5:00 A.M., stopping not only at Gendarmerie outposts but also at the local *champette* or government agricultural station. Haitian hospitality dictated the serving of coffee on such occasions. The Haitians made coffee by roasting the bean practically to charcoal, then beating it into powder which was put into a bag and tied. The bag was dropped into boiling water to which was added a chunk of *rapadeau* or what the Creoles called the first crystallization of homemade sugar.

The result was strong, sweet and very good—but years later doctors attributed an ulcer of mine to these days of Haitian coffee and American cigarettes. There was probably some truth in it because I stopped at three or four of these stations daily to drink coffee and discuss local matters. The managers always seemed delighted to chat with an outsider. I was particularly popular with their numerous progeny who, in return for feeding and looking after my mount, received a corb—a coin worth about a fifth of a cent.

The job called for a considerable adjustment of personal standards—one soon learned never to be surprised by anything. On an early trip I came one evening to the small village of Limbé, unsaddled and went to the local parish house where officers always quartered on marches. No one was there, the house was locked. I slung my hammock on the porch and enjoyed a good sleep, but in the morning found myself without rations to assuage a healthy appetite. At this point a very handsome Haitian, well over six feet, walked up, introduced himself in English as a senator, and asked me to join him for breakfast. Upon my hasty acceptance he said he would bring the breakfast to me.

I had just shaved when down the street came a retinue of servants, the first carrying a table covered with an immaculate white cloth, the second carrying two chairs, and others carrying what proved to be a sumptuous feast.

On a later patrol up north I stopped for the night at Mole St. Nicolas where I was the guest of some Dutch clergy who greeted me warmly because of my Dutch name. After a splendid dinner they said they would have breakfast for me at 4:30 A.M. When I appeared still rubbing sleep from my eyes one of the good fathers offered me a cocktail. I thanked him, but said I couldn't possibly drink a cocktail at this time of the morning.

Obviously surprised he said, "Oh, I thought Americans always drank cocktails before breakfast."

These patrols often meant weeks away from civilization. Once when I was deep in the mountainous north country a hard-riding messenger brought orders from Colonel Cole to return as fast as possible to Cap Haitien. There I learned that my young son was desperately ill in Philadelphia. Colonel Cole had already secured a month's leave for me as well as a reservation on the steamship leaving that evening.

Upon returning to duty I reported directly to him. After thanking him for his help I stammered, "Colonel, I just want to tell you that I have been most glad to serve under you in Cap Haitien. After my experiences at the School of Application I never thought I'd live to say *that*."

He looked up and grinned. "Vandegrift, I have been very pleased to have you here and I never thought I'd live to say *that*." From that day on we got along splendidly.

Soon after Smedley Butler took over the Gendarmerie he transferred me to Port-de-Paix to command the 11th Gendarmerie Company. In addition to training gendarmes and inspecting outposts I was ordered to conduct a district census of civil servants, part of a much-needed over-all reform measure.

The situation made Tammany Hall politics seem like a Sunday-school picnic. Local politicos, I soon learned, had been paying teachers dead for twenty and thirty years. Some living teachers scarcely merited the title: one high school "teacher of English" could not read, write or speak the language—I fired him and returned his pay to the Haitian government. Like most honest reforms, our work proved popular with the bulk of the people but created enemies among local vested interests.

Toward the end of summer Butler transferred me to Port-au-Prince to serve as assistant quartermaster and paymaster of the Gendarmerie, an administrative billet which permitted my family to come to Haiti. The quartermaster, Marine Major Percy Archer, was a splendid officer with a mind like a calculating machine and a willingness to pass on his specialized knowledge to anyone interested. We ran quite a large operation in that we purchased all supplies for the Gendarmerie, contracted for the building and maintaining of barracks besides paying the troops—a payroll of well over $50,000 a month.

Upon Archer's relief early in 1917 I took over his job, a brisk period since I was also studying for the promotion examination to captain. The work, however, proved immensely satisfying. We were building roads, installing communications, teaching sanitation, putting the schools in order with all projects funded from custom revenues collected and distributed by American officials. Progress was slow and we all knew it would be a long pull, but we were making the pull despite immense difficulties at every turn.

But now the war fever mounting at home began to infiltrate our little country. I knew something was up when toward the end of March, 1917, I received secret orders to make a coastal reconnaissance "to ascertain if any submarine base has been established by any foreign power." None had, but by the time I returned to Port-au-Prince we were at war.

The next twenty months constituted the most frustrating period of my life, nor was I alone in my attitude. Regular soldiers all, we had spent our adult lives working and studying and training for this supreme moment and now it became increasingly obvious that we were shunted aside despite the most ingenious attempts and pathetic appeals directly to the Commandant to send us over there. Hope flickered in the autumn when Butler received orders to the States, but his efforts to have us recalled proved fruitless and it was only by the skin of his own teeth that he made it to France, there to be refused front-line duty.

We naturally carried on our duties, but with no great grace. A 1918 fitness report of mine reads under *General Temperament:* "Calm—irritable—forceful—active—bold—painstaking." Sunny Jim had become Cloudy Jim and didn't give a damn who knew it.

Having abandoned all hope I learned late in the summer of 1918, coincident with promotion to major, that I was being ordered home to take a replacement battalion to France. I quickly put my office in scrupulous order for whatever replacement showed up, then sat back to await the actual orders. They arrived in late October. I was turning over my job when the war ended.

Man's only refuge in such moments is personal philosophy. The big one, the war to end wars, had come and gone and I had missed it. This was a personal calamity of tremendous proportions, but there it was and wishing wasn't going to change a thing. In December new orders arrived—I sailed for America, where I was to become an instructor in the Officers Basic School at Quantico.

I had barely arrived in Quantico when the Basic School closed down and I was diverted to Headquarters, Marine Corps, in Washington. There my old commanding officer in Haiti, Percy Archer, persuaded me into General McCawley's quartermaster department, the bait being command of a depot scheduled to open in New York. After I had worked with Archer for about a month Secretary of the Navy Josephus Daniels vetoed the New York depot. Instead I went to the Marine Barracks, Portsmouth, Virginia, known then as the Norfolk Navy Yard.

Postwar confusion immediately claimed my days. Shortly after my arrival and without warning a Navy transport, *Hancock,* presented me with two thousand mattresses. I found a spare mess hall for them, then began writing letters on their behalf—they were still in the mess hall when I departed five months later. So in every other inch of space were the rifles and equipment which thousands of Marines returning from France dropped off on their way through this port.

A postwar economy cycle added to the confusion. My official correspondence consisted almost solely of requests for refurbished furniture, drapery, iceboxes and lampshades for quarters, or pleas for two or three truckloads of gravel or a few hundred pounds of cement. All this red tape made me think nostalgically of Haiti where I had accounted for over a million dollars' worth of equipment a year with a minimum of fuss. Still, I probably would have stuck out the tour but for one incident.

One day a dispatch from Headquarters directed me to go to the debarkation center to select and purchase eighteen horses needed for patrol duty at the Yorktown Ammunition Depot. A most co-operative Army veterinarian helped me in the task and I was pleased with the mounts, excepting one that the vet also was leery about. At his suggestion I took the horse with the understanding that I could swap it if trouble developed.

A few days after the horses arrived in Yorktown the one fellow did go lame. I traded him for another and thought no more about it. Then a letter from General McCawley asked how I could possibly have purchased a horse and traded it for another horse without filling out a fitness report and health record on the first horse.

That did it. All the while I had been dealing with mattresses and lampshades and lame horses, friends in Haiti kept me informed of their situation including the beginnings of a new Caco revolt. Learning of an opening in the Gendarmerie I went to Washington and persuaded Percy Archer to seek my release from General McCawley—no light task since this constituted the prima donna department of the Corps. For some reason, probably the lame horse, the good general acquiesced but since I had to get to Haiti immediately the problem of a Norfolk relief arose. To General McCawley's question of an interim relief I thought quickly: "Holland Smith is there and is perfectly capable of taking this duty." Though the general agreed, Holland never forgot my recommendation —several years passed before it became a joke with us.

When I returned to Haiti in July, 1919, the Caco pot was boiling over—the work of a fiery, French-educated Haitian named Charlemagne Massena Péralte. Having escaped from prison the previous year, Charlemagne subsequently raised a force varying between 2,000 and 5,000 and commenced raiding Gendarmerie outposts throughout north and central Haiti.

Fighting Charlemagne was a greatly expanded Gendarmerie headed by Marine Colonel Frederick ("Dopey") Wise who had won considerable fame commanding the 2d Battalion, 5th Marines, in France. His Port-au-Prince headquarters supervised a Department of the North under Colonel (Marine Major) James Meade and a Department of the South under Colonel (Marine Major) Walter Hill. Each department maintained divisions, each division districts and subdistricts down to small outposts. As a Gendarmerie colonel I commanded a division in the Department of the South with headquarters in Port-au-Prince.

An understrength Marine brigade supported the Gendarmerie. Commanded by Louis McCarty Little, soon succeeded by John Russell, the brigade spotted infantry companies throughout Haiti so that regular troops could come to the aid of Gendarmerie forces whenever necessary.

Despite these measures Charlemagne continued to prosper. By early October his impudence brought him with a good-sized force to a few miles north of Port-au-Prince, from where he demanded the surrender of Dartiguenave's government. When on October 6 his ultimatum was ignored, Charlemagne waited until nightfall and then marched on the capital. We were alerted and about 4:00 A.M. scrambled out to meet the enemy who had reached the center of town as far as the iron market.

With Colonel Hill commanding the gendarmes on the right and with a Marine detachment on our left we moved into a brisk fire fight that quickly pushed the Cacos from the town. Hill now turned the combined forces over to me and I ordered immediate pursuit. Once past the compound of the Sugar Central Company I divided the force, sending the Marines down the main road toward the sea while myself taking the gendarmes along the inboard side. Pushing hard we covered some 17 miles by afternoon. Suddenly we came on the enemy, attacked hard and fast—and took them by surprise, killing a number of them and capturing a great many weapons including a field gun. But most of the Cacos (who never wore uniforms) simply melted into the country-side. Charlemagne was among them.

Charlemagne's days, however, were growing short. The story of his capture, told in detail in numerous sources, emphasizes the worthiness of our Marine NCOs who were acting Gendarmerie officers. Captain H. H. Hanneken, a sergeant of Marines, concocted the plan to get Charlemagne.

Hanneken commanded the Grande Rivière district in Colonel Meade's Department of the North. One day a Haitian named Conzé pronounced himself dissatisfied with white rule and with two other Haitians, one a disgruntled gendarme, left Grande Rivière in favor of establishing a Caco band in the country. Supplied with money from Hanneken's own pocket, Conzé quickly attracted Charlemagne's attention and was made a "general" in the Caco "Army." Conzé next persuaded Charlemagne to attack Grand Rivière where, he reported, Hanneken was so weak and his forces so dispirited that victory was certain. Charlemagne fell for the plot and ordered an attack in force on the night of October 31.

So notified, Hanneken gained secret reinforcements from Colonel Meade, then with his executive officer, Lieutenant (Marine Corporal) William Button, and sixteen hand-picked gendarmes laid an ambush outside of town. To Hanneken's disappointment Charlemagne did not join the attack but waited some distance to the rear not far from Fort Capois.

There was nothing left but to go for it. Taking his small patrol Hanneken worked his way through six Caco outposts and finally confronted the rebel leader in his camp. Before the surprised Cacos could act, the patrol opened fire. Hanneken, an expert pistol shot, personally killed Charlemagne and brought the body back to Grande Rivière. From there it was taken to Cap Haitien and displayed publicly so that no one could doubt Charlemagne's demise.

Charlemagne's death willed the revolt to a lieutenant, Benoît Batraville, who operated mainly in central Haiti. Except for isolated actions, Batraville's activities did not greatly concern my command farther south. We rarely encountered Caco opposition, perhaps because we always traveled armed and with escort. As it turned out Benoît finally was killed in May of 1920 which ended this particular revolt.

Our intended reforms encountered enemies other than Cacos. An honest administration deprived some important Haitians of large sums of money heretofore stolen from the customhouses. Using our campaigns against the Cacos, including alleged brutality, these native dissidents succeeded in having an investigation made from Washington. Fortunately Major General John Lejeune, the new Commandant, and Brigadier General Smedley Butler got wind of this and secretly hurried down to inspect. Upon their return a senatorial team arrived from Washington to tour the better part of the island. At this time I was assistant commander and inspector of the Department of the South and personally escorted the senators through my area. My attitude, and I am sure the attitude of all Gendarmerie officers, was to hide nothing because we felt we had nothing to be ashamed of. The senators took testimony in various small villages and outlying districts. So confusing and contradictory were their findings that they returned with a great respect for our problems and a general belief that we were doing as good a job as possible.

The job was always difficult, usually frustrating. Nearly as great an enemy as either the Cacos or the local politicos was tradition. One day while inspecting a subdistrict I listened to a sergeant interview a boy of about fifteen charged with stealing goats. After the testimony of all concerned, I asked the lad why he had stolen the animals. In great astonishment he replied, "Why, my father stole goats and his father stole goats. It is quite customary in our family and that is all I know how to do." I gave him a lecture, made him return the goats, and put him on parole to the sergeant.

On another occasion I had received professional advice on improving the Haitian method of growing coffee, namely, to clear the bushes of undergrowth. Upon proposing this to a group of mountain farmers I was hotly informed that they were growing coffee in the way of their fathers and grandfathers, and theirs was the correct way. I told them that if they took a hectare of land and raised coffee *my* way and if the yield was smaller than the present one I would pay them the difference. They accepted the challenge and I instructed my district commander to see that they followed my rules. They did and they grew more coffee in that hectare than in any of the neighboring patches. No happy ending, however—this limited success in no way changed their methods.

In a sense our task formed a civil counterpart to the work

of Christian missionaries who were devoting their lives to these people. Although a great many Haitians became sincere Christians, many more paid mere lip service and continued with their voodoo rites and beliefs. Still we unquestionably made progress in those years and though it was very hard work—on occasion I rode thirteen to fourteen hours a day— it was also rewarding.

I was always glad to hit the trail, not only to fulfill official duties but also because I never failed to learn something new about the people and the country. But it also was pleasant to return to my family in Port-au-Prince where we enjoyed a delightful life. A large foreign colony centered around the American Club overlooking the beautiful harbor. In addition to a small diplomatic corps Haiti contained a number of American businessmen, civil servants and Navy and Marine officers. Our entertainments were simple enough, but alto- gether pleasant.

The duty also yielded numerous lessons. As division and later department commander I came to realize the importance of frequent inspections. If these are conducted properly, I know of nothing more beneficial to a command. The subor- dinate must be made to realize that no one is out to "get" him, but rather that an outside eye is often more observant than a local eye that sees the same perspective day in and day out. Then and later I preferred to avoid official channels whenever possible in inspection matters. On one occasion I reprimanded a district commander by informal, private letter. He replied with a very pained personal letter and again by personal letter I explained that these deficiencies had es- caped his notice and there would be no problem if he would rectify them. I heard no more from him. On my next tour of his area I was gratified to see it cleaned up as it had never been before—nor did hard feelings result from the exchange.

I think most of us profited from our long years in Haiti. Whether in the Gendarmerie or the brigade, Marines learned valuable lessons in jungle and guerrilla warfare. We learned many cunning and wily tricks the hard way, but we also in- vented many ourselves. Survival in the field often depended on quick thinking, always on self-reliance. I think it was more than accident that many of our future generals campaigned in Haiti, among them myself, Roy Geiger, Hal Turnage, Dea- con Upshur, John Marston, Jerry Thomas and Lewis Puller.

Puller, who was to become a master of combat patrols, received his schooling in the skirmishes and campaigns attendant upon tracking down Charlemagne and Batraville. He had come to us as a Marine sergeant, the victim of a postwar manpower cut that deprived him of a commission which he now obtained in the Gendarmerie. Walter Hill moved him up the command ladder quite rapidly and when I replaced Hill in command of Department of the South I brought him into Port-au-Prince as my adjutant. His performance here caused me to nominate him for the Officers Basic Course.

Lewis was rather headstrong at this time and that brought him trouble with the entrance examination. As I recall, he took exception to one of the mathematics instructors and handed in a blank paper on trigonometry. He of course failed. The next summer I was in Washington on leave and again arranged for him to be examined. This time he passed and eventually won a regular commission.

I was reminded of this years later when General Lejeune, then superintendent of the Virginia Military Institute, told me, "I believe that any cadet should be allowed one mistake without having it held against him." I felt the same way about young Puller and I believe that his subsequent career vindicated my decision. In Haiti he won the first of five Navy Crosses for valor and went on to become a lieutenant general —in other words, the second chance was good not only for Puller and the Corps but for his country.

Besides developing certain tactical innovations during those years we also pioneered in air techniques. On one occasion two of Roy Geiger's pilots loaded a small bomb in one of the old Jennys and dropped it on a Caco stronghold while simultaneously a ground force attacked. Roy also used his planes to deliver mail and various supplies to patrols. One of his pilots, Captain Francis Evans, rigged a transport plane with stretchers for air evacuation of wounded.

For all these reasons my long tours in Haiti remain among the most pleasant memories of my career. But by 1923 the Marine Corps itself was undergoing interesting evolutions. I thought I should get back to it, and when Smedley Butler suggested I come to Quantico I hastened to comply.

IV

Quantico-China-Washington: I

COMMANDED by Brigadier General Smedley Butler, the Marine post at Quantico was a beehive of activity when I reported aboard in 1923. Thanks to John A. Lejeune, Commandant since 1920, it housed the flourishing Marine Corps Schools consisting of a Field Officers Course, a Company Officers Course, and a Basic Course. In addition to teaching standard curriculums, instructors were worrying about the problems of what years later would be called the amphibious assault.

Lejeune's interest in amphibious development stemmed in part from the Versailles Treaty, which mandated the formerly held German islands in the Pacific to Japan. Both Navy and Marine planners now began to think in terms of a Pacific war against Japan. In 1921 one of Lejeune's most brilliant planners, Lieutenant Colonel Earl ("Pete") Ellis, wrote a remarkable 30,000-word thesis on the subject. He presciently began:

> Japan is a World Power and her army and navy will doubtless be up to date as to training and materiel. Considering our consistent policy of nonaggression, she will probably initiate the war; which will indicate that, in her own mind, she believes that, considering her natural defensive position, she has sufficient military strength to defeat our fleet.

In his blueprint for the future Pete wrote:

> In order to impose our will upon Japan, it will be necessary for us to project our fleet and land forces across the Pacific and wage war in Japanese waters. To effect this requires that we have sufficient bases to support the fleet, both during its projection and afterwards.

Although Ellis lost his life in the spring of 1923 while conducting an espionage mission in the Pacific, his thinking left its mark on the small Quantico staff. Their first discussions and explorations were more groping than substantial, but it was precisely from them that the Marine Corps exists as we know it today.

On the practical side, Butler commanded a newly organized East Coast Expeditionary Force consisting of the 5th Marine Regiment and the 10th Marine Artillery Regiment. Colonel Hal Snyder commanded the 5th Marines in which I served for a short period as executive officer of one battalion before moving up to command the 1st Battalion.

At first we did precious little soldiering. One of General Butler's major missions was to beautify this post—"turn it into the show place of the Corps." Undeterred by such a minor inconvenience as lack of money, Butler since 1920 had turned to with his customary vigor. His ambitions were endless and included a football stadium which, since he never did things halfway, was to be "the world's largest stadium." He somehow had talked the local railroad into donating cement, rails and other material necessary to begin construction. As he assured the Commandant, his Marines could easily do the work.

Many are the stories told about this project which Butler personally supervised. One day he came on three idle bandsmen who told him they could not work because it might damage their hands. "I understand and agree," Butler said. "But henceforth if a single man is working on this stadium there will be a band playing music to improve his morale." And there was.

On another occasion Butler encountered a gunnery sergeant watching some other Marines at work. "What are you doing?" he asked him.

"I'm supervising the work."

General Butler stared at him a moment. "You *were* supervising, Private."

My engineering forays in Nicaragua soon involved me in this task, an immense one since we had to excavate a large quantity of earth with old-fashioned steam shovels. Together with about 150 men from my battalion we worked some eighty days on the stadium (not destined to be completed until after World War II). A fitness report of mine detailed our accomplishment:

> [We] moved 19,307 cubic yards of earth. 200 excavations for concrete pillars were dug. 197 pillars were poured. 30 rails were laid. 381 concrete slabs were placed. Concrete footer was poured for all stone walls laid this year. Grass seed was planted over the sanded field. And field was leveled from side to base wall . . .

Annual autumn maneuvers interrupted this effort. Thanks to the Lejeune-Butler credo of survival by keeping Marines in the news, these maneuvers, one of Butler's brainstorms, wound up with the re-enactment of certain Civil War battles on the original ground, a military pageant attended by President Harding and a large entourage of important persons. In 1921 Butler's Marines fought the battle of the Wilderness in Virginia, in 1922 they re-enacted Pickett's Charge at Gettysburg. In 1923 was scheduled the battle of New Market in the Shenandoah Valley, the Confederate Army being a group of V.M.I. cadets and, because of my Virginian roots, the 1st Battalion, 5th Marines.

In late August our expeditionary force spilled out of Quantico to begin the march to the Valley, a 30-day effort of which twenty-eight days featured a driving, cold rain. Time and again the hard-rubber tires of the old Liberty trucks broke through clay road surfaces with all hands working late into the night to free them. One night, having reined in at the side of the road to see if my battalion was closed up, I heard a voice growl, "Just to think of it—that my grandfather fought four and one-half years to keep this miserable state in the Union."

Gibes from my fellow officers about Virginia roads and weather fell freely in the nightly mess tent. "We don't call this part of the state Virginia," I told them. "This is chincapin country. Virginia begins when we reach Cobham." I knew that at Cobham we would encounter surfaced roads which would end the bulk of our troubles.

Conditions did improve, at least until we reached the summit of the Blue Ridge Mountains where a C.&O. railroad trestle crossed the road. We now discovered that a vertical boiler, a huge monstrosity being hauled solely to provide hot water for the important guests, stood about two inches too high to pass under the trestle. General Butler cantered up to take the problem under consideration. Soon a host of engineers and senior officers were furrowing brows, each of their many suggestions rejected for one reason or another. Finally a tobacco-chewing corporal of mine spat a great wad of juice on the road and said loudly enough for everyone to hear, "Why the hell don't they let the air out of the tires?" This, the perfect solution, proved once again that all brains are not found in brass.

Down in the Valley we conducted regular field exercises prior to the main event. At this time aviation played an integral part in our maneuvers. I had always been interested in the air arm—my thesis at the School of Application in 1909, "Aviation, The Cavalry of the Future," set forth my youthful thinking on the subject and incidentally was marked "unsatisfactory." But Haitian operations proved the importance of aviation, which though primitive continued its military development.

For these services Butler attached a plane to my battalion for both observation and communication purposes. Captain Arthur Paige, a splendid pilot, and I rigged the first air-to-ground pickup of my experience. We set up two poles to support a weighted cord holding a field message. Paige then flew over, caught up the cord and hoisted the message to the cockpit, delivering it to General Butler at brigade headquarters.

For the battle of New Market my battalion became the 68th Virginia Regiment. To liven up the show we issued small black powder bombs whose smoke was supposed to represent cannon fire. I duly led my troops onto the field of battle. A moment later, whether through inadvertence or purpose I don't know, one of these bombs went off under my horse—I very nearly captured the first northern battery by myself.

After a very successful show I was marching my battalion back to camp when we pulled over to let some cars carrying Confederate veterans pass. From one of these an old gentleman leaned out and called to me, "Son, that was a good fight. You did it almost as well as we did." I was about to thank him when one of his comrades said, "You know you're a liar, Jack—they did it a damn sight better."

From New Market we marched back to Washington for presidential review, then watched our football team win a good game over Georgetown, a satisfactory conclusion to a pleasant experience. This was the last but one of the famous re-enactments and I was particularly glad to have participated.

After an interim assignment as post inspector I took over the athletic and morale billet, a challenging job because of our impressive record of football victories for the past several years.

We boasted quite a lineup at this time. Hugo Besdeck of Penn State was our consulting coach, we had a backfield coach from Princeton, and the famous Johnny Beckett coached line. Swede Larson, who invented the roving back technique for Navy, centered a team that at one time or another included Frank Goettge, formerly of Ohio State, Johnny Beckett from Oregon, Harry Liversedge, formerly of California, Sergeant Henry from the ranks of the Marine Corps, Zeke Bailey from Maryland, and Johnny Groves, the famous dropkicker who on a wet field against Lafayette kicked a 42-yard field goal three minutes before the final gun to give us a 3-0 victory.

We played our games away from Quantico, the schedule including Georgetown, Vanderbilt, Michigan State and other conference teams. I talked right hard to get games because, although we filled the college stadiums, we also on occasion hurt the college teams for later conference games. The effort was well worthwhile, however, because we received excellent publicity besides making enough money to support numerous other morale-building activities for the Quantico troops.

Football having gone over so well, I arranged that spring for such college baseball teams as Holy Cross, the University of Vermont, Brown and Lafayette to stop at Quantico to play exhibition games on their way south for spring practice. This gave us a solid afternoon schedule for April and May; we then picked up the southern teams such as V.M.I. and the University of Virginia who were headed north. It was about the cheapest troop entertainment possible because we paid an average $150 a game plus room and board. The men loved it, and I was pleased to have worked it out.

By this time Smedley Butler had temporarily left the Corps

to serve as commissioner of public safety in Philadelphia. I was working now for Major General Eli K. Cole under whom I had made such a poor record at the School of Application. However, the wheel turned full circle: he gave me a series of outstanding fitness reports and, in the autumn of 1925, approved my request to attend Field Officers School. We remained close friends until his death in 1929.

The Field Officers School comprised an eight-month course taught by an earnest and well-balanced group of instructors who knew their jobs. The curriculum reflected the transitory air of the day—we were trying to project ourselves away from the trench warfare of World War I into a war of movement but were not yet ready for amphibious studies. Instead, we concentrated on conventional land strategy, weapons and tactics, the latter proving most valuable to me. I worked very hard during these months and managed to graduate second in the class.

General Cole now decided to send me to the Army's Command and General Staff School at Fort Leavenworth. My orders were in the mill when one day Smedley Butler telephoned. He had finished his Philadelphia job and was back in the Corps commanding Marine Barracks, San Diego. Without offering details he wondered if he could persuade me to forgo a new assignment and come out as his operations officer. He made it clear that he needed me, but said he would request me only if I wished to come. Much as I wanted to go to Leavenworth I of course agreed and within a week was headed west.

General Butler wanted me primarily for moral support. His experiences in Philadelphia had made him a prohibitionist, and a considerable portion of the public (and the Corps) criticized him for it. Prohibitionist or not, when he went to the Marine Barracks at San Diego and found open bootlegging and other questionable activities he clamped down hard. By depriving certain influential citizens of their illegal income he soon became a popular press target ideally suited for the villain's role in the following regrettable incident.

Shortly before I arrived in San Diego a senior Marine officer known to me from Haiti gave a dinner party followed by a dance at the Coronado Hotel. This officer discourteously served drinks in his home even though he knew that his senior guest, General Butler, disapproved. When Butler arrived the host pressed a drink on him, which he refused.

That was all right but later at the dance when the host, now very intoxicated, disgraced his uniform, Butler ordered him escorted from the premises. The next day, with the full concurrence of the Navy district commander, Rear Admiral Robertson, he preferred a court-martial charge—indeed the admiral told Butler that if he did not so charge him he, the admiral, would.

Local papers and certain national papers picked up the story, in most cases telling a lopsided anti-Butler version. The court-martial found the officer guilty and sentenced him to a loss of a few numbers in grade. He was transferred to San Francisco and lost his life a few months later in an automobile accident, thus reviving the story.

All of this combined with the violent political maelstrom of his Philadelphia service left General Butler tired and depressed. Part of the trouble, I believe, stemmed from his discovery both in Philadelphia and in San Diego that vested private interests could form a more solidly entrenched enemy than a bunch of rebels in a Haitian stronghold. From the black-and-white challenge presented by the banana wars he had come up against the gray challenge of public-versus-private interests and did not know how to cope—an ignorance that hurt him as much as the experience infuriated him.

But part of the trouble also stemmed from his commanding a brigade that consisted of the understrength 4th Marine Regiment, altogether a force of only some 600 men quite adequately commanded by the regimental colonel. Even his beautification program—in this case turning everyone to planting thousands of trees on the barren flats of the base—failed to provide sufficient outlet for his fantastic energy. A man of action, Smedley Butler was miserable without it. Fortunately that autumn we got some action—and it proved the necessary anodyne for my old friend.

Back in 1921 a series of mail robberies had finally caused the Postmaster General to ask the President for Marine mail guards. With 2,300 Marines on the job the robberies immediately ceased and the crisis passed. Now in October, 1926, the mail robberies again began. This time the Postmaster General promptly asked for and received 2,500 Marines, the bulk of them formed into the Eastern Mail Guards commanded by Logan Feland at Quantico with the remainder —nearly the entire 4th Regiment—forming the Western Mail

Guards commanded by Smedley Butler with headquarters in San Francisco. I accompanied Butler as his operations officer with additional duties as battalion commander.

Our mission was to furnish armed guards both in mail cars hauling large money shipments and in certain post offices concerned with handling large sums of money. Our routes included all the western states as far east as North Dakota, Colorado, and El Paso, Texas, some 40,000 miles of railroads plus 28 major post offices. We armed our people with .45 automatic pistols, 12-gauge riot shotguns, and Thompson submachine guns. We publicized both their armament and Butler's personal orders, those once given by Spartan mothers to their sons: "Come back with your shields or upon them."

The bandits disappeared as rapidly as they had struck and never did return. In five months only one incident occurred: years before, some bandits had held up a train at the mouth of a tunnel in Oregon. Through coincidence one of our trains stopped in this precise place. After some delay the government mail clerk opened his door to see what was going on. As he did so one of the train's crewmen hollered, "Hands up." Simultaneously a riot gun went off and the man's head would have gone off with it had the clerk not hit the barrel into the air. That ended all practical jokes.

The guard duty earned the Corps many new friends in the western states. In my frequent tours of inspection I was particularly impressed at the attitude of average townsfolk toward the Marines. More than once our men were practically dragged off the streets into private homes and clubs where they received every possible courtesy and, I am pleased to say, replied in kind. Once the crisis ended Postmaster General New cited us:

> Efficiency and courtesy were combined to a degree that could not but evoke a wholesome respect for the Marine Corps, that fine arm of the service which by reason of its training may be utilized in any character of emergency.

Toward the end of the emergency I was recalled to San Diego to take command of the newly organized 3d Battalion, 4th Marines, and equip it for expeditionary duty in

Nicaragua, where rebels again were raising the devil. We had stacked seabags under the arcade at San Diego and were waiting to board ship when new orders canceled the move. Instead of Nicaragua we sailed for China, also a country of crisis.

Colonel Charles ("Jumbo") Hill commanded the understrength 4th Marine Regiment consisting of Major Secor's 1st Battalion and my 3d Battalion. Among the officers were some youngsters destined to be heard from in the following decades: Tommy Watson, Roy Hunt, Evans Carlson, Ray Robinson, Harry Liversedge, Ran Pate and Bob Pepper. About 1,200 in all, we sailed on the old *Chaumont,* reaching the China coast in late February, 1927. We followed the muddy Yangtze River up to the Whangpoo, then worked slowly up its narrow waters pockmarked by myriad native junks bearing wares to Shanghai markets. Some five miles from Shanghai we spotted the silver Standard Oil Company tanks. We moored here to live aboard ship and exercise the troops in the company compound. From here small boats could haul us to the city in case we had to carry out our mission of protecting the lives and property of Americans within the International Settlement of Shanghai.

Dating from the Opium War of 1842, which gave England, France and America trading concessions, the International Settlement steadily attracted other nations until in 1927 it comprised about half of Shanghai, a city of 3,000,000. Britain and Japan dominated the large foreign colony in which some 1,800 Americans constituted the least stake. Mostly businessmen, all foreigners lived very well and together with their families and servants formed one of this century's most unique monuments to international imperialism.

Naturally the Chinese resented this foreign domination as they did other international exploitation. In 1900 fanatical Chinese patriots had tried to drive out the foreigners during the Boxer Rebellion, an uprising put down by an international relief force. Now, a quarter of a century later, nationalism again was running rampant, this time inspired by Sun Yat-sen's revolutionary party, which included a Nationalist army commanded by Chiang Kai-shek. Chiang intended to use it to consolidate all of China into a modern state, free from foreign domination.

Beginning in the south Chiang's forces from 1926 advanced steadily northward. Such was the threat that in January 1927, the American minister, Mr. MacMurray, asked that Marines be landed.

We were not alone. Soon after our arrival a provisional battalion of Marines arrived from Guam and the Philippines. A large force of British including the famed Coldstream Guards were on hand as were considerable French, Italian and Japanese forces.

Owing to the touchy situation, we remained uncomfortably aboard *Chaumont* until late March when the Nationalist vanguard reached the southern outskirts of Shanghai. We landed at once, marched up Bubbling Well Road, and manned posts in the eastern and western areas of the Settlement. From there we sent out patrols without incident. British forces, however, mixed it up as did Communist, White Russian and Nationalist units.

So serious was the situation that Mr. MacMurray appealed to Washington for reinforcements. While a regiment was being scratched up from Quantico, Smedley Butler with a small headquarters sailed from San Diego. During the height of the crisis the senior commander, Major General John Duncan, a splendid British officer, asked us to support him at Markham Road Bridge. Although we were not participating in the perimeter defense manned by other foreign troops, Colonel Hill ordered me to move a small force to this area. The movement completed, my executive officer, Captain Roy Hunt, and I were standing idly by when General Duncan drove up to ask why in the world we were suffering the wind and rain. The upshot of it was that Hunt and I were treated to a most lavish dinner. The crisis proved no match for British aplomb—we spent the evening talking about cotton growing in the American South.

As it turned out, Chiang wasn't as worried about fighting us as he was the local Communists, a series of actions from which we remained carefully aloof. Butler arrived at the end of March, relieved me of battalion command, and moved me to brigade as operations officer. Despite cautionary orders from Washington, we now joined the other international forces in the perimeter defense and also stepped up patrolling by putting troops in armed trucks, all without noteworthy incident.

Having beaten the local Communists, Chiang decided in

May to march north. We were now reinforced by the 6th Marine Regiment including artillery and air units and Butler, anticipating Chiang, sent me to reconnoiter a landing in Tientsin. In early June he split the brigade, bringing the 6th Marines (reinforced) north on the old transport *Henderson,* a neat maneuver that put us a long jump ahead of the Nationalist army.

At this time the United States Army's 15th Regiment garrisoned Tientsin. Many years later one of the soldiers, Charles Finney, described the landing in his book, *The Old China Hands* (Doubleday, 1961):

> A tug brought up the first three lighters of Marines and lodged them, with much banging and clattering, against the concrete rim of the Bund. Lines were thrown ashore and made fast. The lighters were aswarm with young Americans in forest-green uniforms, very dirty, very disheveled. Each man wore a steel helmet and carried a pack, a horseshoe-shaped blanket roll, a Springfield rifle with bayonet fixed, a cartridge belt jammed with shiny .30-06 ammunition clips and an extra bandolier of cartridges over his shoulder. . . . Out of the bowls of their lighters—which had been previously used for transporting coal, and hence were rather sooty—the landing parties hoisted machine guns, Stokes mortars, and 27 mm. [*sic*] howitzers. They did it quickly, efficiently, seemingly without effort, as do well-trained teams. They brought out sandbags; and in something like ten minutes they threw up a horseshoe-shaped barricade, facing the city and sealing off their portion of the Bund. This barricade bristled with weapons. . . . The operation reminded me of a circus's arrival by wagonload, at its show grounds. It seemed at first glance to be nothing but confusion compounded. But it wasn't that at all. It was a well-planned procedure, economically and beautifully executed. Even our critical officers began to be impressed.

Busy as I was, I found this a very educational experience. I was working for one of the sternest disciplinarians in the Corps, Colonel E. B. Miller, who was Butler's chief of staff. A tall, well-built man, Miller already held a reputation from Marine Corps Schools as a pioneer thinker and planner in the embryonic amphibious doctrine. A graduate of Leavenworth, he was a learned, well-balanced thinker who possessed tremendous personal integrity and never hesitated to disagree with Butler, who could be as impetuous as he was imaginative. The colonel was a crusty old devil but he worked hard to teach younger officers what he knew, which was a lot. We had only just landed in Tientsin when he called me in and said, "Vandegrift, a good commander looks ahead. You don't know and I don't know and General Butler doesn't know what is going to happen here. You will therefore prepare a secret plan of evacuation in case it comes to that."

It didn't come to that. We quickly settled down to a garrison routine. Since we were on show twenty-four hours a day to both the Chinese civil population and foreign military forces, General Butler soon turned us into a spit-and-polish outfit. We nickel-plated bayonets, we removed the camouflage from our flat World War I helmets and painted them olive green with a lacquer finish visible about ten miles away, we blancoed leggings and even burnished the eyelets. Important visitors crowded in on us, which meant numerous reviews and parades, not a simple matter in a crowded city particularly for units billeted some miles outside town.

One of these was the artillery regiment whose commanding officer was a genial old colonel, rather stout and not much on walking. To make parade formation he relied on his little Ford which deposited him at the head of his troops two or three blocks from the reviewing stand. Having swaggered past the visitors he was met a block farther on and driven back to camp—mission accomplished.

On the more serious side General Butler set up a rigorous field training schedule which, as always, concentrated on small units. He was a real bug on this and on several occasions remarked to me, "Always remember, James, a regiment that doesn't train from the bottom up isn't a trained regiment."

Besides training, I had my hands full developing various plans which included route reconnaissance and liaison with our various scattered units. General Butler often took me to Peking to visit our Legation Guard, a force of nearly battalion size at first commanded by Louis McCarty Little, later by Colonel Thomas Holcomb, with whom we had to work out plans in case the Nationalists decided to besiege Peking.

To keep tabs on Chiang Kai-shek's movements—our basic mission— we relied on an aviation unit commanded by a fine pilot and gentleman, Tommy Turner, whose premature death a few years later proved a tragic loss to military aviation. Every morning and evening Tommy's pilots, based at the euphoniously named village, Hsin Ho on the Hei Ho, flew their Jennys over Chiang's army moving up from the south and Marshal Chang Tso-lin's army moving west to the Great Wall.

On one of these reconnaissance hops I was flying with an old friend and pioneer pilot, Captain "Nuts" Moore. Returning from a long flight I gave in to the cold and wind and dozed off. I awakened upside down in the middle of a loop. When we straightened out Nuts passed back a note: "I thought you should stay awake."

Moore later involved both of us in an incident that could have been serious. Tommy Turner had proudly told me of the acrobatic work being done by his fliers and asked if they could show off at one of the Tientsin reviews. Butler turned down the idea, but I argued that it would be good for aviation morale. Very reluctantly he gave in.

Came the great day. After a normal fly-by, Moore led the squadron into acrobatics. He stunted beautifully, then put his plane into a steep dive toward the parade ground. Coming out of it he lost one wing, then another. When his body shot from the plane the crowd gasped. Butler turned on me, shook his fist in my face and yelled, "Now see what the hell you have done." I suppose the happiest moment of my China tour came when I saw Nuts floating down in a parachute. Being a fearful ham himself he worked the shroud lines to land himself in front of the grandstand meanwhile shouting, "Whoopee, whoopee."

We suffered another serious incident with aircraft, this one somewhat indicative of the future. During a ground maneuver outside Tientsin we saw Japanese planes observing us. That evening I contacted my Japanese counterpart, told him that General Butler was displeased and would he please fly his planes somewhere else. When they appeared the next day I was ready. Upon receipt of a prearranged signal, Turner scrambled our planes. They came in with the sun behind them, screamed down on the unsuspecting Jap formation, which broke and ran. We never saw them again.

Soon after this I experienced more of the Japanese when I was ordered to Tokyo as observer of the annual Grand Army maneuvers. In the event, there was precious little to observe but I did gain a good idea of their regimental formations and tactics and was extremely impressed with their training. They received and looked after us very well, just as in Tientsin the Japanese officers proved most courteous and correct in their social relations with us.

I returned from Tokyo in time for Christmas of 1927. We were all looking forward to a festive holiday when on Christmas Eve a fire broke out in the Standard Oil plant across the river. Turning out every Marine, we set up a human chain to clear the threatened warehouses of their five-gallon tins of gasoline and kerosene. Simultaneously our engineers built a cofferdam which prevented the burning fuel from escaping into the Hei Ho River where it would have engulfed the hundreds of junks and larger craft and probably spread to the tinderbox city itself.

After working through the freezing night we brought the fierce blaze under control late on Christmas Day, a signal victory which we celebrated by falling into our bunks, filthy clothes and all. The experience made us particularly close friends with the Standard Oil representatives, who donated $10,000 toward furnishing a new recreation hall for the troops besides supplying a new uniform to each officer and man who had fought the fire.

Chiang Kai-shek's forces did not really worry us until the spring of 1928 when his vanguard army showed up in the South. This belonged to Feng Yu-hsiang, the famous "Christian general" who baptized his troops en masse (with fire hoses) and had them sing hymns each night before retiring. Butler sent me out to meet him and explain just exactly what he, Butler, had in mind for the conduct of Feng's troops.

I rode south in an open touring car accompanied by an interpreter and a sergeant and, novel at the time, an air escort which never let me out of sight. Some 30 miles south of Tientsin we stopped in front of the Chinese lines where a young general, Chang Wan Ching, met and escorted me to Feng's tent. Feng, a tall, lean Chinese, received me politely, served tea and listened attentively as I explained what portion of Tientsin was off limits to his forces. Since he outnumbered us about 20 to 1, I was delighted when he agreed to Butler's ukase. He further promised to notify me upon leaving his present billet and to tell me the route he would take to the Chinese portion of Tientsin. As it turned out he was good for his word.

For a Christian general, Feng proved an anomaly. As was the custom with Chinese forces, plainclothes agents preceded the main forces into the city. These men, generally cruel, plundered at will and treated the Chinese folk very harshly.

Soon after Feng's advance, I learned that some of his agents were persecuting the natives in a small village close to one of our defense areas. After confirming the report I hastened to Feng's headquarters. Again he received me most courteously, explained that such acts were contrary to his orders, and promised to deal with the offenders if General Butler would let troops transit our area. Butler gave permission by telephone and I accompanied a platoon to the trouble spot. We caught the looters redhanded. Before I could say anything the Chinese platoon leader lined six of them up and beheaded them, an example to anyone else so tempted. The rest of them he marched back to the Chinese city, lined them against a wall and had them shot.

To our relief Feng wanted peace as badly as we. That summer and autumn, which Chiang Kai-shek spent in consolidating his power in North China, passed without serious incident for us. Our mission was now largely accomplished. In September our first reduction of force began and I sailed for America.

Back in Washington I was ordered to duty with the Federal Co-ordinating Service housed in the old Interior Building. I was a little miffed since I felt that recent duty as operations officer of the largest Marine force since World War I entitled me to a rather more interesting assignment. In answer to my complaint the detail officer said, "General Lejeune picked you for this job. If you don't want it, go in and tell him." That took care of that.

I am glad it did because this independent duty formed one of the most interesting tours of my career. The Co-ordinating Service owed its existence to Mr. Dawes' vice-presidency. Consisting of some fourteen Army, Navy and Marine Corps officers plus engineers from the Bureau of Standards, the Committee was supposed to co-ordinate the material requirements of the various branches of government, thus preventing duplication.

I took charge of all surplus property from World War I plus any property declared surplus by various government departments. I soon learned that if you were giving somebody something you were performing a great service, but when you took something away you performed a great disservice.

I also learned how difficult it was to hold down expenditures. Late in my tour the National Park Service forwarded a requisition for 5,000 double-bit axes for the embryonic CCC program. In turn I offered single-bit axes of which we had 30,000 on hand. Remarking that no forester could use a single-bit ax, the procurement agent refused my offer and sent out specifications for competitive bids. I immediately informed Director of the Budget Louis Douglas, a perfectly splendid and very intelligent gentleman. Logically supposing that CCC recruits could not be considered foresters and could at least learn with single-bit axes, Mr. Douglas had me warn the offending official that if he bought even one double-bit ax he would pay for it with his own money. The episode so amused one of my associates, Captain Walter Bedell Smith, who later became Eisenhower's chief of staff, that forever after he called me the "Ax Man."

After the turbulence of recent years the quiet routine of the Co-ordinating Committee came as a welcome interlude. So did the opportunity to meet and work with such interesting people as Sanford Bates, director of Bureau of Prisons, and Dr. Hugh Cumming, the surgeon general of the Public Health Service, both of whom were kind enough to commend my services. Daily contacts with these and other public officials provided my first real insight into the complexity of national government and its enormous challenge to those charged with its functioning.

During my nearly four years with the Co-ordinating Committee several important developments occurred in the Marine Corps, one of them providing the only personal black cloud of the period. In 1929 General Lejeune retired after eight impressive years in office. His brilliant successor, Major General Wendell ("Buck") Neville, died only a year or so later. Normally the next senior general, Smedley Butler, would have become commandant. But Butler had suffered some run-ins with the Administration and with President

Hoover (with whom reportedly he had crossed swords at Tientsin in 1900). Hoover now appointed the quiet, elderly Ben Fuller.

The appointment nearly broke Butler's heart, but worse was to come. When illustrating a point in a speech that he believed to be off the record, Butler referred to Mussolini as a hit-and-run driver. Unknown to Butler the audience included an Italian diplomat who wasted little time in making a formal complaint. The ensuing international incident brought down President Hoover's wrath: General Butler, holder of two Medals of Honor and numerous other important decorations, was ordered to stand trial by general court-martial.

Ably represented by Henry Leonard (under whom I had served twenty years earlier at Portsmouth) the Butler case brought such strong public support on his behalf that an embarrassed Administration dropped the charges. But all this proved too much for my old friend and mentor. In late 1931 he retired from the Corps—surely one of the most colorful figures in any military service, and certainly one of the major influences in my own life.

V

Quantico-China-Washington: II

UPON reporting to Quantico in the summer of 1933 I returned to a changed and changing Marine Corps. A long-delayed building program had given Quantico new quarters, brick dormitories and even an airfield. It was still the dual home of the Marine Corps Schools and the East Coast Expeditionary Force, the latter commanded by Brigadier General Charles H. Lyman, to whom I reported as personnel officer or F-1.

General Lyman stood over six feet. An intelligent, courteous, and immaculately dressed general, he was one of the most handsome officers in the Corps. He also possessed several idiosyncrasies, one of which centered on haircuts. In his early days he carried a small ruler and if a head of hair rose beyond its dimensions the owner suffered along with the company commander and company barber. The troops for this reason reversed his initials to come out with "Haircut Charlie." He rightfully deplored Marines walking about with their hands in their pockets—if he caught this the Marine had his pockets stitched together.

Lyman ran a tight, well-disciplined force consisting of two understrength infantry regiments, an artillery regiment, engineers and air. Although understrength it was a splendid force to serve in at the time because it reflected the practical application of the new amphibious theories being worked out in the neighboring Marine Corps Schools.

Two years earlier Charles Barrett, Pedro del Valle and a young naval officer, Walter Ansel, had written a treatise called *Landing Operations*. Colonel Buttrick and Colonel E. B. Miller, my chief of staff in China, were now polishing this effort into a definitive manual, a task aided that autumn by General Berkeley and General Russell, soon to become comman-

77

dant, who suspended classroom work at the Schools in favor of committee work on the new manual.

Some very able officers participated in this scrutinizing process which brought arguments hot and heavy to the normally placid Quantico atmosphere. One of these centered on Colonel Miller's desire to abolish the regiment in favor of the British organization of four battalions to a brigade—an idea that I am glad to say was disapproved.

During this period I served additional duty as liaison officer between Quantico and Headquarters in Washington where I worked closely with the operations officer, Stover Keyser. Late that year the over-all effort resulted in a *Tentative Manual of Landing Operations,* scarcely a finished product but one from which a finished product would result in a few years. Upon approving the new manual General Russell also persuaded the Secretary of the Navy to change the designation of East and West Coast Expeditionary Forces to a single title: Fleet Marine Force.

We exercised some of the new concepts in early 1934 during Caribbean maneuvers. Along with other members of the Force staff I went down to Panama where we met the fleet coming from the west coast. I had wondered just how the Navy would react to our plans. At that time a good many naval officers regarded our amphibious ambitions as a supreme nuisance and did not hesitate to tell us so.

My worries vanished when Admiral Horne, commander in chief of the fleet, delivered a brilliant exposition stressing the importance of timing to the amphibious landings of the future. Not only did we have to co-ordinate the landing boats, he told the assembled officers, but perfect co-ordination of naval gunfire and air support was vital if an amphibious assault was to succeed. I have always thought that much of Horne's remarkable insight came from the influence of Lieutenant Colonel Julian Smith, assigned to the admiral's staff to explain what we were trying to do on this exercise.

The actual landing on Culebra Island included such artificialities as simulated naval gunfire and air support, but landing boats were lowered, they did rendezvous and they did cross a line of departure and maintain formations into the beach. We did not exercise logistics nor did the battleships even remain for the final critique; our radios proved completely unsatisfactory and we did not land our small tanks because the landing boats could not carry them. But we accomplished our primary mission of conducting a more or less co-ordinated amphibious landing. In so doing we drew many healthy remarks from ranking naval officers who in some cases reversed previous convictions. Henceforth the amphibious operation remained an integral part of naval operations, and this was General Russell's primary bequest to his Corps.

He also achieved a long overdue reform by instituting promotion by selection. Many indignant screams accompanied the passage of this law which finally cleared away a cord or two of deadwood, permitting in turn long-delayed promotions, particularly of juniors. In 1934 after fourteen years a major I became a lieutenant colonel. Once again I requested a service school, this time the Naval War College. But now my friend and classmate at the Field Officers School, Colonel P. M. Rixey, asked for me as his executive officer at the Legation Guard in Peking. Shortly after my son Archer graduated from V.M.I., Mrs. Vandegrift and I sailed for China.

Beginning in 1905 a Marine guard served in Peking, once the traditional home of Chinese emperors who ruled from the Forbidden City and now the teeming capital of North China. In the autumn of 1935 our unit consisted of a staff, three guard companies and a mounted detachment, something over 500 Marines.

After a pleasant journey including a tourist's stopover in Japan we were met at Chien Men station by Colonel Rixey, his staff, and the Marine band, a pleasant tradition of the China station. A tall, lean man who held himself ramrod straight and faced the coldest Peking weather sans overcoat, Rixey was one of the most gracious officers in the Corps. Having been friends for years we required little time to learn each other's ways, which was fortunate since almost immediately after my arrival our detachment surgeon, Captain Shepherd, United States Navy, ordered him to Peitaiho to recuperate from a bad malaria attack. Our operations officer, Major Graves ("Bobbie") Erskine, was a paragon of efficiency who soon filled me in on the mysteries of life in Peking.

Answering to Mr. Nelson Johnson, the American ambassador, we held a primary mission of protecting the lives and property of American citizens, both diplomats and businessmen, in Peking. Besides furnishing embassy guards we stood ready to carry out numerous emergency plans, each of which was carefully and regularly rehearsed.

The recent upheavals in China coupled with current Japanese ambitions in the North meant a particularly tricky situation for us. I outlined this in a letter to my old friend, Charlie ("Spig") Price:

I believe on my last visit to your house [in Quantico] we discussed the question of the absorption of the Northern Provinces by Japan. It is taking place a little more rapidly than we at that time thought possible. This situation seems to subdivide itself into the following phases:

(a) Japan to exert pressure to assure that only such Chinese officials be appointed as are not only favorable to them but who will be mere puppets in carrying out the will of the Japanese advisers.

(b) To work for an autonomous state of the five Northern Provinces, whose officials will be under the supervision of Japanese.

(c) To declare the five Northern Provinces independent of Nanking and favor a union with Manchukuo.

You can readily see that one step leads to another as a natural sequence. They have been working under (a) for the past few months and have found it unsatisfactory from the Japanese viewpoint. They are at the present writing attempting to form the autonomous state. Yesterday it appeared as though the announcement would be made today. Today there has been a setback. The cause of this could be one of many reasons and to set them forth would make you read through a voluminous intelligence report. Suffice to say that I believe that in the near future it will occur, unless international pressure is such as to prevent it.

Subdivision (c) will be a natural sequel and will follow, but I believed at a later date. To occupy North China as they have Manchuria would put Japan further in the red financially and take a greater military force than they want to throw into that area without endangering their present relation to the Soviet menace in their rear. If for the time being they can accomplish the same object by having North China "voluntarily" establish an autonomous state completely under their dominance they will be far better off. No matter how little one may think of the League, and how little we believe Japan fears action by it, nevertheless the minute they come south of the Wall with troops they become the aggressor and the moral effect, especially in our own country, would be great. How the setting up of this state will affect our status is a question, but I believe it will be an added impetus for our removal . . . everyone seems to agree that should Japan take over . . . and bring Pu Yi down here as Emperor of the North, uniting these provinces with Manchukuo, our situation here will be untenable and we will have to move out.

Neither were we blind to the immense problems confronting Chiang Kai-shek. Shortly after the turn of the year I wrote General Lyman back in Quantico:

> I went to a most interesting review of General Sung's Army on New Year's Day, there being some ten thousand men of all arms in the review. The men in the ranks appeared well drilled, fairly well equipped, and sturdy (they having stood out on the wind-swept plains of Peiping from daylight until ten o'clock with the thermometer hovering around nine above zero, and in wind whistling down from the Western Hills). I couldn't help but think how very unpleasant this outfit and several more like it could make it for our brown friends across the way if properly led and not sold out by those higher up. You have heard me sound off several times on the belief that loyalty down must occur simultaneously with loyalty up—that is one thing which is completely lacking in these Chinese outfits.

Being reasonably sure that whatever move the Japanese made would not be disrupted by the Chinese army described above, we had to prepare for a number of eventualities just as we did in Tientsin years before. Also as in Tientsin, so in Peking daily appearance and performance became tantamount in importance.

Appearance offered almost no problem since by tradition the detachment breathed spit and polish, above all our famed Horse Marines. Riding Mongolian ponies, the Horse Marines constituted our military police force but we used them frequently for show. After troop review each Saturday morning the band broke into "Pop Goes the Weasel" which brought the mounted Marines onto the field at full gallop—a ceremony particularly enjoyed by our frequent Chinese guests.

Crack performance, however, meant field training, no easy matter in this area. During the planting and harvest seasons we were forbidden the countryside which confined field exercises to late autumn and early spring, the winters being generally too cold. A shortage of arable land confined artillery practice to the French range at Tientsin and rifle firing to the range at Chinwangtao—a range that I originally surveyed and helped construct in 1928—and this meant a careful juggling of schedules to keep a necessary troop strength in Peking.

Both Bobbie Erskine and I were bears on training and wanted to extend field exercises into the harsh winter months, a plan not altogether favored by Colonel Rixey. He was a reasonable man, however, and he also was worried about a pneumonia epidemic that had claimed the lives of several Marines the previous winter. When our detachment surgeon, Captain Shepherd, advised him that proper cold weather conditioning could possibly hold down the disease, he gave in. By January I was able to write a friend:

> For the last two months, the crops being out of the ground, we have been able to do some splendid work in combat training, starting with the squad and working up through the platoons. This month we will have company problems and next month battalion problems . . . should we evacuate this place, the outfit here would be a well-trained infantry battalion with enough key men trained in artillery for a pack-howitzer battery.

That winter, one of the coldest in Peking's history, we suffered only two mild cases of pneumonia.

At planting time we shifted our training effort to the rifle range. By this time Charlie Price had come out from America to command the 4th Marines in Shanghai. For the shoot that spring he brought up a team which he declared was going to mop the floor with us. His anticipation changed to chagrin when our much smaller battalion team won both rifle and pistol competitions.

Soon after this Colonel Rixey returned to America. Having

made my number for colonel the previous December, I was now given command of the detachment. Bobbie Erskine moved up to executive officer and Captain Jerry Thomas became my adjutant. Company commanders included Joe Burger, John Bemis and Bob Luckey, officers destined to make a name for themselves a few years later as was a young lieutenant named David Shoup.

Young Shoup was a fine officer, an earnest and conscientious person not easily persuaded from a course he thought correct. Once some friends asked him to help an unfortunate American who somehow had landed in a Peking prison. After thoroughly investigating the case Shoup concluded the man was being unfairly accused. Starting at the bottom of the official ladder he worked to the top, the ambassador. Only when Mr. Johnson turned him down did he admit defeat.

These were a splendid group of officers and because of them I never worried about the appearance or performance of my command. Bobbie Erskine could spot a wayward piece of lint on a rifle from 500 yards. Bobbie, who held a splendid combat record from France in World War I and who later became one of the finest commanders in World War II, was always a severe taskmaster. One day he came to me, mentioned a young lieutenant and said, "I'm certainly disappointed in that young man." I asked why. "I have just inspected him performing his duties as Officer of the Day and found him reading the *Saturday Evening Post.*" I asked what other duties the officer had at the time. "None, but if he has time to read a magazine he has time and should be reading the training manual."

Physically Bobbie was tough as they come and could not tolerate sickness, particularly his own. On one occasion when, as I recall, flu had him down, both Captain Thomas and I attempted to visit him at his home. He wouldn't hear of it— his disease was deadly contagious and he was not permitted to receive visitors. After a few days of this we walked over to his house one morning, brushed aside his number one boy and went upstairs to his bedroom. There lay the toughest officer in the Marine Corps propped up in a huge bed, the spread decorated with little blue bows, in the most feminine boudoir I have ever seen. While Jerry Thomas tried to keep a straight face I exploded in laughter. "Damn it, Bobbie, I'll bet you haven't been in a place like this since Paris in 1918."

I have never seen anyone quite so angry. With great forbearance I refrained from passing the incident around the
Corps—thus undoubtedly preserving our long and fine friendship.

These and a good many other lighthearted incidents
helped ease the increasing tension of our days. By July,
1936, anything could have happened, as I noted in a letter
to John Marston back in Washington:

> I am rather proud of the record of the boys here as
> we seem to maintain friendly relations with everyone and
> so far have gotten in difficulties with none. Our British
> friends have just come through a rather rotten time of it
> in a mix-up with the Japanese. . . .
>
> The question of the Japanese actions in North China
> is growing daily more aggressive in so far as their rela-
> tions with the Chinese and foreign civil population [are
> concerned]. A lot of this, I believe, is due to inferiority
> complex on their part and the endeavor to assert them-
> selves as equals or more than equals of other people . . .
> their enlisted personnel are of a very low order of men-
> tality having been taken from the rice paddies and fields
> not very long ago, and come from the lowest types of
> Japanese peasantry in a good many cases. . . .
>
> So far the Japanese military have been most scrupu-
> lous in their relations with us and a very free and friendly
> feeling exists between the high command of the Japa-
> nese forces here and ourselves. In view of the fact that
> practically none of the junior officers and absolutely none
> of the enlisted personnel speak anything but Japanese,
> any relations between our junior officers and theirs and
> our enlisted personnel and theirs is entirely out of the
> question. As I said early in this letter, the British have
> had trouble, the French have been reported and so have
> the Italians. We so far have escaped. There is a pool on
> with the British, French and Italian commandants as to
> just how soon they will try to hang something on us, so
> in writing the above I have my fingers crossed. . . .

As the American commandant I was by tradition senior
which meant that I presided at the commandants' monthly
luncheon and other meetings designed to iron our various
difficulties. Early in my tour I collided with the Japanese

commandant, Colonel Mutaguchi, over some minor matter and in an exasperated moment told him, "You know, Colonel, your trouble is that you people have an inferiority complex." He regarded me gravely. "It is not so much that we have an inferiority complex, Colonel, as it is that you Americans and British have a superiority complex."

This made me think not a little. Henceforth I went out of my way to be scrupulously fair in dealing with him. I think he appreciated this—at least we never had any personal acrimony in our dealings.

Quite by accident I even won his gratitude. Each year we held an international small-bore rifle competition which for years the Japanese had refused to join, their excuse being a conflict with maneuvers. Thinking it would ease tensions to have them participate in 1937, I told Mutaguchi that we wanted him to put up a team, and that we would schedule the event only when he was free. This caught him off guard but he quickly invented a new excuse: he could not have the rifle range for the hours he wanted. When I assured him he could he thought very quickly: he would enter only if he could supplement his Peking team with shooters from Tientsin. When I told him he could use the Imperial Guard in Tokyo if he wished, he agreed to compete. That year we placed first as always—but I became temporarily unpopular with the other commandants when Mutaguchi's team placed second, an achievement that pleased him no end.

At our last meeting Mutaguchi claimed the final word. Close to the end of my tour he was promoted to brigadier general. When calling to congratulate him I remarked, "I guess that makes you senior to me." He looked at me rather shyly. "To be frank, Colonel Vandegrift, in case the need arose I have always had a commission senior to yours in my safe."

That seems to me to sum up the situation in the Peking of those years: potentially explosive but excepting a few small incidents still tranquil enough to allow us a pleasant albeit a rigorous tour of duty. A large and imposing foreign colony plus a stream of important visitors meant one social occasion after another, most of them providing contacts with interesting and intelligent people, many of whom became my lasting friends. And when duty permitted there was also a fascinating country to explore—I never tired of learning something new about perhaps the greatest enigma of modern times: China.

Early in 1937 my education was cut short when unexpected orders recalled me to Washington to serve as military secretary to the new Commandant, General Thomas Holcomb. It may seem difficult to believe now, but such was the way we saw the world situation in 1937 that I figured this would be my last tour. I was a full colonel with twenty-six years of service and, like most of my contemporaries, planned to retire after thirty years. Deciding to exploit opportunity while it existed, I requested and received permission for my wife and me to return via Europe.

The trip offered still another insight into the Japanese mind, anyway that of Mutaguchi. At Mukden in Manchuria we transferred to a Japanese train for the trip to Manchuli. Upon our arrival the local Japanese commander solicitously met us to offer every possible courtesy. Having learned that we had enjoyed a comfortable trip, he asked if I would mind sending a telegram to that effect to his superior in Peking. I agreed to do so but asked him why. "Because," he said, "unless the commandant receives your wire, heads will roll from Mukden to Manchuli."

Surprisingly, we enjoyed a comfortable trip across Siberia to Moscow, the more so because we wisely carried melba toast and what passed for instant coffee in those days. One afternoon in crossing the Siberian plains I was amazed to see hundreds of parachutes floating down. For some reason the train stopped so I dismounted to watch troops land, fold parachutes and execute an obviously prepared maneuver. I was so impressed that later I reported it to certain officials in Washington only to be told it was an exhibition to impress the country folk. Obviously it was a well-planned mass drop, a technique which we did not evolve for many years.

After a few days in Moscow made the more comfortable by a courteous and brilliant young diplomat, Mr. Charles Bohlen, we continued on to Warsaw, Vienna, Budapest, Venice, Paris and home by boat.

In 1937 Marine Corps Headquarters occupied a wing in the Navy Building on Constitution Avenue. Here I reported to Major General Holcomb for duty.

General Holcomb's fifty-eight years included extensive

expeditionary service and a brilliant combat record in France in 1918. He was well known throughout the Corps as an imaginative planner and administrator. He was a man of medium height and graying hair whose steel-rimmed glasses in no way hid the effect of piercing gray eyes, particularly if they were turned on you.

A quiet firmness and a brain like a calculating machine caused many officers to regard the general as somewhat dour. Only recently a friend of mine in discussing those prewar days asked him what people called me at the time.

"His wife called him Archer," the general (still very vigorous at eighty-three) replied, "his contemporaries called him Archie and his subordinates Colonel."

"What did you call him?"

"Oh, I called him Vandegrift—I was never one for first names."

Having known Holcomb in China and Quantico, I sensed that this briskness concealed a considerable amount of warmth and humility—and I was correct.

The Commandant's office occupied the front portion of the building wing and was flanked on one side by the aides' office, on the other by mine. Various staff sections claimed the rear portion of the building. At the time our organization resembled in some ways the old German concept with staff functions broken into divisions of quartermaster, aviation, operations and training (later plans and policies), adjutant and inspector, and reserve. As the head of operations and training, Brigadier General Holland Smith functioned as a sort of chief of staff although eventually Holcomb used me as much as anyone to co-ordinate staff functions.

The general was not one to waste time with unnecessary administrative routine. When a problem arose he assigned it directly to the concerned division; if it involved several divisions, then Holland or I would farm it out appropriately. Henceforth it became the problem of the division, which was expected to come up with a finished answer; if it was a joint effort, then Holland or I was to have the finished answer. Reasoning that a given problem normally concerned one division more than another, Holcomb saw little value in today's highly touted staff conferences which he considered a waste of time and avoided like the plague.

He did not oversimplify matters. He never hurried his

thoughts on a given problem, and he was perfectly willing to discuss a problem with appropriate division officers during interim phases. Once satisfied with a solution, he accepted it as his decision and responsibility, then stuck to it, often moving mountains in its accomplishment. I learned to respect this willingness to accept total responsibility and the accompanying tenacity of purpose to see a project through more from General Holcomb than from anyone else.

This and other lessons came slowly, in fact after Peking days Washington duty seemed unusually mild. Keep in mind that despite Hitler's excursions in Europe and Hirohito's in Manchukuo, America was just emerging from the worst depression in her history. Washington was far more concerned with domestic than with foreign policy, the armed forces were starved for funds, almost no one was thinking in terms of war. The entire Marine Corps consisted of just over 18,000 persons. Our task at Headquarters remained the task of years: administering our various units which in essence amounted to trying to get two dollars' worth of value out of each dollar received from our pitifully small annual budget.

I struck Headquarters at budget time. Once I had read into the over-all picture the Commandant directed me to work with General Seth Williams on next year's budget. This annual requirement claimed a great deal of his time and he wanted some assistance in lightening the load.

Although from my earlier liaison duty to Headquarters I held a fair idea of its workings, I was certainly naïve as to details. Walking in to Williams' office, I repeated General Holcomb's orders, then blithely remarked, "I wonder if you would explain to me how the budget works. Could you do it this afternoon?" Williams ribbed me about this for years afterward, when we struggled for months over the annual monster.

The budgetary procedure proved the most educational of all activities at Headquarters. Each year we had to submit a proposed budget for the forthcoming fiscal year. This went first to the Navy budget officer, then to the Navy Department, and finally to the House and Senate with each organization ripping it to shreds and putting it back together, not of course during final, formal hearings, but in numerous informal meetings and conferences which generally resolved the most important differences of opinion.

The whole difficulty, then as now, boiled down to money or lack of it, the basic reason for service jealousies. Inwardly I am sure that intelligent officers in each service realized the value of the other services, but when the budget pie was sliced naturally each service wanted the largest share. Before World War II the largest share was small enough, which further intensified ambitions.

Congress could not be blamed altogether for the appropriation famine. Some years ago Mr. Dean Acheson made a talk in which he pointed out that in many cases in a republic like ours the Administration in power could not do as it pleased—it must have a sound, usually obvious cause to gain public approval before taking or even suggesting drastic action. That it did not hold obvious cause to build up the armed forces in 1937-38 was partially the fault of the armed forces, which failed to specify the exact threat that this country faced from foreign enemies. Such an appraisal could only have arisen from sound intelligence; and at that time the armed forces suffered from what psychologists call a mental block when it came to intelligence.

The Marine Corps had no business gathering such long-range intelligence. This was the job of the State Department, the Army and the Navy—and each almost totally neglected it. In turn the true significance of vital international issues escaped in whole or part officers of the armed forces, members of Congress, and the bulk of the American people whose combined opinion is the strength or weakness of a nation such as ours.

In the annual preparation and presentation of his budget General Holcomb not only recognized but respected this nebulous relationship between the members of Congress and the people they represented, and he was good enough to pass some of this understanding and respect on to me.

Under his tutelage I learned that you could have the most urgent need expressed in the most plausible and logical terms for a certain appropriation, but that nevertheless you had to prepare the groundwork very carefully by informal talks with certain Congressional figures.

Here you invariably learned to compromise—for example, to gain one appropriation may have cost you another that was equally important. Or perhaps you could gain half of a requested appropriation for the coming fiscal year but if you waited you could probably win the entire amount in the following year.

Holcomb never asked for the moon and a piece of cheese simply because it would have been nice to have had. Along this line he insisted that his staff divisions justify each of their requests to his complete satisfaction. Once he gave his approval, I prepared a book showing the break-down of requests by each division and the reasoning behind the requests. This book accompanied him to all budgetary hearings, where he often gave dramatic performances in detail, something impossible for chiefs of the larger services. But if his memory failed and the book didn't hold the answer, he never bluffed. I have heard him say many times (as later I would say), "Gentlemen, I am sorry but I cannot answer that question now. I will, however, have the answer for you tomorrow morning."

His careful preparation and honest presentation formed a powerful weapon. More than one congressman told me at the time and subsequently that his vote was favorable because he sincerely believed we were asking only for what we needed. Naturally we sometimes suffered defeats, but we philosophically accepted these as resulting from the intransigent temper of our times when it came to matters military.

To help Congress help us we did what we could to gain public support. The Commandant, however, hated anything that smacked of cheap publicity. Whatever he thought would interest the public he told without fanfare. He appreciated the value of legitimate publicity—when asked to furnish a guard for the 1939 World's Fair we did so even though it created a personnel problem. But when someone at Quantico once dressed some beautiful models in Marine shooting jackets and photographed them at the rifle range the general raised eight kinds of hell.

On the other hand, upon learning that we were to gain several thousand Marines in a coming budget he asked a personal friend, Mr. Sam Meek, a World War I Marine who had served in France and was now with the J. Walter Thompson advertising agency, to poll America to find out what most favorably impressed youngsters and their parents about the Marine Corps. The findings were incorporated into a later and highly successful recruiting campaign.

I once surprised the Commandant with my own public

opinion survey. In 1937 the Japanese sank one of our gunboats, the *Panay*, in the Yangtze River, an incident that some Washington officials believed would fire national indignation into demanding punitive measures against the Japanese. At the height of the crisis I left Headquarters, changed three one-dollar bills into quarters and hailed a taxi. In those days a taxi carried you across metropolitan Washington for a quarter. I made twelve such trips, asking each driver what he thought about the *Panay* incident. I have always assumed that a taxi driver's words reflected other persons' opinions more than his own thoughts and so gave considerable weight to my perhaps unorthodox findings of the afternoon. In fact I informed the Commandant that despite the current hue and cry the matter would drop because the public was just not interested.

"What makes you think that?" he asked.

I told him about my afternoon's work.

He looked somewhat surprised but confined himself to, "Rather odd way of doing things, isn't it?"

Hitler's invasion of Poland on September 1, 1939, began to alter the national air. A week later President Roosevelt declared a limited national emergency which for the Marines meant expansion to 25,000. A year later we called up our small reserve. By late 1941 we counted over 70,000.

Expansion ruled our days beginning in the autumn of 1939. At Headquarters we lived in a limbo of charts each designed to outguess decisions not yet made. For good or ill I was involved in these chaotic years right up to my neck, for in December of that year I made my number for brigadier general. Upon gaining my star in 1940 I became assistant to the Commandant. Henceforth my recent China tour seemed quiet in the extreme.

Because isolationism did not die easily, even after Hitler's move, we trod slowly at first, particularly in the employment of our newly authorized personnel. "Whatever you do, make yourselves look defensive," Admiral Leahy instructed the Commandant.

We could scarcely look defensive by turning our understrength brigades into divisions, yet we had to organize additional units if we were to carry out various missions planned for us by the Navy in case of war.

Aided by his planners Holcomb neatly solved the dilemma

with a unit called the defense battalion. A powerful force of artillery, antiaircraft and coastal defense units designed to hold (but not seize) advanced naval bases, the units nonetheless carried a pleasant potential offensive power not lost on Admiral Leahy. When the Commandant requested permission to form seven such units, which we described as "unsinkable aircraft carriers," Leahy studied the organizational charts carefully and then suddenly smiled. "*Defense* battalions. Now that's what I call *real* war planning."

Real war planning increasingly occupied those busy days. Considering our nebulous position, taken with tremendous shortages of men and equipment, I think we did right well to handle most of the problems that arose. One of these consisted in placing our senior officers where we would derive the most advantage from their particular abilities. Senior officers do not conform to a standard mold, as some people like to think. Certainly in the prewar Marine Corps almost the reverse held true. But here our advantage of smallness became apparent because one or more of us—Holcomb, Holland Smith, Seth Williams and I—not only knew every officer in the Marine Corps but knew a great deal about them. From time to time we erred in their placement; generally, I feel we did not.

The personnel problem did occasionally surprise us. Shortly before our first large inflow of officer candidates I was asked what academic requirements they should hold. I offhandedly suggested my own curriculum at the University of Virginia. "With that criterion," the officer replied, "we'll be lucky to find one eligible person." I then learned that college courses had noticeably changed since my day—particularly in a lack of language and mathematical requirements. Reluctantly I accepted the new standards.

We did keep physical requirements quite high, but I refused to accept an inflexible standard to meet a national emergency. One case speaks for others: a young applicant with a fine education and excellent personality had certain physical shortcomings. Realizing that our expansion would inevitably breed noncombatant jobs, I decided that this man would prove an asset and so waived the requirements. After winning a commission he fooled me by talking his way into the OSS and there serving with distinction in France and

Africa, indeed a wonderful record that in my mind fully vindicated my reasoning.

Hitler's excursion into Poland also eased the appropriations famine. By then we were ready to use whatever money we could get. We had been working on amphibious doctrine for years, our once primitive manual for landing operations was now refined and officially accepted by the Navy as Fleet Training Publication or FTP-167. To carry out its content we needed new and unusual equipment, especially certain types of landing craft.

Since 1934 we had been interested in a landing craft, the Eureka, designed by Andrew Higgins in New Orleans. Although the Navy insisted on developing its own versions, we stuck by Higgins or, more accurately, he stuck by us since we gave him far more moral encouragement than dollars. Tests of the Eureka in 1938 and 1939, which I witnessed, clearly showed its superiority to other models and we were able to give him a small contract in 1940. But even in 1941 when we wanted him to modify his standard design with a retractable bow ramp he had to produce a pilot model at his own expense.

We also were interested in a vehicle brought to our attention by Brigadier General Moses during a hunting trip in the Florida Everglades. Called the Alligator by its inventor, Donald Roebling, it featured a tracked hull that could crawl over land obstacles. Our Equipment Board at Quantico, and particularly Ernie Linsert, tested the vehicle and recommended purchase but in 1938 Congress turned down the Commandant's request for funds. As in the case of the Higgins boat, we were able to let a small contract in 1940.

Unfortunately the neglect of years cannot be repaired with money. As Napoleon liked to say, time is the one commodity that once lost can't be replaced. Materiel procurement is a complicated, lengthy process usually involving a several year "lag" between the time a desire is forwarded and a product fulfilling that desire is in production. Although we received our first Higgins boats and Alligators in 1941, they left considerable to be desired and it was another two years before the bugs were worked out.

But at last we were starting to move. Late in 1940, when the Commandant was on an inspection trip, Rear Admiral Leigh Noyes in charge of Navy ordnance stopped by my office. He thought it a good idea to equip his destroyers and our defense battalions with some of this new and still very secret radar. Together we pleaded the case to Admiral Stark, each of us gaining four of the old SCR-264 sets— this was the beginning of radar in both Navy and Marines. In this and other pursuits we received tremendous help from the new Undersecretary of the Navy, James Forrestal, whose instant grasp of the most complicated issues we found very impressive.

Continuing expansion also posed the thorny problem of physical space necessary to house and train units. On occasion Providence provided the answer. In 1940 a hurricane and tidal wave practically leveled the ancient facilities serving our recruit depot at Parris Island. Hearing of the "disaster" (which took no lives), General Seth Williams and I hurried south. We first stopped at the rail terminal of Yemassee to intercept a contingent of surprised recruits whom we diverted to Quantico. With the help of General Breckinridge and his able assitstant, Lieutenant Colonel Jeschke, we surveyed the enormous damage at Parris Island, flew back to Washington and prepared an estimate which the Commandant hurriedly pushed through the Naval Affairs Committee. As a result we gained a fine new recruit depot in time for the real emergency.

Providence sometimes assumed human form. Realizing that the 1st Marine Brigade, which in late 1940 was sent down to Guantánamo Bay under Holland Smith's command, would soon become a division, we started plugging for a new east coast base, Quantico being too small for training purposes. We eventually hit upon an area around Jacksonville, North Carolina, but for some reason President Roosevelt did not like the proposed site. While Holland's outfit was hacking out a campsite in Cuba at a place called Deer Point, Congressman Woodward visited the area to see his son. Horrified by the primitive conditions, he returned to Washington and laid it on the line to the President—the Marines must have a new training area. With that important help we gained funds to buy the North Carolina site then known as New River. We sent the first units to the wilderness of Tent Camp One in September, 1941. Henceforth it served as one of our principal training bases, a function it continues today as the beautiful Camp Lejeune.

In 1941 we also moved our headquarters to the more spacious Arlington Navy Annex, a labyrinth building on a hill overlooking Arlington National Cemetery. The Commandant's office afforded an excellent view of this national memorial where scarcely a day passed without several old soldiers being laid ceremoniously to rest. One day a visitor asked General Holcomb if the marches and taps and volleys didn't get on his nerves. He reflected a moment. "No, they don't. They would only bother me if I could *not* hear them."

By this time our frantic efforts in numerous directions were bearing fruit. We had a division training on each coast with such progress that they simultaneously were training Army divisions in amphibious warfare. In August, 1941, I witnessed a maneuver at New River which I later described in a letter to Deacon Upshur:

The maneuvers of the First Division, Marines, and First Division, Army, were a great success. There were twelve [battalion] combat teams landed and maintained over a week through surf and by small boats. As it was all within our own area there was nothing taboo and nothing artificial. . . . You will see what I mean when I tell you that they landed four hundred tons of small-arms ammunition and moved it inland for the final stage seven and a half miles from the beach. Little did I think when you and I were bushwhacking in Haiti in 1915 that I would ever live to see the sight of thirty-two transports and cargo ships for the sole use of landing force exercises.

Already in 1940 we had deployed two defense battalions to the Pacific, where units subsequently were trying to prepare defenses on Midway, Palmyra and Johnston Islands. In 1941 we deployed an air group to Honolulu with another remaining on the east coast as part of Holland Smith's new corps. In June we received an emergency request to rush a provisional brigade to Iceland. My old friend John Marston mounted this out in forty-eight hours, a response favorably noticed in Washington official circles.

I spent most of this year traveling since I was responsible for both the New River base program and the Higgins boat program. We were racing against time and knew it, but many people in America did not. On a train trip to the west coast in September, 1941, I sounded out numerous passengers and was appalled at their general disinterest in and ignorance of momentous international developments. One group of educators particularly surprised me by their unrealistic perspective and I spent considerable time discussing the world situation with them.

On the last night of the trip one of them, the president of a small college, approached me in the club car. "You've probably guessed by now that I am a pacifist," he said.

"If being a pacifist means you don't want war, then I, too, am a pacifist," I told him. "But if you think we aren't going to have a war, then in my opinion you are wrong."

"I didn't think so a couple of days ago," he said, "but you have given me an entirely different slant on things. I have just torn up my speech on pacifism and am going to write one more realistic."

"I'm on my way to inspect the 2d Marine Division in San Diego," I told him, "but if I have succeeded in making you face the ghastly facts of our time then my trip already is a success."

That war was coming I was by now certain, though of course I had no idea when. But I had already decided that I did not want to miss this one so I had better leave Washington while it was possible. I had spent nearly four years there, most of the time under considerable pressure, and no one realized this more than the Commandant. When an opening came up for an infantry officer or assistant division commander in the 1st Marine Division, he ordered me to New River to take it.

VI

War

FROM my first day in the division Major General Philip Torrey allowed me carte blanche in training, the traditional task of the infantry officer or assistant division commander (ADC). While still in Washington I had sent Major Bill Twining to New River from Quantico to survey the training problem. One of the brightest young officers in the Corps, Bill delivered his usual comprehensive and incisive report which left no doubt of the task at hand.

At this time the 1st Marine Division existed more on paper than in fact. Its infantry regiments and supporting units such as artillery, engineers and communications were understrength some 12,000 men. New River was largely wasteland. Since their arrival a couple of months earlier the units had been building a billeting area—a most uncomfortable place called Tent Camp One. Few firing ranges existed, almost no roads, but few wooden buildings. In short we were building a camp from scratch and simultaneously trying to organize and train what was to become a reinforced division of over 19,000 people.

I devoted the early weeks to two primary tasks. Instead of command post exercises, designed to test communications between division, regiments and battalions, I stressed small unit training beginning with the squad and working up. With the troops profitably occupied, I again scheduled command post exercises but confined them to headquarters personnel. I simultaneously pushed construction of a variety of live-fire ranges needed for realistic training.

Few of our troops had done any field firing with live ammunition nor experienced artillery firing over their heads, the shells exploding a few hundred yards to their front. Lack of ranges and peacetime safety regulations meant that the troops advanced tactically to a certain point, halted, re-

97

ceived a few rounds of ammunition for point firing only, fired, then advanced, again halted and received more ammunition. I worked hard to change this but probably would not have succeeded but for the events of December 7, 1941.

On that Sunday my aide, Lieutenant Allan Sutter, and I drove to Wilmington for lunch in our favorite restaurant. When the radio announced the Pearl Harbor attack we returned to New River immediately. I have often regretted leaving half a lobster on the table because, as General Torrey and I soon learned, we could do nothing but continue to organize and train.

To us the real meaning of Pearl Harbor lay in the psychological transformation of our troops and those recruits who now joined us by the thousands. From this time no one held the slightest doubt that we would ship out, fight and win. Lethargy vanished, never returned. Suddenly every task from scouring mess gear to stripping automatic rifles in the dark made sense to all hands. Suddenly a great many men realized that they knew not a damn thing about war, that a few of us professionals did, and that their chances of returning safely would improve if they learned what we offered them. They learned fast—in January we began battalion training, in February and March regimental maneuvers. We landed with Army units at New River, we landed by ourselves at Solomons Island off Maryland, each exercise better than the previous one, but each still leaving much to be desired.

War did not dry the swamps of New River nor did it ease the bite of wind or sting of rain and ache of cold nor the monotony of days and weeks in the field. But it helped explain the necessity for these discomforts, and in those hectic months, as the Japanese enemy scored victory after victory in that seemingly inexorable march through the South and Southwest Pacific, the purpose of the division became plain to even the rankest recruit.

On March 23, 1942, I took command of the division, simultaneously receiving my second star. For my ADC I brought in Bill Rupertus from Guantánamo Bay. Capers James became chief of staff with Robert Kilmartin D-1 (personnel), Frank Goettge D-2 (intelligence), Jerry Thomas D-3 (operations and training with Bill Twining his assistant) and young Fred Wieseman D-4 (supply—Fred later became assistant D-4 to Ran Pate, who was senior). Jim Webb commanded the 7th Marine Regiment, Roy Hunt the 5th Marines, Cliff Cates, the 1st Marines and Pedro del Valle the 11th Marines (artillery). Allan Sutter and Ray Schwenke served as my aides, the latter also working at his own request for Jerry Thomas. My personal "family" further included an orderly, Ralph Smith, a cook, Butch Morgan, and a driver.

During the next weeks we progressed well in further filling, equipping and training the units. But now the first blow fell. Merritt Edson, armed with appropriate orders, arrived to comb our units for officers and men deemed suitable for his 1st Raider Battalion—a new organization.

I had known about the raiders in Washington. Neither General Holcomb nor I favored forming elite units from units already elite. But Secretary of the Navy Colonel Frank Knox and President Roosevelt, both of whom fancied the British commandos, directed us to come up with a similar organization. Roosevelt liked his Marines very much, an attitude stemming from his service as Assistant Secretary of the Navy. Often in conversations with General Holcomb he referred to "we Marines." The President also liked military novelties as did his British colleague, Mr. Churchill, and he always took care that "we Marines" would have our share of them. In addition to the raiders we formed parachutist battalions, beach-jumpers, glider units, barrage balloon units and war dog platoons.

Before forming the raiders we sent two young captains, Sam Griffith and Wally Greene, to England to observe the commandos—largely on the basis of their recommendations General Holcomb authorized two raider battalions, one under Merritt Edson on the east coast and one under Evans Carlson on the west coast. Edson's levy against our division, coming at such a critical time, annoyed the devil out of me, but there wasn't one earthly thing I could do about it.

We were just repairing the gap in the 5th Marines when the second blow fell. Headquarters ordered us to flesh out the 7th Marines and one battalion of artillery with the best men, weapons and equipment we possessed. These units, together with a defense battalion, would form the 3d Marine Brigade to sail immediately for Samoa. General Holcomb telephoned me to make these units as combat ready as possible, so I stripped other units mercilessly.

My fear that I had inherited a training division and would

spend the war at New River preparing battalions and regiments for overseas duty proved short-lived. While Webb was still loading out the 7th Marines at Norfolk, Virginia, Stover Keyser, calling from Headquarters about some matter, cryptically added that five days after his birthday something important was going to happen to us. Learning from the lineal list that his birthday was imminent, I sent Jerry Thomas to Washington.

Jerry brought back the details of Operation Lone Wolf, a particularly prescient code name under which we were to ship out immediately for Wellington, New Zealand. Although we ultimately were to serve as the Landing Force of a newly established South Pacific Amphibious Force, we were to train in New Zealand for a minimum six months prior to being committed. I responded to this bombshell by sending Bill Twining to Wellington to contract for suitable camps and otherwise smooth the way for our arrival. I then plunged into the multivarious, generally frenzied activities attendant to shipping out.

Limited ports and ships forced us to split into two groups. Bill Rupertus, with Kilmartin his acting chief of staff, took a second echelon consisting of the 1st Marines and supporting units by rail to San Francisco. I kept the 5th Marines and most of the artillery to my first echelon which on May 20 embarked from Norfolk on the *Wakefield* (formerly the liner *Manhattan*).

We in no way sailed as a combat-loaded force. Various depots shipped much of our supply including ammunition directly to New Orleans where our people manifested it aboard separate cargo ships. None of it was combat-packaged, many items were nonexistent. But considering the requirement, my old friend at Headquarters, Seth Williams, did everything but move mountains to help out. Upon embarkation the state of equipment and supply was considerably superior to our physical state. I made the understatement of my life when I reported to General Holcomb that "the Division has not yet attained a satisfactory state of readiness for combat."

Under destroyer escort we steamed down the now dangerous Atlantic coast, transited the Panama Canal and proceeded into the Pacific. A short way out our guardian destroyers turned back. We next lost our long-range plane

escort, which left us alone with only the vastness of the
Pacific, a zigzag course and our own speed as defense against
discovery by enemy submarines. A few of us shared the terrible truth that life jackets and life boats existed for less
than half our numbers.

Fortunately enemy and weather co-operated to provide an
uneventful if tiresome trip broken only on the last lap. Due
to intense heat we were sailing with hatches open despite a
heavy sea. Suddenly the old girl struck a monstrous swell that
sent tons of water below deck. For a moment I feared panic
but some unknown hero broke the tension by yelling, "Women
and children first."

Early on a Sunday we spotted the New Zealand coast, an
almost perfect pastoral scene of green fields rising to hills
dotted with white sheep and yellow gorse, surely one of the
most beautiful coastlines in the world. My aesthetic appreciation took full rein while we steamed into the beautiful Wellington harbor. It was sharply curbed at dockside where Bill
Twining jumped aboard with the catastrophic news that the
unloading of cargo ships, which preceded us, stood days behind schedule.

"Just what in hell is wrong?" I exploded. "We scheduled
ample time."

"They work differently from us," Twining replied. "They
stop for morning tea, lunch, afternoon tea. If it's raining they
don't work at all."

This was my first introduction to practical socialism. Under the circumstances I didn't much care for it. Here the
Japs hovered within striking distance of Australia and, so
far as I knew, we were the one force designed eventually to
hinder their plans. I knew I was supposed to be diplomatic
but I also realized how badly our Navy was hurting for
the ships lined up in this harbor. "Get our people divided into
working parties," I told my chief of staff. "We'll begin work
this afternoon on the AKs and this ship right here."

We worked that day and night. I thought no more about it
until the next morning I paid an official call on the American
minister, General Pat Hurley. He was a very nice chap whom
I had known casually in Washington. His greeting to me,
though in no way bellicose, surprised me. "Well, Vandegrift,
we are certainly glad to see you here. But you have raised

more disturbance in twelve hours than the Japs have so far in the war."

"What in the world are you talking about, Mr. Minister?"

"About you using Marine labor to work your ships twenty-four hours a day. The dockers are up in the air about it."

"And I'm up in the air about the dockers, Mr. Minister. They must know we're at war because New Zealand has fine fighting outfits on the front at this very moment. Besides, my orders are to get these ships unloaded and out of here as fast as possible. If we have to do it ourselves, we will."

Hurley smiled and congratulated me on getting so much done in a short time. He then took me to call on the Prime Minister of New Zealand, Mr. Peter Fraser. Fraser received us most cordially and did not mention the dockers until we took our leave. Shaking hands with me and with a decided twinkle in his eye he said, "This is off the record because I don't want to lose my job as Labor Prime Minister—but I do want to congratulate you on getting your ships unloaded so expeditiously."

I soon discovered that other New Zealanders worked more realistically than the stevedores. In a remarkably short time a labor force of men and women, drafted for the duration, had constructed quite a good little camp for us, an important project because the New Zealand winter which begins in June was already announcing itself with cold, frequent rains.

The new cantonment, sitting in the hills outside Wellington, consisted of small prefabricated houses. Looking like children's playhouses, each quite comfortably held five men. Covered galleys and messhalls formed part of Bill Twining's specifications, but we did lack a building large enough for division headquarters.

The New Zealand liaison officer solved this one by offering us the Hotel Cecil, a very old building in downtown Wellington. It looked all right to me except for people obviously living in it, a fact I mentioned to the New Zealand escort.

"No problem there," he responded. "They will be out in forty-eight hours."

I was horrified. "You're planning to evict these people on our account?"

"Righto," he said. "This is the only possible site for you." He then assured me that the occupants respected the emergency and therefore would not resent transfer to other quarters.

I was not assured until the next day an elderly, stern-looking gentlemen with a clipped white mustache stopped me in the street. "You are the American general?"

"Yes, I am General Vandegrift."

"Well, sir, I am very glad to meet you. I want you to know, sir, that I have lived at the Hotel Cecil for twenty-six years."

I braced myself for the onslaught, but he suddenly smiled kindly. "I want to tell you, sir, how pleased I am to move from my apartment so that you and your officers have a place to do your job."

I have sometimes wondered how many people would have said the same thing in other streets in other countries.

Most of the New Zealanders reflected the old gentleman's attitude. I found them a virile and very fine people whom I grew to admire and like enormously during our short stay. Their men had gone to war, they suffered a rationing so strict that they used charcoal burners to power their autos and trucks, yet from the beginning they threw open their homes and clubs to share their meager sustenance with their friends, the Marines.

We were quite well squared away and looking forward to a long training period in this fine country when I received a dispatch from Admiral Ghormley up in Auckland—would I report in person as soon as possible?

As Commander, South Pacific, or COMSOPAC, Ghormley was my immediate senior. Shortly after my arrival I had telephoned to arrange an official call but since he and his staff were also newly arrived he asked me to delay this for a few days. I assumed now his dispatch referred to this.

Crowded into my small Lodestar command plane, Jerry Thomas, Frank Goettge, Ran Pate and I were flown to Auckland by my most able pilot, Warrant Officer Petras. Ghormley's chief of staff, Admiral Dan Callaghan, met us and took us to town. There he unloaded my staff at a hotel but hustled me directly to Ghormley's headquarters.

I remembered Ghormley from Washington as an intelligent, quiet but most gracious individual and I was surprised at his harassed, almost brusque manner. We had barely shaken hands when he said, "Vandegrift, I have some very disconcerting news."

"I'm sorry to hear that, Admiral."

He handed me a top secret dispatch. "You will be more sorry when you read this."

I pulled a chair up to his desk to concentrate on the document. It directed Ghormley to confer with MacArthur concerning an amphibious operation against two enemy-held islands, Guadalcanal and Tulagi, in the Solomon Island chain northwest of us. This was to be a naval task force including my division and we were to land on August 1—less than five weeks away.

I could not believe it.

I read the typewritten words again. There was no mistaking their content. Without saying anything I folded the dispatch, pushed it over the desk to Ghormley, and leaned back in my chair.

Ghormley's index finger tapped the orders a moment. Then he looked up at me. "Well?"

VII
Guadalcanal: Preparation

THE READER may better understand my position and subsequent events if I touch on the general points of strategy that dictated this abrupt and fundamental change of plan.

Throughout the twenties and most of the thirties our war planners worked on the assumption of "single" wars which resulted in a series of color plans—for example, the Orange Plan in case of war against Japan. But the advent of the Axis formed by Germany and Japan made them think in terms of a world war and caused them to alter the color plans into a more comprehensive Rainbow Plan.

The Rainbow Plan became solidified in Janaury, 1941, when in Washington ranking American and British officers, the forerunners of the Combined Chiefs of Staff, agreed to a fundamental strategy in case America entered the war. This plan, ABC-1, awarded the European theater priority over other theaters; in other words, we would defeat Germany while maintaining a strategic defensive in the Pacific.

But integral to the Pacific strategy were a series of tactical offensives to be undertaken by the Pacific fleet with both Marine and Army units involved. This portion of the plan, Rainbow Five, became worthless when the Japanese hurt us so badly at Pearl Harbor and began to overrun our bases with their march through the South Pacific. Our task now became one of holding what we could with no thought of immediate offensive action.

This was the situation at the time of the Arcadia Conference which began in Washington a couple of weeks after Pearl Harbor. Arcadia confirmed the earlier strategy of keeping Europe the primary theater, but it also gave the United States primary responsibility for the Pacific theater. Further, it formally established the Combined Chiefs of Staff. To represent the United States on this body, President Roosevelt ap-

105

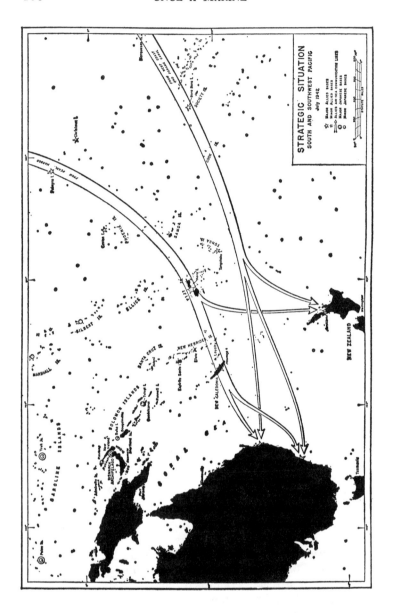

pointed the Joint Chiefs of Staff, or JCS, consisting of General Marshall, General Arnold, Admiral King and Admiral Stark, who was later replaced by Admiral Leahy.

The JCS more or less agreed that the immediate problem in the Pacific lay in keeping open the lifeline connecting Hawaii, New Zealand and Australia. Within the limits of available resources it ordered various ground units to such points along this line as the Fijis, the New Hebrides and Sa-

Organization of South Pacific Forces at the Inception of Task One

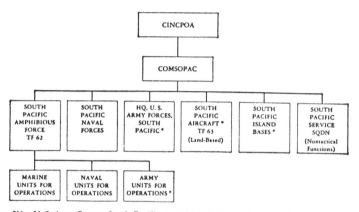

*Hq, U. S. Army Forces, South Pacific, exercised administrative control over Army units.

moa, the last-named the destination of the 7th Marines so precipitately taken from me in April.

To pursue this and future operations in the Pacific, the JCS next divided it into two major commands, the Southwest Pacific Area under General Douglas MacArthur at Port Moresby and the Pacific Ocean Areas under Admiral Chester Nimitz at Pearl Harbor. Nimitz in turn established a subordinate command, the South Pacific, under Vice Admiral Ghormley to whom I was subordinate.

Both Ghormley and I were privy to this general picture. We did not know, although we might have guessed, that to anyone of King's temperament it was gall and wormwood to sit back while the Japanese pushed practically to the shores of Australia and New Zealand. Nor, as we know today, did he hold any intention of doing this. Already in March he was toying with the notion of limited advances to the north-

Organization of Forces for Task One

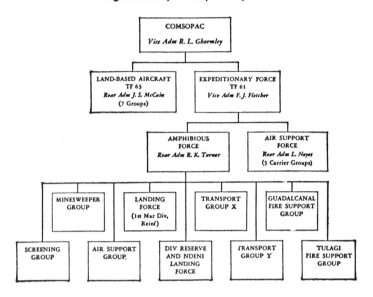

Organization of Landing Force for Task One

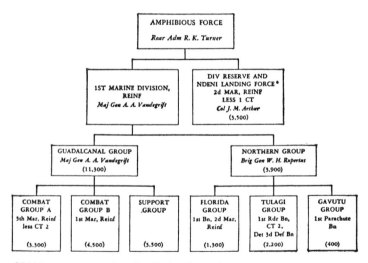

*Division reserve was released to Vandegrift 7–9 August.

west. This idea, farfetched at the time, became more attractive as our units began to defend various points along the all-important lifeline and as our Navy air achieved two striking victories at the battles of Coral Sea and Midway. Although the other JCS members remained cool to King's offensive notions, the top Pacific commanders now placed themselves in the act. Nimitz wanted to strike Tulagi with Merritt Edson's 1st Raider Battalion while MacArthur proposed to assault Rabaul with one amphibious division— plans most fortunately rejected by the JCS.

King's ambitions intensified when intelligence reported the Japanese moving into the Solomon Islands. In June he proposed to strike at Guadalcanal-Tulagi, but in considerably more strength than suggested by Nimitz. From here he reasoned we could push north, finally to take Rabaul. Although his plan met stubborn resistance in JCS councils, he pushed it through.

As finally resolved it called for three phases or tasks. The Navy would command the first, Operation Watchtower, designed to give us the enemy-held islands of Guadalcanal-Tulagi in the Solomons and Ndeni in the Santa Cruz Islands. Tasks Two and Three, the seizure of the northern Solomons and Rabaul, would be under Army command. Marshall and MacArthur at first demanded Army command for Task One but King, pointing out that the Army had no troops ready to move out, insisted on Navy command.

This was why I now sat in Admiral Ghormley's office, my surprise the more great from my ignorance of this recent top-level thinking. I didn't even know the location of Guadalcanal. I knew only that my division was spread over hell's half-acre, one-third in Samoa, one-third in New Zealand and one third still at sea. My equipment, much of it new, had to be broken in; my supply had to be sorted and combat-packaged; shortages had to be determined and filled. After explaining all this to Ghormley I said, "I just don't see how we can land anywhere by August first."

He nodded. "I don't see how we can land at all, and I am going to take it up with MacArthur. Meanwhile we'll have to go ahead as best we can."

I telephoned Jerry Thomas to bring the rest of the staff to Ghormley's headquarters where DeWitt Peck, a Marine colonel serving as Ghormley's plans officer, offered further

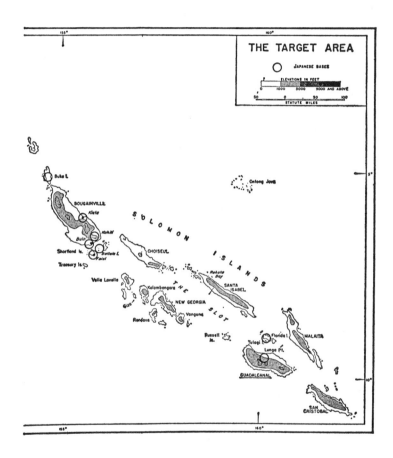

THE TARGET AREA

○   JAPANESE BASES

ELEVATIONS IN FEET

0   1000   3000   9000 AND ABOVE

50   0   50   100
STATUTE MILES

Buka I.

Ontong Java

BOUGAINVILLE
Kieta

Kahili
Buin
Shortland Is.
Ballale I.
Faisi
Treasury Is.

Vella Lavella

SOLOMON ISLANDS

CHOISEUL

Rekata Bay
SANTA ISABEL

Kolombangara
Gizo
NEW GEORGIA
Rendova
Vangunu

THE SLOT

Russell Is.

Tulagi
Florida I.
Lunga Pt.
GUADALCANAL

MALAITA

SAN CRISTOBAL

details. To replace the 7th Marines in our Landing Force the 2d Marines were sailing from San Diego to rendezvous with us in the Fijis. I would also have Edson's 1st Raider Battalion, now in Samoa, and Bob Pepper's 3d Defense Battalion, still in Hawaii. Once we secured the objectives, so the plan stated, Army units would relieve us although these were not yet in the area.

Peck also gave us the allotted shipping for the operation but informed us that Rear Admiral Kelly Turner, the designated commander of the Amphibious Task Force or the force responsible for getting us to the target area, would not arrive in New Zealand with his staff until mid-July. This meant a reversal of the normal planning procedure—from Amphibious Task Force down to Landing Force—with the attendant disadvantages.

So much for our force—what of the objective areas? We soon learned that COMSOPAC's staff knew as much about Guadalcanal and Tulagi as we did, which was nothing. Since intelligence is the basis of all planning, or should be, I sent my D-2, Frank Goettge, to Australia to find out what he could about the Solomons.

Back in Wellington we turned to the problem of combat-loading. This first entailed unloading everything from the ships onto Aotea Quay and sorting it, a task undertaken by Roy Hunt's 5th Marines, hastily moved from their comfortable new camp back to cramped quarters aboard ship.

To complicate matters a heavy rain began and continued for the next three weeks. The commercially packaged supply, particularly rations, rapidly disintegrated until the docks became a slippery mass compounded variously of cornflakes, crackers and prunes. My most vivid memory of this hectic period entails the D-4, Ran Pate, sitting hunched over a desk in a small, leaky shack working 18-20 hour days on cargo manifests while troops a few yards away forcibly and in unmistakable terms defined the science of logistics.

My personal attempts to cheer the troops were not altogether successful nor could I raise spirits by telling them the mission. Only a few members of my staff knew the truth. The others were told, as were New Zealanders, that we were loading out for extensive maneuvers in the Fijis.

Obviously the shipping allotted by COMSOPAC could not

begin to carry all of our equipment and supply, but I was quite upset to learn just how little it would carry. When Pate brought me the sad figures of ship capacity versus division requirements I was forced to some critical decisions. Even after eliminating seabags, bedrolls, tentage, most post exchange supplies, and a good deal of heavy equipment and motor transport, I still had to cut bulk supply—rations, fuel, lubricants—to 60 days and, most tragic, ammunition from 15 to 10 days of fire for all weapons. As stated in the operation order, we would load only "items actually required to live and fight." I dispatched this information to Bill Rupertus, still at sea with the second echelon, and warned him to be ready to transship immediately upon reaching Wellington.

In the middle of the logistics effort Frank Goettge returned from Australia with some very positive results. Colonel Willoughby, MacArthur's intelligence officer, promised to collect and forward what information he could. He also promised photo coverage of both targets and in late July actually prepared a controlled mosaic of the Guadalcanal beaches. Unfortunately these maps were improperly addressed and never did reach us.

Frank also reported the existence of a remarkable Australian intelligence system called the "coast watchers." Before the war the Australian Navy cleverly planted powerful radio transmitters on a number of outlying islands where certain key personnel were recruited to serve as coast watchers in event of invasion. When the Japanese occupied these islands a number of these very brave volunteers took their radios and disappeared into the jungle. There, living like animals, they transmitted frequent coded reports that provided some first-rate intelligence.

From one of them, Martin Clemens on Guadalcanal, we learned of a seaplane base at Tulagi, the construction of an airfield on Guadalcanal, and the location of some guns mounted near one of our designated landing beaches. His estimates of enemy force varied considerably as did all estimates—anywhere from 2,000 to 10,000 on Guadalcanal with a lesser force on Tulagi.

Wanting more precise information if possible, I requested permission from Ghormley to land a small reconnaissance force on Guadalcanal by submarine but he turned this down as "too dangerous."

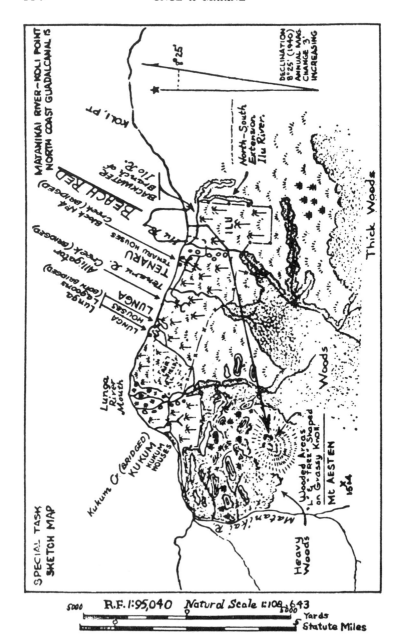

SPECIAL TASK
SKETCH MAP

MATANIKAI RIVER~KOLI POINT
NORTH COAST GUADALCANAL IS

DECLINATION
8°25' (1940)
ANNUAL MAG
CHANGE 3'
INCREASING

8°25'

KOLI PT.

BEACH RED

Block Hd Creek (BRIDGED)

Alligator Creek (BRIDGED)

Lunga Lagoons (BOTH BRIDGED)

LUNGA

LUNGA HOUSES

TENARU

Tenaru R. (BRIDGED)

TENARU HOUSES

ILU R.

BACKWATER
Branch of
ILU R.

North-South
Extension
Ilu River.

ILU

Thick Woods

Woods

Lunga River Mouth

Kukum C. (BRIDGED)

KUKUM HOUSES

Matanikai R.

Wooded Areas
"L" & "Tree" Shaped
on Grassy Knoll

Mt AESTEN
1514

Heavy Woods

R.F. 1:95,040   Natural Scale 1:108,643

5000   5000

Yards
Statute Miles

Goettge also reported some valuable information culled from refugee colonial officers, plantation managers and owners, missionaries and even schooner captains. He brought back eight of these people whom we swore to secrecy and interrogated relentlessly. Some of their information proved invaluable, some worthless and thus dangerous.

One of our recruits produced a crude chart of Guadalcanal which we used to determine critical terrain features such as rivers, forests and heights to serve as reference points necessary for the tactical scheme of maneuver. After our operation plan developed sufficiently to designate Red Beach as the landing zone, I called in a plantation manager who had lived about half a mile from this beach. Pointing to a river, shown as the Ilu River on the chart, I asked its characteristics.*

"Since this is the dry season," he said, "you will have no trouble in fording it."

"It won't be an obstacle?"

"No, it will not be an obstacle."

As it turned out he could not have been more wrong—but this is the sort of "hit-and-miss" information we perforce relied on.

We faced two separate actions. On Guadalcanal, a mountainous island some 90 miles long and 25 miles wide, our interest centered primarily on an airfield which the Japanese were building a short distance inland from the northern coast. Two rivers, designated as the Ilu and the Lunga, flanked this general area. Martin Clemens, the resident coast watcher, warned of gun emplacements around the mouth of the Lunga to the west of the airfield. We further supposed the enemy would defend the beaches immediately north of the airfield and so decided to land on a beach about three miles east of the airfield. King hoped to gain strategic surprise—I was trying for tactical surprise.

At Red Beach, Roy Hunt would land his reinforced regiment (less one battalion), a covering force followed by Cliff Cates landing his 1st Marines in column of battalions. Cliff would then pass through the 5th Marines and push toward

---

* This began a monumental foul-up between the Ilu and Tenaru rivers. Although the river we called the Ilu was the Tenaru and vice versa, I will continue to use the improper names since the error was not discovered or anyway not taken seriously until after the campaign.

Cartographic & Reproduction Unit,Combat Team No.5 1242'

Prepared under the direction of the Commander Combat Team No.5 submitted,and controlled by Map;North Coast of Guadalcanal Island,R.F.1:95,040;14 July,1942

SPECIAL NOTE: This map was reproduced from Special Sketch Map drawn from the information supplied by a man thoroughly familiar with the terrain shown. It is an approximate pictorial representation drawn from this person's memory.It is not to be construed as being an accurate map.

: SYMBOLS :

,'''', ,''', GRASS PLAINS (THICK:4TO 6 FT.HIGH)

,, ↑ ,, COCONUT PALMS AND GRASS LAND

──●── FENCE. (TEN YEAR OLD)

,●,◇◇ DEEP DITCHES,WITH HOLES

≝ ≝ SWAMP   ⊘ KNOLLS

x──x── FIVE STRAND BARBED WIRE FENCES

(GOOD REPAIR)

BRIDGES. 3 TON LIMIT. ONE WAY TRAFFIC

KUKUM,LUNGA,TENARU and ILU,are Plantations

CRUDE SKETCH MAP used in the planning and early operational phases of the Guadalcanal campaign by units of the 5th Combat Team; it is an adaptation of a map prepared by the D-2 Section and typifies the scarcity of reliable terrain information available to the 1st Marine Division when it left New Zealand.

Mt. Austen, or "Grassy Knoll," described by planters as a critical terrain feature "a couple of miles inland" dominating the airfield from the south. The combined force would then take the vital airfield, consolidate its defense and hold until relieved by Army troops brought in from the New Hebrides.

Simultaneously a separate force would strike Tulagi which, together with two tiny islands called Gavutu and Tanambogo, lies about 20 miles north of Guadalcanal; these islands control the sheltered harbor of Florida Island, much larger but so far as we knew not occupied by the enemy. My plan here called for Bill Rupertus to land a small reconnaissance force on the tip of large Florida Island to screen his main force composed of Edson's 1st Raider Battalion, Hill's 1st Battalion, 2d Marines, and Rosecrans' 2d Battalion, 5th Marines, landing on Tulagi's south coast while Williams' 1st Parachute Battalion, sans parachutes, struck Gavutu-Tanambogo.

At the height of planning Bill Rupertus and the second echelon reached Wellington. This convoy naturally had to be unloaded and its equipment and supply sorted prior to combat-loading, all of which added immeasurably to the prevalent confusion on Aotea Quay. Although Cliff Cates' 1st Marines desperately needed some time ashore, not to mention field training, we had to keep them aboard ship to provide working parties around the clock. Rupertus phlegmatically swallowed my briefing of the confused events as he swallowed the daily air.

Despite this activity I continued to study whatever intelligence reports reached us. Learning that B-17s were flying photographic missions over the target areas from Port Moresby, I sent Bill Twining over to go on one of these, giving his special attention to the beaches. Over Guadalcanal a flight of Zeros jumped his bomber. Most of Bill's attention understandably went to the ensuing fight, which cost the Japanese two aircraft, but he did report that the airfield seemed completed and the beaches appeared undefended.

On July 18 Ghormley summoned me to another conference in Auckland. His request to King, made in concert with MacArthur and Nimitz, to defer the operation had been turned down. It being patently impossible to meet the target date of August 1, we drew up a dispatch requesting a delay and sent this to King via Nimitz. King, speaking for the JCS, agreed to delay the landing until August 4; upon our further protest he agreed to August 7—his final compromise.

Ghormley's plan called for us to depart New Zealand on July 22 for the Fijis to rendezvous with Vice Admiral Frank Fletcher's carrier task force and the rest of the Landing Force. Ghormley had given Fletcher local command of the operation, an unfortunate decision since Fletcher was not available during the planning phase. Kelly Turner, who with his staff had just reached Auckland, would command the Amphibious Force whose transports, covered by a group of cruisers and destroyers under Admiral Crutchley of the Royal Navy, would carry the Landing Force which I commanded.

I had known Turner when he was a Navy planner in Washington. A lanky chap who wore steel-rimmed glasses, he resembled an erudite schoolteacher whose didactic manner proved irritating to some people. In Auckland I got along quite well with him since he had not as yet written his plan and perforce relied on mine.

He did seem overly concerned with the Ndeni seizure—a later phase which I thought we should worry about when we came to it—and announced he was keeping the 2d Marines (less one battalion) given him by Ghormley for his reserve expressly for this purpose. I felt this violated the command concepts so clearly laid down in the official manual for amphibious warfare, FTP-167, but told him only that if he retained control of the 2d Marines I could not logically count on this regiment as my reserve and would alter my plan accordingly. With that I returned to Wellington to cope with last-minute details.

Despite the tempo of the past few days in New Zealand, I was reasonably calm and cheerful, partly I suppose to maintain the subterfuge of embarking for maneuvers, partly because I am by nature optimistic. For my own peace of mind this was just as well. Beginning at Koro, the tiny Fiji island where we rendezvoused on July 26, I received a succession of surprises, none pleasant.

That afternoon Turner, I and several staff officers risked a heavy sea to transfer to the destroyer *Dewey* which had brought Dan Callaghan from Auckland. She had also stopped in the Fijis to pick up Read Admiral John McCain, who commanded all of Ghormley's land-based aircraft, Laverne ("Blon-

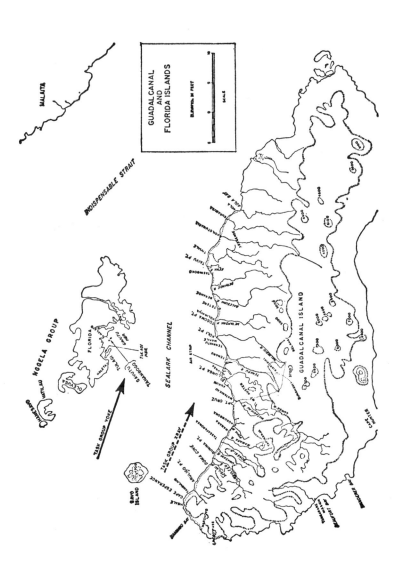

die") Saunders, who commanded the Army Air Corps' B-17s and Bill Twining.

The *Dewey* hauled us to Fletcher's flagship, the *Saratoga*. McCain being senior, custom dictated him to leave the small ship first. Just as he caught hold of the Jacob's ladder someone aboard the *Saratoga* opened a garbage chute and covered him with milk. He managed to retain his hold but a startled officer of the deck soon faced one mad little admiral.

Fletcher received us in the wardroom. I had never met him. He was a distinguished-looking man but seemed nervous and tired, probably the result of the recent battles of Coral Sea and Midway. To my surprise he appeared to lack knowledge of or interest in the forthcoming operation. He quickly let us know he did not think it would succeed. To his arbitrary objections, expressed forcefully, we replied as best we could but obviously failed to make much impression.

Suddenly Fletcher interrupted Turner to ask him how long he would take to land my troops on Guadalcanal. Turner told him about five days. Fletcher said he was going to leave the area in two days because he refused to risk air attack against his carriers for a longer period.

My Dutch blood was beginning to boil, but I forced myself to remain calm while explaining to Fletcher that the days "of landing a small force and leaving" were over. This operation was supposed to take and hold Guadalcanal and Tulagi. To accomplish this I commanded a heavily reinforced division which I was to land on enemy-held territory, which meant a fight. I could hardly expect to land this massive force without air cover—even the five days mentioned by Turner involved a tremendous risk.

Although Turner heatedly backed me, Fletcher curtly announced that he would stay until the third day. With that he dismissed the conference.

Both the sea and my temper were roiling on our return to the *McCawley*. This time we attempted transfer by breeches buoy, Frank Goettge being the guinea pig. One look at his husky frame flopping around in that damn contraption convinced me that the old-fashioned Jacob's ladder was safer— the crew finally poured some oil alongside and we made it aboard.

During the next four days we worked hard inspecting the new units and ironing out various support plans such as air and naval gunfire bombardment, ship-to-shore communications and debarkation plans. On July 28 I wrote home:

> We had landing exercises today. It took too long to get the boats out and too long to get the troops in the boats. We bring them back on board tomorrow and we have another exercise when we hope to correct any mistakes made today. The sea is entirely different in a little boat than in a big ship. You would be surprised to see how agile the old man has become. I've been up and down so many cargo nets that my leg muscles are getting like those of an Alpine guide.

These rehearsals did not work out well, mainly because hidden coral prevented the boats from reaching the beaches. Although I later described the rehearsal as "a complete bust," in retrospect it probably was not that bad. At the very least it got the boats off the transports, and the men down the nets and away. It uncovered deficiencies such as defective boat engines in time to have them repaired and gave both Turner and me a chance to take important corrective measures in other spheres.

But I can't admit to being pleased when we weighed anchor late on July 31. I shuddered to think what would happen if those beaches turned out to have been defended in strength. Consoling myself that a poor rehearsal traditionally meant a good show, I went below for dinner.

VIII

Guadalcanal: Execution

GRAY CLOUDS mercifully covered the last lap of the voyage until darkness took over to protect our final run east between the Russell Islands and Guadalcanal. A few hours after midnight on August 7 our transports split, one group taking Rupertus' force north of Savo Island to Tulagi, one group taking us south of Savo to the waters off Guadalcanal.

We sounded reveille at 3:00 A.M. We dressed and ate breakfast and by first light lined the rails of the *McCawley* to watch Crutchley's cruisers and destroyers and Fletcher's dive bombers commence bombardment of the landing area.

In a short time I broke radio silence to talk to Bill Rupertus. He reported numerous enemy targets including a nest of Japanese seaplanes in Tulagi harbor burning from the bombardment. Observation planes reported little enemy activity in either area. Rupertus planned to land his first assault troops at 8:00 A.M. and I decided to land mine shortly after 9:00.

While Roy Hunt's two battalions were on their way in, Rupertus again reported—a company landing on Florida Island and the first of Edson's raiders, led by his executive officer, Sam Griffith, landing on Tulagi were meeting no opposition. I could not yet tell what was happening on my front since at Turner's insistence planes were laying smoke designed to mark the beaches but only obscuring them. Observation planes continued to report slight if any enemy activity but I felt better only when Hunt's battalions reported themselves ashore on schedule and moving rapidly inland against no opposition.

Roy Hunt landed his CP about half an hour later and reported his units in temporary defenses several hundred yards inland with his 1st Battalion pushing west down the beach as planned. With the perimeter formed, Cates' 1st Marines began landing, again an efficient operation conducted in remarkably short order. Passing through Hunt's units, Cates' people struck out for the Ilu River. Described by a plantation manager as "easily fordable," the Ilu turned out to be a deep lagoon which halted Cates' advance until engineers bridged it by using amphibian tractors for pontoons.

The Tulagi landing was progressing well. In late morning Rupertus reported the raiders running into opposition, but Edson was ashore confidently taking matters in hand—accordingly Rupertus was going ahead with the Gavutu landing, scheduled for noon.

At this critical point Turner received a coast watcher message warning of enemy air on the way to Guadalcanal. While his transports moved into emergency evasive action, Fletcher's planes formed high to the north to jump the enemy force of Betty bombers and Zero fighters that struck shortly before noon. The brief but furious action turned a placid sky into a panoply of planes screaming through air pockmarked by ships' defensive fire. It ended decidedly in our favor—only one destroyer taking a bomb.

With unloading again underway I sent Capers James and Bill Twining ashore to set up an advanced command post, or CP. I was getting ready to join them when another coast watcher report moved Turner into evasive action. This time dive bombers struck us but once again Fletcher's planes and ships' gunfire drove them off with no damage to the transports.

In midafternoon I moved my CP ashore. Our landing craft picked its way through myriad traffic infesting the blue inshore waters to add cargo to cargo already piling alarmingly on the white sand beach.

There in the humid heat Marines stripped to dungaree trousers were trying to cope with the boxes and crates that had to be man-handled out of the small boats, then carried up the beach and sorted into diverse supply dumps. George Rowan, commanding the short party responsible for the work, told me he was getting behind and needed more people. These could come only from the regiments, a levy patently impossible at this critical time. Finding myself literally between the devil of the enemy and the deep blue sea I told Rowan to carry on as best he could—I would help him at the first opportunity.

My major concern centered on the two regiments. I set out for them on foot followed by my orderly, Corporal Smith, who carried a 12-gauge shotgun. On the beach west of the main perimeter I found the 1st Battalion, 5th Marines, moving as if it were about to encounter the entire imperial army. I gave the battalion commander hell. In Hunt's CP I asked him to go down there personally and get the troops moving—the day's objective was the Tenaru River, about two miles west, which I wanted defended by nightfall.

At Cates' CP I learned that his right battalion was bogged down in an immense rain forest west of the Ilu River. Our informants in New Zealand had failed to report this obstacle, a fetid morass so thick with overgrowth you couldn't see Mt. Austen or anything else from its depths. In working their way through it the troops, in poor condition from the weeks aboard ship, seemed about done in by the heat and high humidity. I saw nothing for it but to order Cliff to halt and dig in for the night.

Back at my CP, a rude installation under some shell-shattered coconut palms off Red Beach, I found disturbing news from Bill Rupertus at Tulagi. That afternoon he and Edson had lost radio contact but now Edson was reporting heavy fighting and expected darkness to bring enemy attacks in strength. On Gavutu Bob Williams' parachutists had struck a real hornets' nest. Despite severe fighting in which Williams was wounded, the parachutists were still trying to cross the causeway to Tanambogo. Knowing Rupertus very well I knew he did not tilt at windmills so sent my acting D-1, Jim Murray, to Turner requesting him to release a battalion of the force reserve to Rupertus.

After a hasty meal of cold rations I turned to the next day's plan. Earlier that day my staff and I while still aboard ship had been disconcerted by the appearance of Mt. Austen. What a plantation manager described as a hill a couple of miles inland looked in Jerry Thomas' words "like Mt. Hood" and obviously lay several miles farther inland than reported. We decided to forget about it for the time being. Instead we ordered Cates to shift northwest out of the rain forest, then push west to the airfield. Simultaneously Hunt would hold what he had to the east and south while his 1st Battalion pushed west to the Lunga River, crossed it and struck a Jap camp reported at Kukum.

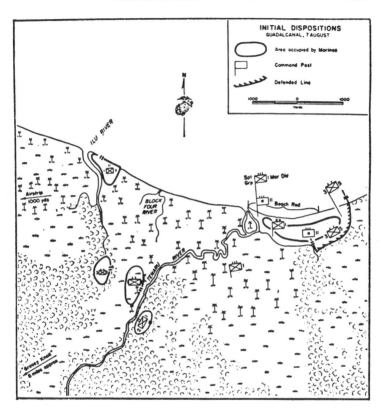

By the time we sent out the order Jim Murray returned—
mission more than accomplished since he had persuaded
Turner to release both of the remaining battalions to me. It
was now very late. Accompanied by staccato bursts of small-
arms fire—the work of my trigger-happy Marines—and the
raucous cries of jungle birds disturbed from their night's
repose we settled down to cope with dispatches that failed
to respect man's need for rest.

On the morning of D + 1 we began to suspect that the
intelligence picture was the reverse of what we believed—
that is, more enemy seemingly occupied Tulagi and those
islands than Guadalcanal. From Rupertus we learned that
Edson's people spent the night holding against a series of
attacks in strength, an ugly battle still being fought. Simultaneously the reserve battalion landed and was fighting on

Gavutu-Tanambogo where a determined enemy already had cost us heavy casualties and would cost us more.

Contrarily, on Guadalcanal no enemy had struck our lines during the night; morning air reconnaissance reported nothing alarming and a few laborers captured by our patrols told interrogators the enemy had fled west.

Here was an opportunity I wanted to exploit. When later in the morning Frank Goettge and I found our units in the Tenaru area again moving as if a Jap defended every bush I decided on drastic action. Calling together a group of officers I told them, "There isn't a damn thing up ahead and I'll prove it with my own reconnaissance." We moved off fast in the jeep, followed a trail off the beach nearly to the airfield and returned, having met scattered small-arms fire in only one area. After that the patrols moved out more vigorously but nonetheless ate up the morning working toward the Lunga.

After briefly inspecting the other units I returned to the CP to worry about the supply situation on the beach. As explained earlier, we landed at Red Beach hoping to avoid the enemy. In consequence we were building supply dumps three miles east of the area which we would defend once we took the airfield. To straighten this out I prevailed on Turner to move his transports west opposite the field, bring them in closer, and furnish ships' working parties to augment the exhausted pioneers.

Just as his ships were getting underway a coast watcher report warning of enemy bombers dispersed the movement. This time the Japanese fliers, armed with torpedos, came in low over Florida Island to elude Fletcher's fighters high over Savo. From a vantage point above the airfield, which we had just reached, we watched them racing in only 20 to 40 feet above the sea. Turner's disciplined gunners waited for proper range, then cut loose. Time after time we saw planes about to release torpedos blasted into explosive flames. The actions left the transport *Elliott* burning, an enemy plane having spun into her hold.

When the transports resumed unloading late in the afternoon we were quite well consolidated ashore. The airfield was ours. Instead of the finished field anticipated we found that the enemy, working from either end, had left a several hundred foot gap in the center. He also left a considerable amount of construction equipment which coupled with that aboard the transports would soon, we hoped, provide a finished airfield.

We had obviously surprised the enemy. West of Lunga River we found the village-camp of Kukum deserted with every evidence of the Japanese fleeing in panic at our approach.

Here we captured large stocks of food and supply. The food, mostly rice but including cases of canned Alaskan crab, salmon, mushrooms, beer and sake, would supplement our daily ration of two meals for weeks to come.

Some of the supply proved disconcertingly impressive. Captain Brown, my division surgeon, pronounced the Japanese surgical kit superior to ours—he and his principal surgeon, Lieutenant Commander Keck, used Japanese instruments for the rest of the campaign. They also possessed a far superior hospital tent, one interlined with mosquito netting so the canvas sides could be raised without exposing the occupants to insects. The compact first-aid kit carried by their soldiers included a filter tube for water purification and salt tablets, both of which we lacked, and a bug repellent superior to ours.

In a letter a few days later to General Holcomb I described our haul:

> A power house, an alternate one, a radio receiver station with six sets with remote control to a sending unit 3 miles away, innumerable pieces of machinery such as generators, engines, pumps, etc. 9 Road Rollers, over 100 trucks so far found of the Chev 2 ton types, Anti-air guns, loaded and locked—can you beat that. Tons of cement, some fifty or sixty thousand gals. of gas and oil and double that much destroyed by bombs. All were in pipes underground [Air raid] warning sets, 2, and hundreds of other items.

That afternoon of our second day ashore Turner sent in a Coast Guard party under Lieutenant Commander Dexter who began turning Lunga Point into a miniature naval operating base. Adding to my satisfaction with the day's events, Bill Rupertus reported Tulagi secured and the situation favorable on Gavutu-Tanambogo. That evening, sitting in a camp chair outside my new CP by the airfield, I scrawled the following note home:

The fighting is now over and we have the place we set out to take. The outfit did beautifully in a very trying situation. I am feeling well and very fit after a night in the jungle, and the worry of what was going to happen to the men. The show opened before dawn and we got in without their knowing it. At first it was exciting but then came the anxious hours of waiting to hear how things turned out on all sides. It went as planned. I deeply regret the men lost and wounded, but we had to expect that and it was less than expected.

My optimism proved premature.

Toward dark a message from Turner summoned me to the *McCawley*. Supposing the conference concerned unloading procedures, I thought little about it as Jerry Thomas and I walked to the beach and tried unsuccessfully to find a *Mc-Cawley* boat. The boat we took valiantly hunted the headquarters ship through the blacked-out fleet. About 11:00 P. M. we stumbled on a Coast Guard transport whose captain put us on the right track to the *McCawley*.

Turner's chief of staff, Captain Peyton, and his Marine officer, Henry Linscott, met us and took us to the wardroom where we found Turner and Admiral Crutchley, who commanded the cruiser-destroyer covering force. Jerry and I were pretty tired but these two looked ready to pass out. Over a cup of coffee Turner told us of a dispatch received several hours earlier which warned him that an enemy task force consisting of three cruisers, three destroyers and two seaplane tenders was heading our way. In his opinion, the force was steaming for Rekata Bay on Santa Isabel Island some 150 miles northwest of Savo. From here, he guessed, the enemy would launch new attacks against the Expeditionary Force on the following day.

He next showed us a dispatch from Fletcher to Ghormley intercepted a few hours before:

Fighter-plane strength reduced from 99 to 78. In view of the large number of enemy torpedo planes and bombers in this area, I recommend the immediate withdrawal of my carriers. Request tankers sent forward immediately as fuel running low.

This was the Koro conference relived except that Fletcher was running away twelve hours earlier than he had already threatened during our unpleasant meeting. We all knew his fuel could not have been running low since he refueled in the Fijis—a tidbit of knowledge that solved nothing. Here was a *fait accompli,* and we knew it. Basing his words on his superior's decision, Turner said he thought to take his transports out the next morning. What did I think?

I told him, "We are in fair shape on Guadalcanal but I don't know about Bill Rupertus on Tulagi. He has been fighting ever since his landing and I doubt if he's gotten much supply ashore. I must certainly check with him first."

Turner peered over the rim of his glasses. "I thought you would want that," he said. "I have a mine layer standing by to take you over there."

Admiral Crutchley broke in. "I'll take you to the mine layer myself. My barge is lying alongside."

At my protest he said, "No, no, I insist. Your mission is much more urgent than mine."

As it turned out this was not the case—he only just reached his flagship when the enemy task force which Turner supposed was far to the north struck his covering ships.

Upon disembarking from the *McCawley* I wrenched my old football knee when a rung of the Jacob's ladder gave way. It swelled quickly and by the time we reached the mine layer, *Southard,* I was limping. Crutchley and I shook hands. He evidently envisioned what the withdrawal of the transports meant for he said, "Vandegrift, I don't know if I can blame Turner for what he's doing."

The skipper of the *Southard* took us to a tiny wardroom for coffee. We were well underway when a sailor's voice blasted the bridge tube: "Commodore, you better come up here. All hell's broke loose."

We shot topside, I moving more slowly than the others. The sailor was right. Flares covered the channel area to our stern. A constant boom of heavy naval guns penetrated the still air. Sailors on deck cheered at sudden enormous explosions. We all felt elated—we were sure our forces were winning. By the time we reached Tulagi the action was over. We did not know that the Japanese fleet discussed only a couple of hours before in Turner's wardroom had caught us by surprise. We did not know that we had witnessed the worst naval disaster in American history, the battle of Savo Island, which cost the U.S.-Australian force five cruisers and one destroyer sunk and others damaged. These ghastly hours claimed 1,300 Allied lives plus some 700 other casualties.

Bill Rupertus and his staff met us aboard the *Neville,* a transport hastily converted to a hospital ship. Calmly and with confidence my assistant commander related details of the incredibly severe two-day fight on Tulagi and Gavutu, the latter still not secured. My news of the pending naval withdrawal upset him because he held little idea of the amount and kind of supply landed—only that it wasn't much.

The executive officer of the *Neville,* a wiry little lieutenant commander named Swigart, told us that if we could handle the supply ashore he would get everything possible off this and other ships by sailing time. I will always be grateful to this energetic and helpful naval officer who proved good for his word.

While the staffs worked out details, Bill and I went below to see the wounded Marines. The pathetic sight of rows of helpless men, some of them only boys, brought home the crushing responsibility of command. Some of these Marines were in a bad way but the spirit they displayed deeply moved me and made me terribly proud. When I was satisfied that everything possible was being done for them I returned topside.

There we listened to staff estimates and decided that Bill could make it on his own for a few days, a decision sent to Turner by dispatch. Despite my swollen and aching knee I slept a little on the return trip to Guadalcanal, where we met the *McCawley* and other transports returning from the eastern end of the island. While Peyton and Linscott transferred back aboard, Turner stood on the lower bridge of the *McCawley* shouting to me through a megaphone. There had been a heavy battle. He did not know the details but Crutchley's covering force was badly hurt. Turner was sailing his transports as soon as their boats finished picking up survivors from our sunken ships.

Waving off, we returned by small boat to the beach. In my CP I brought Capers James up to date and asked him to call in the division staff and commanders down through battalion level. I read dispatches until the officers assembled. It was 9:00 A.M. Some of the transports were calling in their boats prior to getting underway. Very shortly we would fight alone.

IX

We Stand Alone

SINGLY or in pairs they straggled to my CP, the colonels, lieutenant colonels, and majors on whom so much depended. They already were a sorry-looking lot with bloodshot eyes and embryonic beards and filthy dungarees. They were tired. They did not talk much as they slumped to the wet ground under the coconut palms and huddled over their knees against rain hissing on a pathetic fire. Some smoked, others sipped black coffee from aluminum canteen cups and swore when the hot metal touched chapped lips. Most of them watched the beach and the parade of small boats landing survivors whose semi-naked bodies black from burns and oil of the sunken ships claimed the ministrations of our doctors and corpsmen. Even as they watched, the cruiser *Chicago,* her bow shot away, limped past transports busily hoisting landing craft to their decks.

Sometimes a commander can withhold bad news, sometimes not. I told these officers of the major naval engagement whose outcome we did not yet know. I told them of Fletcher's carriers precipitately retiring, which meant that the transports were leaving. According to Ran Pate's best estimate, less than half of our supply was on the beach; all of our heavy equipment remained aboard the transports; God only knew when we could expect aircraft protection much less surface craft; with the transports gone the enemy would shift his attacks against us and we could expect surface attacks as well.

Then I ordered them to relate these unsavory facts to their junior officers, NCOs and men. But they must also pound home that we anticipated no Bataan, no Wake Island. Since 1775 Marines had found themselves in tough spots. They had survived and we would survive—but only if every officer and man on Guadalcanal gave his all to the cause.

Jerry Thomas took over to detail three immediate tasks: construction of a main line of resistance (MLR), completion of the airfield, removal of supply from the beaches to dispersed inland dumps under the concealing palms.

In this initial phase my biggest fear centered on a landing against our beaches, although I worried nearly as much about an attack against my left, or western, flank, the enemy having retreated in that direction. To compress my perimeter and lend weight to the priority areas I pulled in my right, or east, flank from the Ilu to the Tenaru. Beginning 600 yards inland Cates' 1st Marines, less one battalion, refused this flank to the beach, then dug in along the beach to the Lunga River.

At the Lunga he tied in with Hunt's 5th Marines who carried the perimeter up to Kukum and around it back to the Lunga to tie in with the LVT company.

Del Valle, ably assisted by his executive officer, John Bemis, backed this 9,600-yard MLR by emplacing his 75mm and 105mm howitzers in central positions which enabled them to register anywhere on the line. Pepper emplaced his 90mm antiaircraft guns northwest of the airfield. Bob Luckey dug in his 75mm half-tracks north of the airfield, ready to move forward to prepared positions on the beach. Behind them I retained the tank company and an infantry battalion as division reserve.

To defend the remaining 9,000 yards, mainly of heavy jungle running south from my CP and then east behind the airfield, supporting units, primarily artillery, engineers and pioneers, manned outposts tied together by roving patrols. Beyond the perimeter Hunt and Cates established observation posts besides pushing out daily patrols.

Simultaneously unit commanders furnished working parties to move the supply up from the beaches, sort it and store it in protected dumps. All of this called for a great deal of improvisation since most of our sandbags and all the barbed wire remained aboard the transports. Moreover, the units received almost no help from the engineers busy with the equally important task of finishing the airfield.

Besides other abandoned equipment the enemy obligingly left us two small gasoline trains with hoppers. At first we laughed at the Toonerville Trolley appearance of the trains but soon found that without them we never could have moved over 7,000 cubic yards of fill to make the field operational by August 12—an immense accomplishment due mainly to the excellent work of my engineer officer, Frank Geraci, my air officer, Ken Weir, and a lot of sweat from a lot of willing Marines.

These activities were well underway by late afternoon of August 9 when Bill Rupertus reported all objectives in his area taken and the situation well in hand. Although he was continuing to patrol Florida Island and other smaller islands, his victory was obvious and I cited his splendid men in a division bulletin:

> The Commanding General desires to transmit to all hands here on Guadalcanal the good news that has reached us from Tulagi. Our comrades there have added the name of a splendid victory to the long roll of battle honor of the Corps. Striking from the sea they assaulted and conquered a series of organized positions defended in great strength by a wily and determined opponent. The fight was carried to the enemy at all times and in all places and he was driven from every place he held by the resolute attack of men who were not afraid to die. God favors the bold and strong of heart; the Commanding General is grateful to inform you that casualties, while severe, were less than at first believed and by no means disproportionate to the results achieved. We salute the officers and men of our Division who carried through the Tulagi operations to so brilliant a conclusion.

Our own patrols to the east and south reported negatively on August 9, but one of Hunt's small patrols in attempting to cross the Matanikau River southwest of Kukum ran into an enemy force, losing one officer killed and several men wounded—my first combat casualties on Guadalcanal despite a noon air raid that tumbled us into slit trenches and foxholes. Our suspicion of a Japanese force to the west was confirmed the following day when Hunt sent out a larger patrol which again encountered enemy opposition on the Matanikau.

General Rupertus, reporting no further discernible enemy in his area, radioed a list of priority supply requirement. By this time I held a pretty good idea of our own supply situation so we raised Ghormley's new headquarters in Noumea to report our needs. Air power being the priority need, I urged him to send the planes in as scheduled.

Hoping to counter the adverse affect on morale of day and night air attacks, I began making morning tours of the perimeter. I started about 10:30 and talked to as many troops as possible. Not only did this allow me to keep a personal eye on the command but because the enemy usually struck at noon a definite tension began building up in late morning and I thought it a good idea to show the troops that the division commander was out and about. I repeated the tour in the afternoons whenever possible.

By August 11 the full impact of the vanished transports was permeating the command, so again I called a conference of my staff and command officers. I emphasized our progress, particularly in sending out aggressive patrols which were our only eyes and ears, and told them to spread the word of the remarkable progress on the airfield. I again stressed that we could and would hold. I ended the conference by posing with this fine group of officers, a morale device that worked because they thought if I went to the trouble of having the picture taken then I obviously planned to enjoy it in future years.

Enemy air attacks infuriated all of us. That afternoon one of them interrupted my writing a report to General Holcomb. I continued:

> Just ducked into the side of a hill as six Jap Zeros came sailing by at low altitude, guns blazing, no casualties. I wonder why we (U.S.) are the only ones with short-range fighters. These come from 450 miles away. They climb and maneuver well. When the bombers came down the other day, 44 of them, they had fighters over them.

Prospect of survival brightened considerably on the following day when a PBY piloted by Rear Admiral McCain's aide lumbered to a stop in the muddy airstrip which we decided to call Henderson Field in honor of a Marine pilot killed at Midway. McCain sent him over to learn if the field was operational. Although the unmatted strip lacked taxiways and other refinements, the young pilot pronounced it suitable for fighter operations, a particularly courageous and optimistic decision in view of the day and night air attacks and, as of the night before, surface bombardment by destroyers. McCain also wanted to know when he could visit me to discuss air matters. I blessed him for his attitude, which brought a great deal of encouragement to the Marines.

A tragedy quickly blighted our morale boost. On the previous day Frank Goettge, my intelligence officer and old friend, reported that, according to a captured Japanese warrant officer, hundreds of Japanese troops were roaming the jungle west of us ready to surrender. Frank tied this intelligence in with a patrol report of a group of Japanese waving a white flag on the west bank of the Matanikau. Frank proposed personally to lead a patrol to this area.

Initially hostile to his request, I unfortunately gave in but cautioned him to avoid a regular engagement. By the time he lined up his force—some twenty-five Marines including a Navy surgeon—it was late Sunday afternoon. Without notifying us at division headquarters, this very brave officer decided to push ahead and make a night landing on the other side of the Matanikau.

Just after daybreak on Monday, August 13, a naked, badly cut and exhausted Marine crawled into the perimeter. This was Sergeant Charles Arndt, who with two others escaped the ambush which struck Frank's patrol. Roy Hunt immediately sent out a reinforced company which landed west of Point Cruz to beat its way east back to our lines. It found no trace of Frank's patrol nor did we ever find a trace. The following day I wrote home:

I write this with a heavy heart. We lost Frank Goettge. In addition to being a splendid and brave officer, Frank was a fine shipmate . . .

Following hard on the Goettge disaster came ominous news from another direction. One of Cates' patrols probing to the east happened on to a missionary Catholic priest from Massachusetts who reported native rumors of an enemy force farther east.

We were still pondering this unsettling report when confirmation arrived in the person of Captain Martin Clemens, the coast watcher who strolled into our lines after spending months in the Guadalcanal hills literally surrounded by enemy. Clemens brought with him a small and loyal group of native scouts including Sergeant Major Vouza, a retired member of the Solomon Islands constabulary. At the outbreak of war Vouza, a black and bandy-legged little fellow, as were all the natives, reported to Clemens and accompanied him into the hills. There they recruited a goodly force of natives who hated the Japanese because of cruelty to the islanders. Clemens and Vouza trained these young men as scouts and when Clemens offered me his and their services I was delighted to accept. Vouza later rendered superb service as did all the scouts—of the entire coast watcher organization I can say nothing too lavish in praise.

Clemens, a famed athlete in his undergraduate days at Cambridge, was a remarkable chap of medium height, well-built and apparently suffering no ill effects from his self-imposed jungle exile. He sat on a ration box in my CP to describe the original Jap landing on Guadalcanal, our own landing, and subsequent events. His skill at eluding the enemy and getting valuable reports back to listening stations was fantastic, as was the teleradio that made this possible. Our radios were practically worthless and I asked Clemens how in the world he kept his working in this wet, humid climate. "I just wait until morning," he said, "open it, dry it off and by afternoon it works."

My international command received further reinforcement on the following day when McCain took a terrible chance to send in a small convoy of destroyer escorts carrying aviation gasoline, ammunition, bombs, tools and spare parts plus a good-sized Seabee unit to help the engineers further improve the airfield for the planes we hoped would soon arrive. One of the officers brought me a letter from McCain. After discussing a scheme to build a PBY anchorage at either Lunga or Tulagi, thus allowing these lumbering old amphibians to be used for night torpedo operations, he also promised some B-17 bombers to give daylight coverage. He then went on to the most important matter:

> The best and proper solution, of course, is to get fighters and SBDs [dive bombers] onto your field. *Long Island* [a small carrier] arrives Vila the early morning of the 17th. Trained pilots will be put aboard and she will proceed to fly-away position off south tip of San Cristobal. Planes will be flown off to reach field between 4 and 5 in the

afternoon probably the 18th, and if not the 18th, the 19th, of which you will be duly advised. As I understand she has one squadron of fighters and one squadron of SBDs . . .

They could arrive none too soon. The mounting ground threat kept me almost constantly preoccupied. Martin Clemens confirmed the existence of an enemy force of unknown size to the east. A subsequent dispatch from Turner reported indications of a massive Japanese attack building against us. Knowing that Bill Rupertus faced no such threat on Tulagi, I asked him to ready the 2d Battalion of the 5th Marines along with the raider and parachutist battalions for transfer to Guadalcanal. I also asked Roy Hunt to make a probing action in strength across the Matanikau and Cates to send a similar patrol east and souheast. Clemens agreed to send Vouza and a patrol to the south to work its way west deep behind the perimeter.

On August 18 three of Hunt's companies kicked off, two attacking the village of Matanikau and one landing west in the vicinity of Kokumbona in order to catch any enemy fleeing in that direction. In a two-day action this force waged several sharp fire fights which cost the Japanese some sixty killed at a loss of four Marines killed and a small number wounded. I was especially pleased at the action of the company officers who calmly and bravely pursued the action. Captain Spurlock, commanding Company L, unexpectedly faced the first banzai bayonet charge of the war and thoroughly disrupted it.

Simultaneously Captain Brush, commanding Company A, 1st Marines, pushed east toward Koli Point while Sergeant Major Vouza and his patrol disappeared into the bush country on his right. Brush ably ambushed a group of about thirty-five enemy and wisely wasted no time in collecting the map cases and personal papers from the bodies already identified by uniforms as officers of the imperial army. These documents showed that the Japanese had pegged my position to a T, undoubtedly from observation posts on Mt. Austen, the massive eminence that, stolid and green, rose tantalizingly from the reach of my meager forces.

Certain of my staff wanted me to use a portion of these forces to probe eastward to clarify the uncertainty aroused by the new intelligence. After considerable thought I rejected any such plan in favor of conservation: having taken the airfield, I would hold it with what force I had. I did, however, order every possible measure to further fortify my east, or right, flank along the Tenaru. Del Valle quickly and efficiently reregistered his artillery along this line.

This was my position when late on August 20 Pepper's antiaircraft gunners for once relaxed at the sound of aircraft. From the east flying into the evening sun came one of the most beautiful sights of my life—a flight of twelve SBD dive bombers led by young Lieutenant Colonel Dick Mangrum. I was close to tears and I was not alone when the first SBD taxied up and this handsome and dashing aviator jumped to the ground. "Thank God you have come," I told him.

Following Mangrum's flight, Captain John Smith led in nineteen Grumman Wildcats, the stubby little fighters that were to turn the tide in the Pacific air war. With the arrival of Charley Fike, the group commander, Cactus Air Force set up operations in the Pagoda, an unfinished building bequeathed to us by the enemy.

This concluded phase one of the operation—an American victory. I knew not what vicissitudes the future would hurl at us on Guadalcanal. No doubt they would fall fast and heavy That evening I joined my Marines for a bath in the Tenaru River. From the brown water I looked up at a young Marine positioned behind a 30-caliber machine gun guarding our relaxation. Somehow he epitomized everything that all of us were working for. Somehow he caused me to face the future with sublime confidence.

X

Battles Land and Air

HOPING to get a little sleep before the visit of "Louie the Louse," the Jap plane which alternated with "Washing Machine Charlie" to bomb us usually about midnight, I turned in early on August 20. Shortly after midnight I was awakened, not by Louie, but by a field telephone. Jerry Thomas reported a call from Al Pollock, commanding the 2d Battalion of Cates' 1st Marines: one of his listening posts on the east side of the Tenaru River had exchanged shots with enemy patrols and withdrawn. Jerry correctly alerted all units—there was nothing to do but wait.

About 2:00 A.M. a green flare exploded the clammy air of the eastern night into a bedlam of rifle, machine gun, mortar and artillery fire. Huddled over the field phone in the operations dugout we waited anxiously for the first reports. A commander feels enormously helpless in such a situation. He can only rely on the thoroughness of measures already taken, on the courage of his men and on the two slim wires that connect him to the scene of action or on runners whom he dispatches to the scene.

Fortunately our wire held good. We soon learned from Cates that this was no probing action but a full-scale night banzai attack. At terrible cost in lives the enemy briefly penetrated Pollock's line but he quickly restored it with his reserve and was now calling down artillery fire. Violence rocked the hours of darkness but what I most feared, a simultaneous attack against my west, or left, flank, failed to materialize— Roy Hunt continued to report a quiet front.

Soon after dawn when Jerry Thomas and I reached Cates' CP the issue no longer stood in doubt. Pollock's people had beaten off a second major attack, this time from north of the river's sandspit. After laying down a heavy mortar barrage, enemy infantry stormed across the river, struck our wire

139

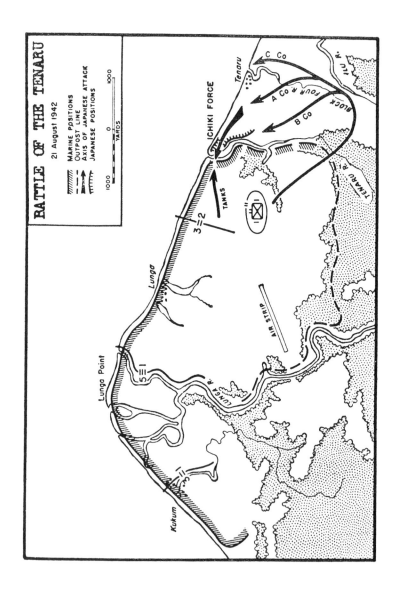

BATTLE OF THE TENARU
21 August 1942

MARINE POSITIONS
OUTPOST LINE
AXIS OF JAPANESE ATTACK
JAPANESE POSITIONS

1000   0   1000
YARDS

C Co
Tenaru
A Co
FOUR R COR
BLOCK
B Co
ICHIKI FORCE
TANKS
3 ≡ 2
Lunga
5 ≡ 1
Lunga Point
LUNGA R.
AIR STRIP
TENARU R.
ILU R.
Kukum

and were decimated from enfiladed machine gun fire and del Valle's artillery.

Thanks to Sergeant Major Vouza we now held a pretty good idea of the enemy force. During the night's action Vouza, bleeding from a dozen wounds, crawled into Pollock's front lines. Soon he was gasping out his story to Martin Clemens: the enemy had surprised his patrol, captured him, interrogated him without success, then tied him to a tree to torture him unmercifully and finally leave him for dead. His face a pulp from rifle butts smashed into it and bleeding from bayonet wounds in the throat, shoulders and chest, he chewed through his ropes and on hands and knees crawled through the battle to reach our lines and gasp out valuable information on the strength and dispositions of the attacking enemy.

To eliminate this force Cates and Thomas suggested sending a battalion south across the Tenaru to strike the enemy's left flank and rear, pushing him into the anvil formed by Pollock's defensive line. The plan sounded good to me. To accomplish it I released my reserve battalion commanded by L. B. Cresswell. We also sent Pollock a company of engineers who worked throughout the morning, often under fire, laying a minefield across the sandspit and restoring the shattered defenses.

It is frustrating to remain away from the scene of action no matter how much trust and confidence you hold in your subordinate commanders. To while away the long morning hours I forced myself to dictate dispatches and letters. Each time Jerry Thomas hove into view I looked expectantly at him; each time he maddeningly offered only the phrase, "Nothing yet."

Shortly after noon Cresswell reported his battalion in position, ready to attack. Jerry and I hurried to Cates' CP. By the time we arrived our planes, which had landed only the previous day, were strafing the compressed enemy while artillery crashed through the coconut groves to take an equally deadly toll. We were also learning more of the enemy's habits —Marines responding to cries for help from wounded Japanese were either treacherously shot by the wounded or blown up by hand grenades concealed on their bodies. I later wrote my reaction in a report to General Holcomb:

I have never heard or read of this kind of fighting.

These people refuse to surrender. The wounded will wait until the men come up to examine them and blow themselves and the other fellow to pieces with a hand grenade. You can readily see the answer to that . . .

The answer was war without quarter, so I offered Cates a platoon of light tanks to finish off the action. Moments later we watched the little tanks, their 37mm guns firing canister shot, splash through the surf and emerge to run across the bodies covering the sandspit. I described the action to General Holcomb:

[We] sent tanks with infantry down the line on them; it was a slaughter, those they did not shoot they ran over. The rear of the tanks looked like meat grinders. There is a story going around that the tanks would then hit a coconut tree, thus knocking out a sniper or snipers and the riflemen would shoot them when they lit.

By now other stories were filtering upward—true stories of human bravery on the previous night. Stories of a badly wounded young lieutenant who could no longer fire but remained slumped in his foxhole unjamming automatic rifles for others; stories of an infuriated Marine who threw aside a jammed weapon to kill three Japanese with a machete; stories of a corporal named Al Schmidt who, almost completely blinded, stayed on to fire his machine gun; stories of men responding to the acid test with courage which etched their deeds onto that long scroll of the noblest deeds of man.

We beat the Japanese at the Tenaru. The attack cost them some 800 dead with only a handful escaping to the jungle. Our own casualties came to 100 with 43 dead.

But casualties rarely tell the stories of battle, the sacrifices involved or the extent of the victory. And this was the case with what even then we began calling the battle of the Tenaru. In but hours its psychological effect grew out of all proportion to its physical dimensions. Yesterday the Jap seemed something almost superhuman, a kind of mechanical juggernaut that swept inexorably through the Philippines, through the Dutch East Indies, over the beaches at Guam and Wake Island, through the jungles of New Guinea. True, we had beaten him at Tulagi and Gavutu but to us on Guadalcanal this victory stood remote, difficult to grasp because it was foreign to the immediacy of ourselves.

But today *we* had beaten the Jap. The Jap no longer seemed superhuman. The Jap was a physical thing, a soldier in uniform, carrying a rifle and firing machine guns and mortars and charging stupidly against barbed wire and rifles and machine guns. We stopped this Jap, decimated his ranks, and I hastened to pass the word in a division letter:

> The Commanding General desires that all personnel of the Division be informed concerning the results of the Battle of the Tenaru River which commenced at 0200 August 21 and was terminated at nightfall of that date.
>
> The 1st Marines and supporting units, when their defensive position west of the Tenaru River, north coast of Guadalcanal, Solomon Islands, was assaulted under cover of darkness by a well-trained, well-equipped enemy landing force of about 700 men * whose mission was to seize the airport west of the river, defended their position with such zeal and determination that the enemy was unable to effect a penetration of the position in spite of repeated efforts throughout the night. The 1st Marines, counterattacking at daybreak with an envelopment which caught the enemy in the rear and on the flank, thus cutting off his withdrawal and pushing him from inland in the direction of the sea, virtually annihilated his force and achieved a victory fully commensurate with the military traditions of our Corps. The Commanding General conveys to the officers and men who carried through this outstanding operation the salute of all officers and men of the Division.

Confidence is a vital factor in a unit. It was wondrous to see the infectious wave of confidence that swept over the Marines on Guadalcanal. On this note I ended my report to General Holcomb:

> The men are fine, in good spirits and thank God still in good health. These youngsters are the darndest people when they get started you ever saw.

---

* Over 100 enemy dead drifted onto the beach in the next day or two.

Our war switched to the air. The day after the battle of the Tenaru we learned that a large Japanese task force was standing toward the Solomons. That afternoon one of McCain's PBYs sighted a group of enemy transports estimated within maximum range of our planes.

The chilling thought of heavy ground reinforcement called for the most drastic action. Charley Fike, Dick Mangrum and I decided to risk our small air force in an all-out attack. From the Pagoda I watched Mangrum lead his dive bombers aloft followed by Smith's fighters. I wondered how many would return.

They all returned and very soon because north of Florida Island they ran into heavy weather. The pilots were very upset by this abort; I was, too, but tried to hide my disappointment and comfort them as best I could.

The next morning we picked up another sighting report from one of McCain's PBYs, but neither our planes nor those from Fletcher's carriers operating to the south could find the enemy. That afternoon a flight under Commander Harry Felt from the carrier *Saratoga* landed at Henderson, fuel tanks nearly empty. I now commanded a joint air force, a squadron of Army P-400s having flown in from Espiritu Santo.

On August 24 Smith's F4Fs ran into a large enemy flight and knocked down 10 bombers and 6 Zeros at a loss of 4 planes, the pilot of one parachuting to safety. Fletcher's force also struck a Japanese carrier but the carrier *Enterprise* caught hell and retired south, which forced a flight of SBDs and TBFs from her deck to land on Henderson Field.

With the situation desperate our luck changed radically and dramatically. A search-and-strike flight returning to base the following morning struck the Japanese transport force. Minutes later Marine and Navy fliers left a cruiser burning and, more important, a large transport helpless in the sea. Army B-17s followed this strike, sunk another large transport and damaged a third to send the enemy in retirement north —very welcome news to me and obviously to others:

From COMSOPAC [Admiral Ghormley]—all your shipmates in the South Pacific give three loud cheers.

The enemy struck back hard the following day but while

our small perimeter shook from his bombs our fighters caught him on the way out to flame 13 bombers. Just before dark two days later Dick Mangrum's dive bombers stumbled on to four of his destroyers, sank one and severely damaged another.

Smith came back into his own the next day, his F4Fs knocking down 8 Zeros, and on the following day another 14. Unfortunately the Army's highly vaunted P-400 proved practically worthless for any kind of altitude fighting. After a number of these went down I ordered them confined to close air support and reconnaissance flights.

This series of hot air actions proved no less significant than had the preceding battle of the Tenaru. Enemy fliers had established a myth of invincibility centering around the famous Zero fighter. In ten days American pilots completely shattered this myth, an achievement I cited in a division letter of the time:

> The Commanding General desires that all personnel of the 1st Division and attached units be apprised of outstanding efforts made by and the conspicuous successes obtained by VMSB-232, VMF-223, VS-5 and 67th Fighting Squadron (USA), all of which were stationed at Guadalcanal, Solomon Islands, during all or a portion of the 10-day period from 21—30 August 1942.
>
> During this period one or more of the above-named units have contacted the enemy on the sea or the air eight times. Sustaining losses themselves which were far below what might be expected in view of the results obtained they have destroyed 16 enemy twin-engine bombers, 5 single-engine bombers, 39 Zero Fighters and 3 destroyers in addition to which they have hit and probably destroyed 1 cruiser, 2 destroyers and 2 transports.
>
> Operating under difficulties from an unfinished advance air base with limited facilities for upkeep and repair these units have without regard for the cost sought out the enemy at every opportunity and have engaged him with such aggressiveness and skill as to contribute conspicuously to the success of the Allied cause in the Solomon Island Area. The Commanding General takes pleasure in conveying to the officers and men of the above-named units in behalf of the officers and men of the 1st Division

appreciation and felicitations for their outstanding performance of duty.

Higher echelons quickly noted by dispatch the significance of the achievement:

The Under-Secretary of the Navy [Mr. James Forrestal] joins with me in saying to your hard-hitting fliers, "well done again." Ghormley.

And:

CINCUS [Admiral King] to Vandegrift for his fliers—Many happy returns Sunday and congratulations—Keep knocking them off. CINCPAC [Admiral Nimitz] congratulating.

The victory exacted a heavy toll, not only in fliers killed and planes shot down, but in general fatigue of airmen and crews. Although our supply line was beginning to shape up a trifle, we lacked much equipment essential to running an air operation of this size. We still fueled by hand, loaded machine gun belts and bomb racks by hand and cannibalized shot-up and bombed aircraft for spare parts.

Our limited rations, mainly captured rice, miserably failed to provide the high protein diet prescribed for altitude flying. The pilots also suffered from diseases endemic to us all, mainly dysentery and fungus infections. Jap air and surface raids, day and night, disrupted badly needed rest to the extent that I began to wonder how much longer my fliers could keep going.

Still, our position showed signs of improving. Coincidental with Mr. Forrestal's visit to Ghormley back in Noumea, Nimitz' logistics officer, Admiral Bill Calhoun, flew into Guadalcanal. At last I was talking to someone from a higher echelon who understood our problems, particularly how the lack of heavy equipment hindered our airfield maintenance. Upon his departure from the island Bill told me, "Archer, I'm going back to Espiritu Santo where I'll stand on that dock and see that the heavy material you need is put aboard ship and sent to you. I promise you this."

That is exactly what happened. From then on we began

to receive bulldozers, graders and forklifts, though not until much later in the number needed.

I did not know it at the time but our situation dramatically impressed Mr. Forrestal, who upon his return to America forcefully presented our need for additional aircraft to the highest levels.

By August 30 the 19 F4Fs which had flown in but ten days earlier were reduced to 5 that could fly. But now Colonel Bill Wallace, who had been with me in China in 1927, led in a squadron of 17 F4Fs and another of 12 SBDs, and assumed command of the air operation.

Admiral McCain also flew down for a short visit, thereby fulfilling a promise made when we separated a month earlier in the Fijis. At that time I told him, "I have one bottle of bourbon and will save it to celebrate your visit."

I now opened this bottle, sufficient for about one drink each for us and our staffs. We were toasting his visit when the siren announced enemy bombers. Later that night a Japanese cruiser tossed the normal ration of shells at us; the next morning enemy air again struck. During this attack McCain and I sat in my little dugout. He was a scrawny little fellow with very sharp features and intense eyes. At the height of the bombing he fixed me with his eyes. "By God, Vandegrift, this is your war and you sure are welcome to it. But when I go back tomorrow I am going to try to get you what you need for your air force here."

In a subsequent dispatch to Ghormley, MacArthur, Nimitz and King, he outlined our situation then called for:

> Two full squadrons of P-38s or F4Fs in addition to present strength should be put into Cactus [Guadalcanal] at once with replacements in training to south. . . . The situation admits of no delay whatever. . . . With substantially the reinforcement requested Cactus can be a sinkhole for enemy air power and can be consolidated, expanded and exploited to enemy's mortal hurt—The reverse is true if we lost Cactus—If the reinforcement requested is not made available Cactus can not be supplied and hence cannot be held.

McCain did not add that even with air reinforcement the issue would remain in considerable doubt. Despite our air victories the enemy had landed and was continuing to land substantial ground reinforcements to our east and west—information reported by Clemens' scouts and partially confirmed by our ground and air patrols.

To meet the mounting threat in late August I began moving troops over from Tulagi, asking Turner to replace them with the rest of the 2d Marines—nearly 1,000 troops—still at Noumea. I also made it clear to Turner and Ghormley that I needed the 7th Marine Regiment, still at Samoa, as soon as possible.

In early September Bill Rupertus loaded-out Edson's raiders. En route to Guadalcanal the always perceptive Edson landed patrols on Savo Island. Discovering no enemy, the raiders re-embarked on two destroyer-transports and landed at Lunga that evening. Unfortunately the skippers decided to cruise out the night instead of trying to return to Tulagi. Early in the morning a Japanese surface force caught them in Sealark Channel and sank both ships with a considerable loss of life.

XI

Crisis

EARLY in September my old friend Roy Geiger arrived to take over the Cactus air operation. A Parris Island classmate of mine in 1909, Roy was one of America's great air pioneers. He was a splendid chap, taciturn and solid and very hard to catch off base. Once squared away in his tent by the airstrip he reported to my CP to deliver a mailbag described as "fan mail" from Admiral Nimitz. The admiral's thoughtful gesture turned out to be a case of Johnny Walker Scotch. Knowing I drank bourbon Roy said, "Archer, I have a case of bourbon and will trade you level even though mine are quarts."

We loaded the precious Scotch in a jeep and drove to his tent. He rummaged around, quietly at first, then frantically. At last he admitted the awful truth. Someone had walked off with his bourbon. Although I gave him two bottles of Scotch, his chief of staff, Louis Woods, reported him in bad temper for some time.

I welcomed such interludes because they helped to relieve the tension of our days. On another occasion of some important visitor, Roy Hunt thoughtfully donated a half dozen good-sized bass to my mess. At dinner he explained how Bill Whaling had caught these and went on to build Bill into some sort of Daniel Boone. Finally one of my suspicious staff officers turned to Bill: "Just how did you catch these bass?" Bill turned brick-red. "Hell," he said, "I dropped a hand grenade in the Lunga and up they came."

These simple jokes passed through the command to give everyone a much-needed laugh. Once I was sitting with my staff listening to the 7:00 P.M. news broadcast from San Francisco. After the news the program switched to a USO show whose audience went wild when the announcer introduced Paulette Goddard. I turned to my operations officer.

149

"Jerry, just who the hell is Paulette Goddard?" Before he could answer the disgusted voice of a Marine came through the night air: "Now ain't that something—the old man's never heard of Paulette Goddard."

We listened to Tokyo Rose with considerably more amusement than to some of our own news broadcasts which tended to paint too black a picture of our situation on Guadalcanal. Defeatism is a terrible disease in a military organization. It can spread faster than dysentery or malaria. Because of that I always tried to display confidence during my daily tours of the perimeter. When, for example, I saw an emplacement protected by only one or two strands of wire, I would say cheerfully, "That will hold anything they can throw against us."

I tried to offer a similar confidence to our correspondents. Quartered with our junior staff officers these varied in numbers depending on the availability of transport aircraft. Persons such as Dick Tregaskis, Bob Miller and Bob Brumby accompanied us in the original landing. Others came and went on ships or planes. From the beginning of the campaign I let them go where they wanted and write what they wanted so long as it came within logical security confines. I refused to tie up my meager staff by publishing canned communiqués, and I refused to tie up my limited time by holding scheduled press conferences, although I made it clear that any correspondent could come to me at any time with any question.

The press later complimented me for this policy which did produce good copy and, later, good books by Tregaskis, Sherrod, Hersey and others. It wasn't as charitable as it sounds—the only radio available to them was under our control. I did not know, incidentally, that higher echelons were drastically censoring their copy.

The reinforcements from Tulagi somewhat freed my tactical hand. When in early September Clemens' scouts reported a Japanese force in the vicinity of Tasimboko I decided to send Edson's raiders to investigate.

Merritt's small task force put to sea on the night of September 7. As he was about to land the next morning, two of our transports escorted by warships pulled into view from the south. Evidently thinking we were landing in strength, the considerable Japanese force took to the jungle, permitting the raiders to land unopposed. Edson quickly attacked the enemy's base camp, which he destroyed after seizing some arms and a large number of documents.

The documents suggested that a considerable Japanese force based on Tasimboko was moving southwest behind our perimeter. One morning Edson and Thomas came to my CP, unfolded a map and said they believed they knew where the enemy was going to hit us. I asked them where. In his respectfully disapproving way Edson said, "The ridge you insist on putting your new CP behind."

He referred to a ridge about 2,000 yards south of the airfield. Here the terrain, after sloping down from Mt. Austen, began to level off either into jungle or to foothills and chopped-up ridges covered with high, tough kunai grass. The ridge indicated by Edson and Thomas dominated this immediate terrain complex. Its spine, running northwest to southeast for about 1,000 yards, sprouted four vertebrae-like spurs, two on each side.

For some time I had been getting tired of jumping from bed several times a night and having shrapnel from Japanese bombs and surface shells whistling through my CP. Wanting a more protected location, I found a spot beneath a hind spur on this ridge where engineers were now building a new CP.

But assuming the presence of a Jap force in the area the ridge obviously represented a danger. We blocked it by moving up Edson's composite battalion of raiders and parachutists. On September 10 Edson put his raiders on the forward spur, which sloped several hundred yards down to the Lunga River; he put the parachutists on the left forward spur, where they tied in with units on their left. Del Valle registered in his artillery, shifting a battery of 105s just south of the airfield to give better support. I brought my division reserve, the 2d Battalion of the 5th Marines, south of the airfield and asked Cates to back it with Cresswell's battalion.

Simultaneously, despite some profane staff arguments, I moved into the new CP about 100 yards behind Edson. This was no act of courage—I simply wanted a good night's sleep. I described my new location in a letter home:

The Engineers said that I had been living in the mud long enough, and they have built a pavilion about 3 ft. off the ground, 35 ft. long by 18 ft. wide. Capers [my chief of staff] and I sleep in one end and the other end is the office and sitting room. It is in the jungle and this morning at sunrise the white and red parrots and the large macaws were all around.

I have some Jap wicker furniture and will in a few days have a Jap icebox run by kerosene if we can make it work. The pavilion is built of Japanese wood and the mats by our bed are Japanese too, and some of the mess gear is also Japanese. So you see, they did well by us.

Two vicious air raids during the day interrupted these moves besides depleting our already depleted air force. But by evening the troops were digging in and Geiger's (and my) spirits were raised by an incoming flight of twenty-four F4Fs taken from the carrier *Saratoga* presently in drydock for extensive repairs.

My first visitor to the new CP was Kelly Turner, who flew in the next day. That morning Jap air hit us hard. Soon after Turner's arrival the sirens again sent us to shelter. Turner seemed to be under a strain—and after the air raid I learned why.

In my CP Turner reached inside his shirt, pulled forth an ordinary Navy communications form and passed it to me. A staff estimate of the situation drawn for and approved by Ghormley, it gave the unpleasant details of a very strong Japanese amphibious force concentrated at Rabaul and Truk. Forward area air strengths were included along with other facts suggesting the enemy would launch a huge amphibious effort against us in two or three weeks.

This was bad enough but I read next of Ghormley's situation—his shortage of ships and airplanes, his lack of supply. Compared to the size and strength of the enemy this meant, according to the staff paper, that the Navy no longer could support the Guadalcanal operation.

I handed the message to Jerry Thomas. Turner produced a fifth of Scotch from his bag and poured three drinks. Jerry finished reading and looked at me. "Put that message in your pocket," I told him. "I'll talk to you about it later, but I don't want anyone to know about it."

Turner indicated the glasses. "Vandegrift," he said, "I'm not inclined to take so pessimistic a view of the situation as Ghormley does. He doesn't believe I can get the 7th Marine Regiment in here, but I think I have a scheme that will fool the Japs."

This began a discussion primarily concerning the deployment of the 7th Marines, when and if they should ever reach Guadalcanal. I knew from previous experience that Turner held certain strategic and tactical ideas which so long as they pertained to naval operations were valid enough. When he got into the work of the generals, however, he should have saved his time. In this instance he favored the quaint notion of sprinkling little groups of the 7th Marines all over Guadalcanal. I argued vigorously against this but when we broke up that night the issue remained cloudy.

Turner apparently thought we were worrying unduly about the vulnerability of our perimeter and the Japanese attacks against us. Having suffered our daily air raid, he next tasted our night life. About midnight Louie droned over, dropped his flare, the signal for Jap ships to begin a two-hour bombardment, part of which combed the ridge uncomfortably close to where we were sheltering behind a small row of sandbags.

In the morning I showed Turner the results of the night attack including the pitiful and bloody annex of our field hospital, struck by a large Japanese shell. I think he was impressed. Anyway at the airfield he said, "When I bring the 7th Regiment in I will land them where you want."

I walked back to the CP with my operations officer. "You know, Jerry," I told him, "when we landed in Tientsin, China, in 1927, old Colonel E. B. Miller ordered me to draw up three plans. Two concerned the accomplishment of our mission, the third a withdrawal from Tientsin in case we got pushed out." We walked a bit farther. "Jerry, we're going to defend this airfield until we no longer can. If that happens, we'll take what's left to the hills and fight guerrilla warfare. I want you to go see Bill Twining, swear him to secrecy and have him draw up a plan."

I went to the Pagoda then and took Roy Geiger for a walk. I told him of Ghormley's estimate, said I did not agree with it—we were going to stay here come hell or high water, Navy or no Navy. "But," I said, "if the time comes when we no longer can hold the perimeter I expect you to fly out your planes."

Roy turned to me. "Archer, if we can't use the planes back in the hills we'll fly them out. But whatever happens, I'm staying here with you."

Throughout September 12 enemy air repeatedly struck us. That night his warships steamed down the Slot to scream shells into the ridge, a repetition of the previous night.

But this time the bombardment lifted in about thirty minutes. Probing actions began against Edson's lines. I spent the night by the operations telephone close by. The enemy came in slowly, pushed back Edson's right, hurt his left. Aided by del Valle's artillery firing on preregistered targets in the jungle, Edson held. Shortly after dawn he restored his right flank.

With the issue far from resolved enemy air struck us hard that morning. After the raid I went to Edson's CP. Nonchalant as always, he greeted me with his quiet grin. "They were testing us," he told me. "They'll come back tonight." He spent the day moving back his front, tying in automatic weapons, improving fields of fire and laying more communication wire. At his request I moved my reserve battalion closer to his lines. Again enemy air interrupted these activities, as I noted in a letter home:

> Another Sunday—and what a way to spend it! Planes roaring away overhead, Jap Zeros darting in and out of clouds and our boys chasing them. One of our pilots, Major Smith, has shot down 13 Japs crates to date.

That night Louie flew down on schedule to drop his green flare. Before he droned off all hell broke loose, first with a pounding destroyer bombardment from Sealark Channel followed by an attack in force against Edson's ridge. For nearly two hours our artillery and mortars fired into advancing waves of enemy as determined to take the ridge as Edson was to hold it.

Grouped around the telephone on the side of the hill, Thomas, Twining and I followed the action. About 11:00 P.M. the Japanese attacks diminished. Jerry said, "Looks like we've won the first round."

About then Ken Bailey, shortly returned from a Noumea hospital from which he had taken French leave, came back to report that his Marines were out of grenades. While staff officers scurried some up, headquarters personnel got them to the ridge where Bailey, crawling on hands and knees, distributed them to foxholes.

After a slight respite the Japanese came in again. We were greatly heartened by listening to Edson's inspiring epithets hurled at his people as the battle progressed. Cries of "banzai!" vied with the screams of macaws to claim the heavy humid air already alive with profanities in both languages. By now del Valle's artillery was firing so close to our front that the earth constantly reverberated from the shock of the exploding shells.

Sometime after midnight Cates called to report a heavy attack against Bill McKelvey's battalion dug in on the upper, Tenaru. Cliff reported him holding—welcome words since Thomas already was feeding my reserve to Edson unit by unit. It was all I could do to hear Cates' words for the crescendo of battle to our front.

Suddenly a terrific mortar barrage fell on our position and knocked out communications to Edson. Thanks to the work of my communications officer, Ed Snedeker, who on this and many other occasions constantly exposed himself to work alongside his men, our telephone was quickly repaired. Although Edson was still holding, he had ordered some parachutists on his left back to prepared defenses—a difficult move skillfully executed by Captain George Stallings.

Had the enemy pressed this assault God knows what would have happened, but once again he drew back. More than this, as he had done the night long he continued to announce his next two attacks with copious numbers of flares to give our artillery perfect targets. Jeff Fields, commanding one of our artillery battalions, later described this vital action to me in detail. Altogether the 105mm howitzers fired 2,000 rounds during these vital hours, many of them at distances no more than 1,600 yards—a tremendous contribution to the victory brought by dawn.

And shortly after dawn Geiger sent up his Army P-400s to complete the carnage. It was still early when I was standing in front of my CP reading messages. Hearing some shouting including several cries of "banzai!" I looked up to see

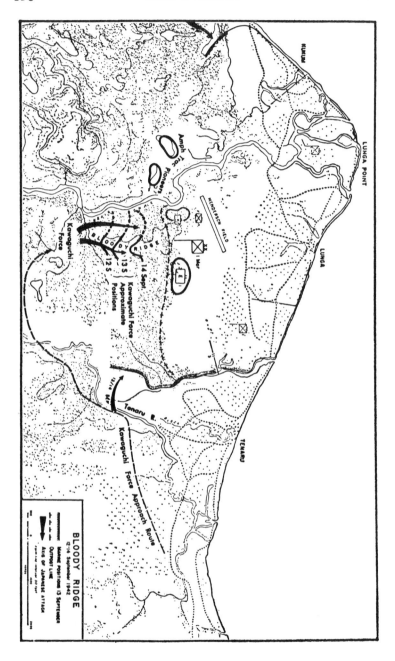

BLOODY RIDGE
12-14 September 1942

two Japanese soldiers and an officer swinging a samurai sword. The officer threw his sword at a Marine, then fell from a shot fired by Sergeant Major Banta. A Marine corporal tried to fire at one of the soldiers. His pistol jammed and he dived at his enemy. Just as he hit him with a flying tackle shots rang out and both Japanese fell dead. To this day I don't know who fired.

Some hours passed before I knew our precise position. While patrols roamed the area to flush and kill Japanese, Edson received his casualty reports. From a penetration on the east flank against a very brave engineer unit protecting the artillery we lost 4 killed and several wounded. The main defense cost us 263 casualties of whom 59 were killed. We counted over 600 dead enemy on the ridge, another 200 on the Tenaru. Today we know that this battle decimated an entire Japanese brigade because they carried off hundreds of wounded, most of whom died in their grim retreat through the jungle to the west.

That day I knew only that we could claim an enormous victory. I tried to put something of the pride and humility which I felt into a division letter:

. . . during the period from 1930 [7:30 P.M.] on the 13th to 0600 on the 14th the enemy launched a series of ferocious assaults . . . each culminating in fierce hand-to-hand combat in which both attacker and defender employed bayonets, rifles, pistols, grenades and knives. The Parachute Battalion, hastily reorganized into two companies after its withdrawal from the main line of resistance, counterattacked the enemy advancing on the left of the reserve position to extend that position to the left and to straighten the line then being held by the Battalion Reserve. This counterattack was carried out successfully in that the enemy was forced to withdraw into the edge of the woods fronting the reserve position, his flanking movement which had threatened the whole position having been halted. During this courageous attack the Parachute Troops suffered casualties estimated at 40 per cent.

Throughout the night the Eleventh Marines supported the Raiders and Parachutists by nine hours of almost constant artillery fire of the greatest accuracy and effectiveness, and greatly assisted them in standing off the attacks of the enemy. The morning of the 14th found the enemy retreating and the reinforced Raider Battalion in complete control of the field of battle.

Almost without exception the officers and men engaged in this action proved themselves to be among the best fighting troops that any service could hope to have, and in extending to them the salutation of the officers and men of the Divison the Commanding General wishes to state that he considers it a privilege and an honor to have had troops of this caliber attached to his command.

In addition to this citation and to approving many other recommendations for decorations for the supreme sacrifice, I recommended Major Ken Bailey and Colonel Merritt Edson for Medals of Honor—which were awarded.

XII

"Are You Going to Hold This Beachhead?"

WE HAD been on Guadalcanal for over five weeks. We were still eating two meals a day, mainly of Japanese rice. Many of us suffered from dysentery and fungus infections and more recently from malaria, a disease we had not known was endemic to the island. Against this dreaded fever we force-fed the troops with atrabrine, a preventive pill that tinged the skin yellow, nauseated the stomach, and caused the ears to ring.

Day by day I watched my Marines deteriorate in the flesh. Although lean Marines are better than fat Marines, these troops were becoming too lean. Some of my units were shot, certainly the parachutists, by now scarcely over a company, which I replaced with the 3d Battalion, 2d Marines, from Tulagi.

Shortly after the battle of the Ridge I received a welcome reinforcement—the 7th Marine Regiment, which sailed from Espiritu Santo on September 14. Kelly Turner's audacious move cost the Navy heavily. In only a few minutes a Jap submarine torpedoed the carrier *Wasp,* a battleship and a destroyer. On the same day enemy air and surface attacks hit us very hard.

But on September 15 enemy attacks against us suddenly ceased. Two days later I wrote home:

> Things have quieted down entirely and we all have gotten two nights of sleep which we severely needed . . .

On the morning of September 18 Turner's transports, miraculously unscathed, began loading-off at Lunga Point. The bonanza included over 4,000 fresh Marines complete with supporting units, motor transport, heavy engineer equipment and ammunition. A separate convoy landed a large amount of aviation gasoline sorely needed by Roy Geiger's fliers.

With considerable reluctance I ordered what was left of the parachutists aboard these ships along with my other wounded. Although the parachutists were never to jump during the Pacific war, they rendered brave and invaluable service first at Gavutu, then on Guadalcanal, actions which together cost them over 50 per cent casualties.

I now made a change in my command lineup, a very difficult task. Several weeks earlier General Holcomb had written that the Corps, now 157,000 strong, would reach 223,000 by the turn of the year. As one result we were promoting officers in wholesale batches. A recent list promoted nine of my lieutenant colonels to colonels which put me seven colonels over strength—the Commandant directed me to return these senior officers to the States, where he needed them to organize and train new regiments.

I had served in the Corps long enough to know that any method employed to select the officers for transfer would cause hard feelings, and I was not wrong. My thoughts on the subject are obvious from a letter of the time to Colonel Robert Kilmartin, a very old friend:

> My dear Killy,
> This is a very hard letter for me to write and I believe you will accept it in the way that it is meant. We now have fourteen colonels in the Division, Jerry Thomas just having received a field promotion to that grade. We have orders from the Commandant of the Marine Corps to send all excess officers, over and above our authorized allowance, back to the States at the earliest practicable date so that they may be used to organize and command new units now forming. This has worried me greatly as I hate to lose any of the colonels in the Division.
> •After careful consideration I thought that the fairest way to do it was to send them out in accord with the date on which they joined the Division. This, I believe, is the fairest to everyone and certainly is beyond criticism as to favoring one person or another. . . .
> You have done excellent work and it will give me great pleasure in putting it both on your fitness report and in a letter of commendation.

The change of slate left me with Jerry Thomas as chief of staff. Jerry had done superb work for me, particularly in planning and executing the Guadalcanal-Tulagi operations. So had Bill Twining, whom I moved up to the operations slot. Pate remained D-4 and Buckley, who replaced Frank Goettge, the D-2 with Jim Murray D-1. I turned the newly arrived 7th Marines over to Colonel Sims. Cliff Cates kept the 1st Marines. I moved Edson into command of the 5th Marines and let him take Lew Walt, an exceptionally able and brave raider officer, along as a battalion commander. The splendid work of Edson's executive officer, Sam Griffith, on Tulagi and Guadalcanal caused me to give him command of the 1st Raiders. By rights Pedro del Valle should have gone home but I could not consider losing his services—I also recommended him for promotion to brigadier general because I believed a division artillery commander should wear that rank.

The Commandant further directed me to send home other surplus officers. As I wrote Kelly Turner:

> I have gotten rid of some of the older lieutenant colonels and replaced them by younger lieutenant colonels and in some instances majors who are much younger and who have shown by their actions here an aggressive spirit and conduct in pushing patrols and handling their battalions in the jungle. I feel as we now stand, after the changes are made, that we are much stronger than we were before.

About this time Admiral McCain also received orders to Washington. I hastened to write him a fond letter of farewell:

> I think too much of you to congratulate you. I can think of nothing worse than to be in Washington at this time. Your friends here will miss you, but we will know we have a friend in court who will render a sympathetic ear when told that we need more fighter planes.

He replied:

> What I hate most is the breaking off of my close association with yourself and the tough eggs under you.

In a final paragraph he reminded me of all he had tried to do:

The planes must find these ships that run in and hit you at night and must strike them before dark. Should I die now, those words will be found engraved on my heart.

McCain referred to the destroyers and barges called the Tokyo Express which almost nightly brought enemy reinforcements to Guadalcanal, movements which we did everything in our power to prevent. We were just not strong enough to stop them from landing troops at their will. Even if this will were confined to the night, the night was still ten hours long. Geiger worked miracles with his planes, asking and receiving more than we possibly could expect from our fliers.

Despite their exhausted condition the pilots kept a keen sense of humor. One of their favorite stories concerned an F4F pilot cut off by a flock of Japanese Zeros. Undaunted the pilot radioed the rest of his flight: "Hey, fellows, come on over; I've got twelve of the bastards cornered."

Competition also ran high, particularly between fighter pilots. About this time our leading ace, Marion Carl, was shot down and presumed killed. We were pleasantly surprised five days later when he walked into the perimeter, a native scout having picked him up, succored him and returned him by small boat. When he reported for duty Geiger told him that in his absence Smith's tally had risen to fourteen enemy planes—two more than Carl's record. Carl looked at Geiger: "God damn it, General, you'll have to ground Smith for five days so I can catch up."

McCain's very able relief, Rear Admiral Aubrey Fitch, visited me on September 19. After a pleasant chat I turned him over to Roy Geiger and settled down to a long talk with Mr. Hanson Baldwin, the military correspondent for *The New York Times* whom I had known in Washington and who rode in with Fitch.

Hanson passed on some disconcerting information. The people of America, he told me, were not getting a true picture of Guadalcanal. As opposed to the tiny perimeter which we were defending and the rugged quality of our lives, which he instantly recognized, the American public saw us strongly entrenched, occupying most of the island. At the same time he explained, it was no secret around Washington that top officials viewed our position with mounting alarm, a tone of defeatism which he heard more strongly expressed in Ghormley's headquarters.

I told Baldwin I could neither understand nor condone such an attitude. Within a month we had stopped Japan's march across the Pacific besides hurting her badly. Her air and surface fleets were suffering as much if not more than ours. I did not know Japan well but I doubted if her industrial capacity could begin to repair such losses as readily as our own.

Every indication, I continued, suggested that our advance into Guadalcanal had caught Japan away off guard. The messages intercepted by our intelligence pointed in certain cases to mass confusion at top command levels. More important was the confusion of her acts in fighting us. I told him of the blind, crazy assaults against our Tenaru position which revealed how fanaticism could produce tactical blindness. I explained the recent battle of the Ridge, pointing out the futility of the enemy's trying to hold a co-ordinated attack plan after spending days marching through jungle which often limited progress to less than a mile a day. I went over our present positions, telling what I could. I admitted our problems but claimed our strengths, particularly the fantastic esprit displayed by officers and men.

When I had finished he looked at me in the probing way of a professional journalist. "Are you going to hold this beachhead?" he asked. "Are you going to stay here?"

I answered, "Hell, yes. Why not?"

He seemed impressed with what he learned—to my surprise he termed it an exclusive story—and when Fitch left a short time later Hanson accompanied him. His subsequent stories in *The New York Times* began to enlighten the public vis-à-vis our true position as well as our determination to hold; much later the series won him a well-deserved Pulitizer prize.

Shortly after this vist Major General Harmon, USA, flew down to spent the night. I received him warmly because his visit concerned our eventual relief by an Army division which he hoped to have ready before too long. Harmon painted a bleak picture of life in the higher echelons. He said he would never place an Army division on Guadalcanal under Kelly Turner's command (and he never did). He abhorred the pessimism increasingly displayed by Ghormley and certain of his staff, and he vigorously criticized the supply situation in Noumea which Hanson Baldwin had described as chaotic.

Since he was a very capable professional officer, I was pleased when he agreed to my tactical dispositions. In walking through some of these I mentioned how a lack of cutting tools hindered our efforts. After a moment's thought he perhaps unwittingly put a verbal finger on the enormous changes wrought by this war: "We have plenty of cavalry sabers up at Noumea. I'll send you a shipment. You can sharpen them—they will make splendid machetes."

Shortly after Harmon's visit I wrote Kelly Turner my thoughts on our relief:

> I know you favored sending the Division to Noumea in event of an immediate relief as had been planned before the occupation. This, of course, has been no Russian front but the men have been, and I imagine will continue to be, under a constant strain of both aerial and surface craft bombardment—this, together with the hardships of the jungle, I feel warrants a change in the plan, and I earnestly recommend it. The Division will have to be entirely refitted in clothing, the equipment gone over, and rehabilitated before another offensive. The men will need to get to a place where there are recreational facilities and a real change of atmosphere. I do not feel that this is available at Noumea. It was found in the World War that units pulled out of the line and taken to a perfectly safe place with comforts and conveniences, but yet lacking in recreational and amusement facilities, were not near as fresh as those who went back to an area where those things were available. I realize that it is a long jaunt to Wellington or to Auckland, but I strongly recommend for your consideration that when and if this Division is pulled out of this place, it be sent to one of those two places so that we can rebuild and re-equip. The Division will not need combat training while in this area but will need, after a prolonged period of living in foxholes, to have disciplinary drills, long marches, in order to weld together a compact, well-trained outfit.

With my forces numbering over 19,000 I felt an almost luxurious freedom of action. Wishing to enlarge the perimeter as far to the west as the Matanikau River, I approved a plan described to Kelly Turner on September 24:

> To the west we have patrols down as far as Matanikau River, coming back through a jungle path that the Japanese had cut about a mile and a half inland. This morning, at dawn, Lieutenant Colonel Puller is taking his battalion [1st Battalion, 7th Marines] and cutting his way to the southwest until he hits the large grassy mountain [Mt. Austen] which we have so often talked about and which was mentioned in our attack order. I am sure that there is an observation post about the center of that ridge, and he is to go down it until he gets to the western end of it. Tomorrow or next day I plan to send a battalion out to Kokumbona where they will dig themselves in for protection at night and operate from there, particularly to the westward and up the (Native Track) trail which leads from Kokumbona southward to Beaufort Bay. I don't of course intend to send them over the mountains at the present time. I do, though, want to scour the country from that trail eastward to our installations. Not only so that we will know there is no one in it, but also to familiarize ourselves with that country.
>
> With reference to the installation here and defense area, we are maintaining our right on the Tenaru as it is a strong and natural boundary. We are pushing our west boundary out to a ridge line which gives us a strong position, and our rear we have pushed out to another ridge line which makes us feel safe in that direction. We are handicapped by a lack of cutting tools but hope that some are on the *Betelgeuse* [a transport scheduled for early arrival]. We are making fine progress, I think, in cutting approaches through the jungle to our lines, and cutting a field of fire in front of the lines where such cutting is necessary. After our two experiences of the Tenaru and the attack on the rear, I feel confident that if we can have fifty to one hundred yards of clear space in front of us, well wired, mined, and booby-trapped, that our fire and grenades will stop any assault they can make, certainly long enough to throw in our reserves for a counterattack.

Should they attack again, I feel certain it will be from the west and south, and perhaps with augmented personnel of the forces now in the vicinity of Cape Esperance. We are keeping them under constant observation by the P-400s, who daily visit them and strafe or bomb whatever is in sight.

This iimited operation began on September 24 when Puller's battalion marched south to the upper foothills of Mt. Austen, fought a number of contact engagements and turned west to the Matanikau. Finding the river defended in considerable strength he marched down its east bank to the coast.

Hoping to box in the force uncovered by Puller, I sent Sam Griffith's raiders south to the upper Matanikau, there to cross and come in behind the enemy while the 2d Battalion, 5th Marines, attacked across the bar at the mouth with Puller's battalion landing from boats on the other side of Point Cruz.

The action, commanded by Merritt Edson, backfired when the raiders ran into severe opposition. In the ensuing fire fight Ken Bailey, Griffith's executive officer, who won the Medal of Honor at the battle of the Ridge, was killed. In an attempt to envelop the enemy later in the afternoon Griffith himself was severely wounded but refused to relinquish his command.

Believing the raiders had crossed the river and started to fight toward the coast, Edson sent the 2d Battalion across the bar of the Mantanikau and simultaneously pushed Puller's battalion west for the Point Cruz landing. Both attacks ran into enemy concentrations which repulsed them with severe losses to us.

Back at division headquarters we held a fair idea of what was going on. When Edson radioed for air support to help the battalion that was all but surrounded at Point Cruz we hastened to comply. But now an air raid, the first since September 15, hit us very hard and temporarily knocked out communications. Puller, who stayed back to help Edson, fortunately got aboard a destroyer which steamed to Point Cruz and evacuated his battalion.

We concluded the action late on September 27. It taught me a big lesson: the danger of overconfidence. Obviously the

Matanikau area held a far stronger enemy than I had suspected. I still wanted to move against him, and I would. But
next time I would move more slowly and in much greater
strength.

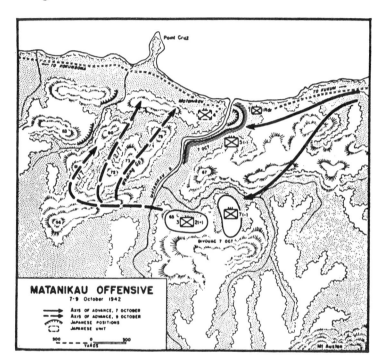

XIII

"Nothing but Artillery . . . ."

MY DISAPPOINTMENT with the Matanikau operation was somewhat assauged on September 28 by a dispatch from General George C. Marshall, Army chief of staff. I hastened to publish his encouraging words to the command:

> Heartiest congratulations from the Army on the magnificent job you and your men have done. I am filled with admiration for the way the task was carried through, the gallantry, the technique, the fortitude and the general evidence of superiority over the enemy.

I did not publish another communication of this date, a letter from Kelly Turner, who again tried to assume the role of ground commander. After reviewing my situation as he saw it he wrote:

> Based on the foregoing conjectures, now would seem to be the time to push as hard as possible on the following items: (a) continue clearing out all the nests of enemy troops on the north side of Guadalcanal, initial operations continuing to the westward. I believe you are in a position to take some chances and go after them hard. I am glad to see Rupertus is cleaning up Florida Island; and believe he should establish detachments on Sandfly Passage, the north coast, Matumba Bay at the eastern end of Florida, as soon as justified. Here we are working up a scheme to start out within a few days with the two APDs available and two companies of the Second Raiders, to attack the Jap outposts entrenched at Cape Astrolabe, Malaita; at Marau Bay on Guadalcanal, and at Cape Hunter. We want to co-ordinate these operations with you, and get your approval of our plan; therefore the

Commanding Officer of the Second Raider Battalion, after conference with me, will shortly fly up and see you and go over our plans with you. One question to decide, is whether or not to leave small detachments of the Second Raiders at these places; at a later time, we would relieve them with other line troops.

With the recent Matanikau operation only too fresh in my mind I bluntly replied to what I privately deemed nonsense:

From [Puller's] reconnaissance it is estimated that the Japanese are now holding this river line [the Matanikau] in force of about fifteen hundred men as an outpost line of resistance. Information received from a captured prisoner, a copy of his testimony which is enclosed with this letter, would tend to show that we may expect an attack in force from additional troops to be landed some time around the first of October when the moon is favorable to such landing and operations. If the testimony of this prisoner is true, and an additional division is landed to the west of us and puts down a major push in depth through our west or southwest lines, they are now so thinly held and our reserves so few that it could well be dangerous to our position.

I regret that Major Bailey of the Raiders was killed and that Lieutenant Colonel Griffith, the present Commander of the Raiders, was wounded in the shoulder. I have talked the question over with Edson, its previous Commander, and I believe that with the losses sustained in both officers and men of this battalion, and the strenuous work that they have done, that they should be returned to Noumea or some other place for rebuilding. If this is done, I urgently recommend that the Second Raider Battalion be sent in to replace them as we will need all the strength we can get for this next push which I feel sure will be a major one.

Turner failed to realize that the enemy was slacking off only until he could land sufficient troops to make another assault against the perimeter. We knew the Tokyo Express nightly was landing troops west of the Matanikau; late in September we received disturbing information that long-range artillery, 150mm howitzers, was being landed as well. This would put us, particularly Henderson Field, under constant artillery bombardment which lacking sound-flash locating equipment and long-range guns, we could not possibly counter. More than ever I desired to push across the Matanikau to deprive this area to the gathering enemy. My last attempt proved conclusively the need for additional strength. In turn I needed every unit available in rear areas, and to use the 2d Raiders for Turner's purpose seemed ludicrous.

Fortunately I did not stand alone in my thinking, General Harmon for one agreeing. On the last day of September another potential ally flew in: Admiral Chester Nimitz, commander in chief of the Pacific Ocean Areas.

The flight almost cost America one of her finest naval officers. Nimitz' B-17 got lost and only by chance happened on to our island. It landed in the rain which as usual turned the field into a quagmire. I was not exactly sorry since I wanted Nimitz to see what we were up against.

In the afternoon I took my guest on a tour of the perimeter, pointing out our positions and explaining the reasons for them. Realizing the effect of his visit on morale, I introduced him to the regimental commanders and to as many officers as possible. He was particularly impressed with Edson's ridge and our description of the battle. Geiger and Woods briefed him in detail on the air operation, then at his request I took him to the hospital to visit and chat with our wounded.

The grim appearance of the command noticeably impressed him and when I pleaded for a suitable rehabilitation area once we left the island he promised to arrange it. That evening he said he wished to decorate some of the command and asked me to prepare a suitable list.

After as pleasant a dinner as possible, we sat down for a long talk in my CP, once again moved back from the ridge. In view of Kelley Turner's newest notions, I wanted to impress upon Nimitz what I regarded as my main mission—holding the airfield. Subsequent events suggested that I succeeded, but I don't think I had to work very hard. Admiral Nimitz was a very perceptive officer who recognized logic when he saw it.

Later in the evening over a drink we relaxed into general conversation. "You know, Vandegrift," he said, "when this war is over we are going to write a new set of *Navy Regulations*. So just keep it in the back of your mind because I will want to know some of the things you think ought to be changed."

"I know one right now," I told him. "Leave out all reference that he who runs his ship aground will face a fate worse than death. Out here too many commanders have been far too leery about risking their ships."

He smiled but did not comment.

Early the next morning a small group of officers and men formed in front of the CP. Nimitz gave them a nice little talk, then pinned on decorations. I was very proud and pleased and was about to thank him for this thoughtful gesture when he asked me to step forward. Before I knew what was happening he read a citation awarding me the Navy Cross and then pinned the medal on my shirt. I publish the citation because it was intended as much for the officers and men of the division as for me.

> For exceptionally meritorious service to the govenment in a duty of great responsibility as Commander of all ground troops engaged in the attack on the Solomon Islands on August seventh, nineteen hundred and forty two. He, in spite of much enemy opposition, led his command with great courage and superb determination to the end that all objectives were captured and opposing enemy forces destroyed. His conduct throughout was in keeping with the highest traditions of the naval service.

After the informal ceremony I took Nimitz to Henderson Field quickly because it began to rain hard and I did not want the mud to hold back his departure—I was scared to death the noon air raid would drop a bomb on him. At the field he decided to make the return trip in the nose of the B-17, a position normally reserved for the bombardier. He crawled in, the engines started, the big plane taxied to the far end, revved up and moved down the muddy runway. I did not like the plane's pace and I saw from Roy Geiger's face that he did not like it either. Just after the point of no return the pilot shut off his engines and hit the brakes. The bomber slithered maddeningly along, stopping finally with its nose hanging over the edge of the field not far from the trees.

After the rain stopped and the field dried a little the pilot tried again. This time the admiral's aide briskly put him in the back of the plane where he belonged. I was pleased to get him off safely because he appeared impressed with what he had seen and heard. Perhaps optimistically I interpreted his cautious remarks to mean additional air, ground and sea reinforcement for us—nor was I wrong.

A few days after Nimitz departed we kicked off the new Matanikau operation. Our tactics resembled those of the earlier one, but our forces did not: nearly two regiments heavily supported by artillery. On October 7 our plan sent the 5th Marines to the mouth of the Matanikau with the 7th Marines less one battalion inland some 2,000 yards. To lead this latter advance I put Bill Whaling in command of the 3d Battalion, 2d Marines, reinforced by his special scout-sniper unit. Our plan called for him to cross the river, then wheel to the right. Behind him Hanneken's battalion would continue further west and wheel right, and finally Puller's battalion moving still farther west before turning. With Puller holding on the coast west of Point Cruz the 5th Marines would push west from the river to complete the pincers.

While deploying, the 5th Marines ran into an enemy force defending the sand bar at the river's mouth. Simultaneously and greatly to our surprise Whaling hit another force *east* of the river—in other words, while we were attacking the enemy he was on the way to attack us. When Edson called for help I sent him a tired company of raiders, all I could spare, which he used to hold the enemy at the sand bar.

By the morning of October 8 these forces stood ready to attack. Unfortunately a cloudburst, which among other things grounded our aircraft, caused me to postpone the operation for twenty-four hours. That night the enemy struck the raiders, who killed sixty of them and cleared the way for the 5th Marines.

A priority message from Ghormley received that afternoon proved more vexing than the torrential rains. According to his intelligence, a large enemy task force was bearing down on us—we could expect anything. Although an Army reinforced regiment would soon join us, I could not risk my

Guadalcanal—"From the brown water I looked up at a young Marine positioned behind a 30-caliber machine gun. . . ."

The fantastic Sergeant-Major Vouza. *Below*, the battle
of the Tenaru—"Yesterday the Japs seemed something
almost superhuman. . . ."

Bougainville—the landing at Empress Augusta Bay. *Below and next page*, enemy dead and smashed Marine landing equipment on the beach at Tarawa.

Marines attack at Kwajalein and Roi-Namur in the
Marshall Islands.

Saipan, June, 1944. The tactical problem.

Next page, Tinian landing: "An example of a model operation."

Saipan: Tactical troops take a break on a jungle trail.
Below, the end in sight.

Peleliu, October, 1944. General Rupertus to General Vandegrift—"This terrain which we had to finally pocket the remaining Japs in was the worst I have ever seen. . . ."

Next page, Iwo Jima, February, 1945.

Holland Smith (*right*) and Bobbie Erskine on Iwo. *Below*, the beach at Iwo Jima on the afternoon of D-day, February 19, 1945.

Iwo Jima: the walking wounded. "That the issue was resolved in our favor was due to a fighting spirit unexcelled in the history of warfare. . . ."

Okinawa, April, 1945. *Left,* Pfc. Harry Kizierian after 12 days of heavy fighting. *Right,* Major General Tom Shepherd—"I did not know of a better division commander in the Corps." *Below,* Okinawa aid station—"There is no royal road to Tokyo."

exposed perimeter for the time foreseen in the original attack plan. I did, however decide to go ahead with a limited version.

On October 9 the three battalions pushed across the river, turned right and began moving toward the coast. Puller's battalion soon met heavy opposition answered by our artillery that drove the enemy into his guns, a fearful carnage more than compensating for our disappointment. Once the battalions reached the beach they turned east, passed through Edson's 5th Marines and returned to the perimeter. I had planned to keep the 5th Marines along the Matanikau but in the confusion someone in operations ordered Edson back. Fortunately I learned of this in time to contact Edson and tell him to stay where he was. We backed him with Bob Luckey's Special Weapons Battalion. This ended the action, which cost us 65 killed versus over 700 enemy dead.

On October 13 transports landed Colonel Bryant Moore's 164th Infantry, a reinforced Army regiment numbering about 3,000 well-equipped troops. As happened when Turner brought in the 7th Marines, the covering force for the transports found itself in heavy action but this time gave better than it took. Atlhough the transports arrived unscathed, the soldiers were still disembarking when enemy bombers welcomed them to Guadalcanal.

A new weapon took over from the bombers—the 150mm long-range howitzers, one of the reasons I had tried to push west of the Matanikau. Fortunately engineers and Seabees had completed an alternate airfield some 2,000 yards east of Henderson. Geiger hurriedly moved his fighters and dive bombers to this strip, which we called Fighter One.

When the big guns started talking I saw my cook, Butch Morgan, grab his World War I helmet which he affected along with a bushy red mustache—he strongly resembled the famous cartoon character Old Bill of the first war. "Where are you going?" I asked.

"Bombs."

"No, those aren't bombs. They're either howitzers or guns."

Butch reflected a moment. "Hell, nothing but artillery—I'm going back to work."

As if air and artillery bombardment weren't enough for the new and untried soldiers, sometime after midnight Louie droned over to drop his flares. When the alert sounded

I went to my dugout, a trench hacked out of a coral ridge and fitted with a long bench and telephone connection to the operations dugout. Moments later Jerry Thomas, the division surgeon, Captain Brown, and Bud Schwenke tumbled in after me.

Jerry listened to the exploding shells. "By God, those aren't five-inchers they're throwing in."

He was correct. Enemy battleships were firing 12- and 14-inch shells at us—the only action in the Pacific war where Americans found themselves on the receiving end of these monsters.

I could do nothing to disrupt the raid. We owned no night fighters; our artillery could not reach the ships. Like everyone else in the perimeter I sat out the bombardment, hoping against a direct hit on my dugout.

A man comes close to himself at such times. People have since asked me my attitude toward shell shock or combat fatigue cases. Being a good Presbyterian I could only reply, "There but for the grace of God go I."

This probably requires amplification. Unless the reader has experienced naval or artillery shelling or aerial bombing he cannot easily grasp a sensation compounded of frustration, helplessness, fear and, in case of close hits, shock.

One night quite early in the Guadalcanal campaign a doctor and a chaplain, both fairly senior, were in my CP discussing combat fatigue. The doctor could not understand it. "Look at us," he said. "We're all much older and we aren't touched by it." The chaplain averred that faith was the true defense. As is my wont when dealing with experts, I kept quiet.

That night a shell from an enemy destroyer burst close to the doctor's dugout. He was not wounded physically, but his mental hurt caused the division surgeon to evacuate him. A week later a shell struck close to the chaplain's dugout— again, he was not wounded but had to be evacuated the next day.

Another case disturbed me more than these two since both doctor and chaplain recovered. One morning after a terrible shelling a young infantry officer, who earlier was brought to my attention for his meritorious behavior under fire, came to my CP. With tears running down his face he said, "I am awfully sorry, sir, but I know I cannot stand another shelling and I do not want to crack up in front of my men." I could not doubt his sincerity. I turned him over to Captain Brown, who recommended we survey him home.

A year or so later when I was in Washington he came to me asking if he could have another chance. When I agreed he requested a three-week delay before his orders were written. I thought no more about it until a young Navy doctor called on me to explain that this officer could not go into a combat area. Naturally I asked why.

"Because he asked me to accompany him to a naval gun-fire proving ground and I agreed," the doctor said. "We went there, pitched tents not far from the impact area and stayed for a week." Placing a report on my desk he concluded, "He obviously cannot take it—and don't ask me why." I did not ask because I knew. It is not a matter of physical build, stamina, faith, courage or what have you. It is a matter of man, and thus fortune.

Fortune, too, is elusive. One night during a Jap naval shelling one of our eager combat photographers climbed a ridge, set up his camera and commenced taking time exposures of enemy gunfire flashes. During his madness he hollered to a salty Marine sergeant who was crouched in the lee of the ridge, "Come up and see this. It's terrific."

"No, thanks," the sergeant returned.

"Oh, come on. If your name is on one you'll get it."

"Yes," the sergeant agreed, "but I don't have to be damn fool enough to reach up for it."

Now in my dugout during this incredible pounding I, like the walrus in *Alice in Wonderland,* thought of these and many things. Suddenly during a lull after thirty minutes of vomiting destruction Jerry Thomas spoke up: "I don't know how you feel, but I think I prefer a good bombing or artillery shelling."

I nodded. "I think I do—"

A terrific explosion cut off my words. I was sitting toward the end of the bench. The concussion bowled us down like a row of ten pins. I ended on the floor, unhurt except in dignity. We learned later that the shell struck next to del Valle's CP close by us.

For over an hour the shells rained down. Huge fires sprouted around Henderson Field. Field telephones brought gloomy preliminary damage estimates but ensuing air attacks made damage control out of the question.

At daybreak I hastened to Roy Geiger's CP. It was a terrible mess. The Pagoda was half wrecked and Roy told me he was going to knock it down since he figured the enemy was using it for a registration point. The shelling cost us forty-one killed. Shells tore up or fired several supply dumps, destroyed over thirty SBDs, half as many F4Fs, and damaged most of the others. Roy's people already were working desperately at Fighter One to put some planes in the air. Two of these eventually took off, spotted a large task force of transports coming down the Slot and ran for home pursued by Zeros now claiming the air as Japanese ships insolently claimed the sea. Clearly we were facing the anticipated enemy effort. I dispatched to Ghormley:

> Urgently necessary that this force receive maximum support of air and surface units.

I should have saved my time. That night enemy ships again threw everything they had at us. In the morning we saw enemy transports calmly discharging troops and supply off Tassafaronga to the west. By a maximum effort Geiger launched a dozen SBDs in midmorning; later, B-17s from Espiritu Santo came over for more runs. This pathetic effort at least caused the enemy to beach four transports and withdraw two more to the north.

So desperate was our situation that Geiger's personal pilot Jack Cram, rigged two torpedoes under the wings of Roy's command plane, an old PBY. Cram sent one of the torpedoes into a beached transport and returned with Zeros clustered around his tail. He made a successful landing (and received a Navy Cross for this fantastic display of bravery).

Throughout the day bravery ruled, not alone in the efforts of the Henderson fliers but also in those of the transport pilots who flew in 55-gallon drums of aviation gasoline and spare parts from New Caledonia. A fresh squadron of F4Fs reached us in the afternoon as did the seaplane tender *Mac-Farland,* carrying aviation gasoline.

The enemy was hurting us and he knew it. That night his ships returned to strike us once more. In the morning I sent a priority dispatch to Nimitz, Ghormley and Turner:

Despite destruction of four hostile transports and departure of remaining two estimate that enemy landed about ten thousand troops yesterday on Cactus with considerable equipment and supplies bringing total force ashore to at least fifteen thousand. . . . Our force exceeds that number but more than half of it is in no condition to undertake a protracted land campaign due to incessant hostile operations and labor connected with the development of this base over a period of ten weeks. . . . The situation demands two urgent and immediate steps: take and maintain control of sea areas adjacent to Cactus to prevent further enemy landings and enemy bombardment such as this force has taken for the last three nights; reinforcement of ground forces by at least one division in order that extensive operations may be initiated to destroy hostile force now on Cactus.

Enemy air hit us throughout this day and also caught *MacFarland* which managed to limp into Tulagi harbor. In a letter of October 17 Bill Rupertus gave a picture of what these brave sailors endured in the enemy-infested waters:

She "blinked" us last night and called for all boats. We sent all of our boats to her, one YP to tow her in and protected by two PT boats. She is now here at Sasapi anchored—we took off about 100 uninjured, about 30 wounded and 5 dead. The wounded have very small fragmentation wounds in the legs, and faces only very badly burned—in a few cases I saw the faces were jet black which indicates their clothing protected them from the burning blast (all except the face) and the "daisy cutter" effect of the small bombs put the wounds in the lower part of the body, i.e. the legs. A great number are momentarily deaf.

In the same letter Bill involuntarily emphasized the paucity of resources at our combined disposal but also displayed his usual cheerful outlook:

Now what's the next priority to send you? Shall we send the battery (I Battery of Pack Howitzers) you asked for, or do you want the remaining gas we have here—it won't be more than 3,000 gallons, maybe 2,000. The bold YP which was aground over there jettisoned almost all of its diesel fuel so I can't use him until some ship gives him some fuel. We have two good PT boats, one without torpedoes . . . and one (the flagship) having fired her torpedoes and is badly leaking partly backed in a slip at Sasapi. Tell Thomas to send me a short radio "Send battery on YP tomorrow" if that is what you now need. In a way I feel like a grocery proprietor! "What'll you have, madam!" We all know that you can lick hell out of those Japs if the Navy keeps those damn night movements away. And if you need us, too, there are still Marines here.

XIV

Frustrations East and West

BETWEEN these momentous events of October we lived a simple existence in which small comforts assumed large importance. On October 5 I noted in a letter home:

> To add to the civilized aspect of things, the captain of one of the ships gave me an electric fan, and my shower is finished, too. My, this place is getting too comfortable. I'm afraid we will get too soft.

On October 8 I wrote:

> This is a miserably wet and rainy day. Was out all morning and got soaked to the skin.
>
> Yesterday afternoon had a hot shower, believe it or not. This is how it works: we have a tank that "our friends" left us. Have put it on a hill about 150 yd. from the tent. We use one of their pumps to pump the water from the river to the tent; also their pipe to run it through, not only for the shower but also for the galleys. The pipe runs on top of the ground. If you want a really hot shower, you bathe around 3:30; if a cold one, you take it in the early morning.

And on October 11:

> Field Harris . . . has just flown in. We also have staying with us two Army colonels and a New Zealand colonel. This place is now getting on the tourist route and our privacy is fast disappearing.
>
> I fear the rains will start soon and then we will have mud up to our necks. We expect a ship in shortly and do hope it will have some mail in it for us. I am well. . .

My daily routine did not greatly vary during this interim period. Shortly after the 7:00 P.M. news broadcast from San Francisco I retired. Night bombardment or no, I arose at 6:00 A.M. After a cup of coffee with Jerry Thomas I showered, shaved and dressed in as clean khaki tousers and open-neck khaki shirt as circumstances allowed. We breakfasted in a small staff mess. Occasionally my headquarters aide, Guy Tarrant, scrounged such luxuries as cold storage eggs and canned ham from a ship in return for a Jap rifle or sword. Most of the time we ate powdered eggs which I could not take, probably because in 1927 in China we anchored opposite a powdered egg factory—the stench being unforgettable.

After breakfast I read dispatches, discussed them with my chief of staff and operations officer, and issued the necessary orders of the day.

As soon as possible I began an inspection of the perimeter. Although I purposely wore khaki to be recognized, I wore a pith helmet because the steel helmet which I carried on my arm gave me a devil of a headache.

In each sector I visited regimental headquarters, checked over the map situation, and went on to battalion headquarters and down to companies and platoons, front lines and outposts. This way I talked to a lot of Marines, encouraging them to sound off and showing an interest in their problems. They were a salty lot, bronzed and lean, their dungarees practically in shreds. They held the enemy in terrible contempt. They laughed at Louie the Louse and Washing Machine Charlie and even at the new long-range howitzers which they called Pistol Pete. They joked about nearly everything but their humor didn't fool me. They were tired men. I wanted desperately to get them off the island.

They accepted their fate with marvelous equanimity. One popular story concerned an automatic rifleman who decided he would get surveyed back to the States by pretending to be crazy. One day he ran to his first sergeant, grabbed him and said, "Top, I've been watching you—you're crazy as a loon." Figuring the first sergeant would report him as a victim of combat fatigue, he was greatly surprised when the senior noncom regarded him gravely and finally replied, "I think you're right. I am crazy. I'd better go in and ask the old man for a survey."

My orderly, Corporal Smith, pulled a trick illustrative of

the spirit of these Marines. One morning he asked me if he could take a ride in an airplane providing some pilot would let him aboard. I agreed and forgot about it until he failed to turn up the following day. He finally appeared that evening.

"Where in the world have you been?" I asked.

"Well, sir, you told me I could take an airplane ride so I found this B-17 and Colonel Twining* said can you shoot a waist gun and I said yes so we flew to Rabaul and bombed hell out of it and got jumped by Zeros and I shot hell out of the waist gun and here I am."

On another occasion when I was inspecting the Matanikau sector I noticed a Marine whom I remembered talking to back at New River. By no stretch of imagination had he looked eighteen years old, so I called him over and asked him his age. "I am eighteen, sir."

"Where do you live?"

"I am eighteen, sir."

"What kind of school did you attend?"

"I am eighteen, sir."

"Now that we have that firmly established, suppose you answer my questions."

He did and I let him rejoin his unit. This was the boy I now recognized manning a Matanikau outpost. He was more gaunt than formerly but when I approached him he smiled and said, "I am still eighteen, sir."

These daily tours served still another purpose in that they allowed me to keep a finger on the over-all health and welfare of the command. By mid-October malaria, despite the suppressive atabrine tablets, was taking an alarming toll. I did not mind the atabrine but most of the troops did; despite the most rigorous supervision, a number of them refused to swallow the medicine and paid the price. Others acquired the fever despite the pills. It is no fun asking a man to carry on with a 103-degree temperature, but we were asking exactly this—still another reason why I daily hoped for relief by the Army.

This was not to happen for some time but on October 18 we did receive a greatly needed morale boost: a dispatch announcing Ghormley's relief in favor of Bill Halsey. I held

---

* This was Bill's brother, Nathan Twining, who was flying out of Espiritu Santo.

nothing personal against Ghormley, whom I liked. I simply felt that our drastic, imperiled situation called for the most positive form of aggressive leadership at the top. From what I knew of Bill Halsey he would supply this like few other naval officers.

A few days later our cup brimmed over. Late on October 21 the Commandant of the Marine Corps, General Thomas Holcomb, flew in with several members of his staff. His visit put me in two minds. One, I looked forward to seeing him both because I could talk to him about many problems and because I knew he would inspire the troops as no one else could. Two, I was scared to death each moment he was on the island and only hoped that he would avoid the casual shell or bomb.

Holcomb brought along his director of aviation, Ralph Mitchell, his operations officer, Walter Rogers, his engineer officer, Bill Riley, his communications officer, Phil Berkeley, and an aide, Lieutenant Colonel Brunelli. After giving the group a briefing we paired each officer with his opposite, dined them and retired, I taking General Holcomb to my CP. We were just about asleep when the most God-awful noise—one resembling Washing Machine Charlie at low altitude—sent us racing to the bunker. A moment later Jerry Thomas called us out. "Believe it or not," he explained, "that was Bill Riley snoring."

In the morning I took the party on a tour of the perimeter. I wanted the Commandant's reaction to my positions because I regarded him as the best tactician in the Marine Corps.

The arrival of Bryant Moore's new regiment had caused me to reorganize my defense into five sectors. We started the tour with Sector One north of my CP, 7,000 yards of beach on either side of the Lunga River held by Pepper's 3d Defense Battalion, units of the Special Weapons Battalion, AmTracs, Pioneers and Engineers. Pepper's right, or eastern, flank joined Moore's 164th Infantry holding a 6,500-yard line south along the Tenaru, then curving west and stopping short of Edson's ridge. This line tied in with Sector Three held by the 7th Marines less one battalion, a 2,500-yard front stretching to the Lunga River. It tied in with Cates' Sector Four, the 1st Marines less one battalion, which held 3,500 yards of a jungle line merging into Sector Five. Edson's 5th Marines took over from here to the sea where their line curved back into Sector One.

To the west two independent battalions supported by artillery and 75mm half-tracks held a position from the mouth of the Matanikau inland to Hill 67.

This was essentially an "interior lines" defense. The bulk of del Valle's artillery was positioned and preregistered to fire on targets in any sector. I held an infantry battalion in reserve along with most of the tank battalion. In turn, regimental commanders held a third of their strength in regimental reserve and so on down through companies.

General Holcomb easily took in all the details. As usual he spoke only when necessary, his eyes alert behind steel-rimmed glasses. He was most interested in descriptions of the various actions and paid numerous compliments to officers and men.

Back in my CP we relaxed a little before dinner. I was pleased when he offered his impressions. "Vandegrift, I think you've done a good job. I don't see how you could spread yourself out or cover any more territory than you have with what you have."

After dinner he filled me in on the Washington scene and spoke of various developments both inside and outside the Corps. "You know, I turn sixty-four next year," he remarked. "If the President wishes me to stay on, I shall stay."

"I certainly hope that is the case," I told him.

He studied me for a moment, then dropped a real bomb. "If he wishes me to retire, I am going to recommend you as my successor." Brushing aside my thanks he continued, "If he approves, I promise to keep you fully informed before you take over."

With that he returned to the local situation, questioning me closely about command relationships. I told him my problems and added, "The quicker we get the Navy and particularly Kelly Turner back to the basic principles of FPT-167 [our manual of amphibious doctrine] the better off we are going to be."

He nodded, then told me something I hadn't known—Turner's attempts to break up certain regiments into battalion-size raider units, recommending to Nimitz and King in the process that Marines be limited to such sized units in the future. King sent Holcomb this document, which earned

Turner a reply amounting to a thinly disguised reprimand for interfering in Marine Corps matters without even consulting his local Marine commander.

At Halsey's request I flew up to Noumea with the Commandant and his party on October 23. I stayed with Turner aboard the *McCawley*. After dinner we went over to Halsey's flagship, the *Argonne,* to join Halsey, his chief of staff, Miles Browning, Holcomb, Turner, Harmon and General Patch, who commanded the Army's American Division slated eventually to relieve us on Guadalcanal.

Halsey sat smoking until we settled around a table. He opened the conference with a few brief sentences, then asked me to outline my position on Guadalcanal. I reviewed the campaign to date, hitting the major points and bringing him up on our present positions and knowledge of the enemy. I impressed on him the poor physical state of my command— the inevitable result of two and a half months of restricted diet, sleepless nights and disease. I described what frequent surface and aerial bombardments meant to the troops, how the critical shortage of planes and materiel was hurting us, and the deadly effect of the constant run of Jap ships to our feelings. I told him that to hold we simply had to have air and ground reinforcement, that our people were practically worn out. Besides fighter and dive bomber squadrons we needed at a minimum the rest of the American Division and another regiment of the 2d Division. I quoted casualty figures in the 5th and 1st Regiments and gave the latest malaria figures which amounted to six or seven hundred cases in the past week.

After Harmon and Holcomb vigorously defended my statements, Halsey asked Turner for his views. We listened to a depressing story of lack of shipping and attendant difficulties in getting supply to the beleaguered island.

Gray eyebrows bristling, the compactly built Halsey drummed the desk a moment with his fingers. He abruptly turned to me. "Can you hold?"

"Yes, I can hold. But I have to have more active support than I have been getting."

He nodded. "You go on back there, Vandegrift. I promise to get you everything I have."

Halsey canceled the Ndeni operation on the following day, a decision I welcomed. He also signed a dispatch to Admiral

King written by General Holcomb. This recommended that naval officers in their command relationships with Marines subscribe to the principles established in FTP-167, specifically that when ashore the Landing Force commander must hold a parallel rather than a subordinate command to the Expeditionary Force commander. It also called for a separate Marine headquarters in Noumea to better represent our needs at this echelon.

Much later I learned that General Holcomb followed this dispatch home across the Pacific. In Pearl Harbor Nimitz showed it to him and asked his opinion—he gave it and Nimitz endorsed it favorably. In Washington King showed it to him and asked his opinion—he gave it and King approved the dispatch and returned it to Halsey. I mention this only because the document charted the future course of Navy-Marine command relationships in the Pacific.

Besides doing us all a world of good on Guadalcanal the Commandant's visit resulted in another improvement. Coincidental with his arrival on the island came the first V-letter. Bill Twining looked at it closely, pondered and observed, "I don't see why it is any easier to send a *little* envelope through the mail than a *big* one."

"I don't either," I agreed, "and I'm damned if I understand why the Navy takes so long to get any size envelope here from the States."

Back in Washington the Commandant remembered this complaint and discussed it with Admiral King. They finally learned that the Navy in San Francisco was keeping ship movements so secret that no one gave the schedule to the fleet post office. King changed this to our considerable benefit.

I returned from the Noumea conference to find the division actively engaged. I described the action in a letter to General Holcomb:

I returned to Cactus and found the enemy, on the night before, had made an attack in which he had piled up, and for the ensuing days he kept hammering away at our defenses. I feel that we have really put three of his regiments on a noncombatant status. One regiment drove in from the southeast, and 1,200 of them were buried in the vicinity of the wire and in the assembly areas where our artillery got them. Another regiment attacked from the south in two columns of a battalion each, we think, and of this number over 600 were killed. Another battalion came in from the southwest, succeeded in pushing a part of Hanneken's battalion off a ridge which Hanneken proceeded to retake, and got 62 of them in the wire, and about 150 down in the hollow in front of it. This ridge, by the way, was just west of the position of the Fifth Regiment down in the jungle that you went over.

The position on the southeast was right at a corner where I told you was a machine gunner's paradise, and it certainly turned out to be one. The third regiment . . . just west of the Matanikau River . . . pushed 12 tanks across the sand bar of the river, or at least they attempted to. Eight of them were stopped cold before they reached the line; one of them got through and behind the line. It evidently stopped for orientation over the foxhole of one of the men, who reached up, put a hand grenade in the tread, pulled the ring, ducked, and blew off the tread. This allowed the half-track which had stopped most of the oncoming tanks to back up. The remaining tank got going on one tread and wheeled around into the water and was completely demolished. Realizing that tanks do not go off by themselves, a concentration of thirteen [artillery] batteries were placed in the woods across the river and walked back. They knocked out over 650 of them.

The enemy's southern attack fooled me. Before I left Guadalcanal I was convinced from intelligence reports that the main enemy attack would come across the Matanikau. One of my last orders transferred Hanneken's 2d Battalion, from the southern defensive line, or Sector Three, west to the independent force dug in along this river. Unbeknownst to us, even at that time a strong enemy column was worming its way through the jungle to strike at this weakened sector.

Fortunately on October 24—I was still in Noumea—a massive downpour impeded the movement and disrupted enemy communications. What was to have been a co-ordinated attack became a series of separate attacks, the first of which struck Puller's battalion shortly after midnight. Roy Geiger, commanding in my absence, at once began feeding in units of Bob Hall's 3d Battalion, 164th Infantry. Both Puller and Hall performed excellently in executing this maneuver made the more difficult by night, rain, mud and a determined enemy. Fighting with Marines, the Army squads, platoons and companies more than justified their existence in the ensuing hours. So did Marine Sergeant John Basilone who fought his machine guns with such skill and bravery that I recommended him for a Medal of Honor, later awarded.

After a horrendous day of wild air actions in which a relative newcomer, Joe Foss, became an ace, the enemy struck again in the night, both against Puller's and Hall's positions and against Hanneken's lines to the west. There the Japs made a serious penetration, but the following day Hanneken's executive officer, Major "Tex" Conoley, rigged together a force of clerks, cooks and bakers and restored the line— not the last time this would happen in the Pacific war.

The total action cost us 90 killed and 100 wounded. We buried about 2,000 enemy corpses, most of them fronting Puller's sector. Torrential rains followed by hot sun made it imperative to get the bodies underground quickly, a problem solved by having bulldozers dig mass graves.

The extent of the enemy's upset can be measured by a captured order in which General Hyakutake, commanding all Japanese forces on Guadalcanal, somewhat prematurely established the procedure for our surrender. Once the perimeter was overrun, I and my staff were to be escorted to the mouth of the Matanikau where I would formally surrender Guadalcanal. We would then be flown to Tokyo and paraded through the streets, presumably to delight the populace.

Hyakutake's disappointment spelled our victory. I hastened to cite all participating units by special division bulletins such as the following to the Army's 3d Battalion:

The Commanding General commends the 3d Battalion, 164th Infantry, U. S. Army, for the effectiveness of its operations against the enemy on 24, 25 and 26 October, 1942. The 1st Battalion, 7th Marines, occupying a defensive sector of a width of 2,500 yards situated to the south of the positions of the 1st Marine Division (reinforced) on Lunga Point, Guadalcanal, British Solomon Islands, having been attacked by a numerically superior enemy force at about 1000, 23 October, 1942, the 3d Battalion, 164th Infantry, then in Regimental Reserve, was ordered to reinforce the line. Moving by a forced march at night through rain and over difficult and

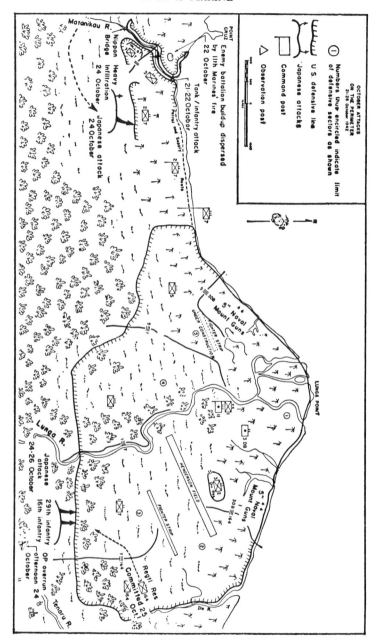

OCTOBER ATTACKS
ON THE PERIMETER
21-26 October 1942

① Numbers thus encircled indicate limit
of defensive sectors as shown

⊔ U.S. defensive line

□ Command post

▽ Observation post

Japanese attacks

unfamiliar terrain it arrived in time to prevent a serious penetration of the position and by reinforcing the 1st Battalion, 7th Marines, throughout its sector, made possible the repulse of continued enemy attacks throughout the night. The following day, having been assigned the left half of the sector formerly occupied by the 1st Battalion, 7th Marines, the 3d Battalion, 164th Infantry, so occupied and prepared the position that when the main effort of another enemy attack was directed at it on the night of 24 and 25 October, 1942, it was able to hold the position without serious loss to its own personnel, although heavy casualties were inflicted upon the enemy forces. The 1st Division is proud to have serving with it another unit which has stood the test of battle and demonstrated an overwhelming superiority over the enemy.

The significance of the bulletins was not lost on Admiral Nimitz, who sent me this message:

Reports of your successful land actions have thrilled all of us—Express my appreciation to your Marines in the front lines and to your Army troops for the way they have backed up and re-established the lines by their counterattacks—We feel that you have welded a combination that will be more than a match for the enemy.

Meanwhile massive events developed at sea where an enormous Japanese task force was bearing down on us from the north. To meet the enemy, Rear Admiral Thomas Kinkaid was approaching from the south with two slim carrier groups built around the *Enterprise* and *Hornet*. Upon receiving sighting contacts on October 25, Halsey made his first major tactical decision as COMSOPAC. His dispatch to Kinkaid which we received on Guadalcanal inspired us all by its aggressive brevity:

Attack Repeat Attack.

Kinkaid fought what was later named the battle of Santa Cruz during the day of October 26. The action-packed hours claimed grave casualties and damage from both sides including the loss of our precious carrier *Hornet*. Tactically a standoff, the engagement at least drove the Japanese fleet back to Truk.

I did not know it but I now gained a powerful ally in my fight to hold Guadalcanal. On October 24 the President of the United States overrode the supreme strategy which was giving priority of men, materiel, ships and planes to the European theater. In a memorandum of that date to the Joint Chiefs of Staff he wrote:

> My anxiety about the Southwest Pacific is to make sure that every possible weapon gets into that area to hold Guadalcanal, and that having held it in this crisis that munitions and planes and crews are on the way to take advantage of our success.

I understand that he also authorized *Time* magazine to go ahead with an issue featuring my portrait on the cover. It appeared in early November and the story pleased me because it seemed to bring the real meaning of the campaign home to the American public. I doubted if the authorities in Washington would permit us henceforth to continue operating on our only too familiar shoestring.

Halsey already was doing his best in Noumea to carry out his promise to me. Having canceled the Ndeni operation he diverted the 1st Battalion, 147th Infantry, to Guadalcanal with the remaining battalions of the regiment to follow. I was also to receive Hall Jeschke's 8th Marine Regiment from Samoa, part of Evans Carlson's 2d Raider Battalion, units from two Marine defense battalions, a large Seabee contingent and some heavy artillery units including 155mm gun batteries which could answer the 150mm Pistol Petes. Nor did Halsey neglect vital air support. Toward the end of October and in early November I received the first squadrons of Marine Air Group 11 with the others to follow. I also brought over most of John Arthur's 2d Marines from Tulagi.

Halsey's reinforcement plan contained one major flaw: he committed part of the force to a landing at Aola Bay, nearly 50 miles east of Lunga, there to build an airfield—a project proposed by Turner over a month earlier. Two factors forced me to fight it: after reconnoitering the area my engineers found it totally unsuitable for airfield construction, something Martin Clemens had told me in the first place;

secondly, the project required a security force which I needed badly at Cactus. I also needed the Seabees to help build a new airfield, Fighter Two, west of Kukum.

Unfortunately Turner persuaded Halsey to accept his plan, which cost me an Army infantry battalion, half the raider battalion, a defense battalion, and all the precious Seabees. Turner saw the light a couple of weeks later and canceled the project—but this didn't help me at the time.

Despite my loss, the other reinforcement gave me riches beyond the dreams of avarice. Tactically my situation resembled the period following the battle of the Ridge when we had beaten the enemy but could not pursue. This time I could pursue. We turned west.

XV

End of an Epic

TO DISRUPT the temporarily beaten enemy before he could consolidate his old positions, I wanted to move west of the Matanikau River to an area around the Kokumbona-Poha River. By pushing to this line I would force Hyakutake to use landing beaches much farther west besides freeing Henderson Field from Pistol Pete's harassing fires.

We gave the operation to Edson's 5th Marines, Arthur's 2d Marines less one battalion, and Whaling's Group composed of the scout-snipers and the 3d Battalion, 7th Marines—altogether a powerful force supported by artillery, air and surface craft. Such an attack force was certainly new to the Guadalcanal veterans; I could scarcely believe myself that we could muster it.

With Whaling's Group on the left, Edson kicked off on November 1, his troops crossing the Matanikau on bridges built by the engineers the preceding night. His battalions rapidly punched through to the Point Cruz area where on November 2 Lew Walt wheeled his battalion north to the coast to complete envelopment of the enemy position. As I reported to General Holcomb:

> In this pocket they killed to the last man 350 odd Japanese and captured three cannons, nine thirty-seven millimeter guns and thirty-two heavy and light machine guns.

While the 5th Marines closed in here, I pushed the 2d Marines west and simultaneously sent Frank Richards' Army battalion to Edson for his reserve. As was earlier the case, we seemed well on the way to accomplishing the mission when Halsey warned that the Tokyo Express was landing a reinforced regiment at Koli Point *to my east*. To paraphrase Hamlet I now lacked gall to make oppression bitter particu-

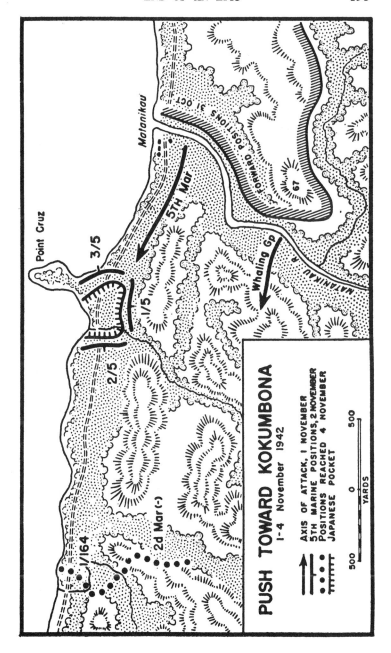

Point Cruz

Matanikou

FORWARD POSITIONS 31 OCT

67

MATANIKAU R

3/5

5TH Mar

1/5

Whaling Gp

2/5

2d Mar (-)

1/164

PUSH TOWARD KOKUMBONA
1-4 November 1942

→ AXIS OF ATTACK, 1 NOVEMBER
━━ 5TH MARINE POSITIONS, 2 NOVEMBER
•••━ POSITIONS REACHED 4 NOVEMBER
•••━ JAPANESE POCKET

500   0   500

YARDS

500

larly since the 8th Marines had not yet reached Guadalcanal.

To meet the new threat I sent Hanneken's battalion on a forced march east. Edson relinquished command of the Matanikau operation to Arthur whose 2d Marines plus one battalion dug in west of Point Cruz. Edson's regiment returned to the perimeter which was further strengthened on November 4 when Jeschke's 8th Marines together with heavy artillery units began landing.

Hanneken lost contact with division headquarters on the first day of his march. On the following day we learned that he had walked into a severe fire fight and was now fighting a withdrawal action. After sending him air support and starting surface craft to the area, I sent Puller's battalion in boats around the sea flank while Moore's 164th Infantry marched in from the south—an operation commanded by Bill Rupertus.

While these units atempted to join Hanneken now west of the Nalimbiu River, I received permission from Kelly Turner to send Carlson and his two raider companies at Aola Bay to the west to try to cut off any enemy force escaping our envelopment action.

Terrain, general fatigue of troops and combat inexperience of the Army units delayed the envelopment sufficiently for the main Japanese force to escape west. Bad luck further plagued the inconclusive action: Bill Rupertus succumbed to dengue fever and Lewis Puller was wounded by shrapnel. With Rupertus knocked out I gave command to Ed Sebree, ADC of the Americal Division, who brought the units back to the perimeter while Carlson's raiders continued to fight a series of actions to the southwest.

I was not particularly surprised by the conclusion of this hastily improvised plan. As I wrote General Holcomb on November 6, during the action:

> If we can do that [envelop the enemy], and they don't slip through our fingers, we will immediately start the push again westward. We will start it anyhow on about the 10th or 11th after the arrival of another Army regiment. The Americal Division is moving in rapidly, and I understand the 43d [Army Division] is to follow them at which time I understand the First Division, then troops of the Second Division are to be evacuated. Tired though they

were and greatly depleted by malaria, we having had 1,500 cases, the First Division, reinforced has certainly given one damn good account of itself during the past ten days.

Meanwhile my command was undergoing almost daily changes. Against my and Roy Geiger's wishes, Halsey pulled him back to Espiritu Santo to command the wing and Louis Woods took over. The handful of original pilots had long since departed. They would scarcely have recognized a Cactus air force that even included special photographic aircraft busily mapping the western half of the island. Thanks to the newly arrived heavy artillery, Pistol Pete no longer coughed lethally at Henderson Field whose operations overflowed to Fighter One and the recently finished Fighter Two west of Kukum.

On November 8 Admiral Halsey flew in like a wonderful breath of fresh air. During a tour of the area he showed extreme interest and enthusiasm in all phases of the operation, concurring with my existent positions and future plans. More important, he talked to a large number of Marines, saw their gaunt, malaria-ridden bodies, their faces lined from what seemed a nightmare of years. I believe then and there he decided to get us out as fast as possible.

Halsey's fine sense of humor demonstrated itself that evening when he complimented me on the dinner and asked to see my cook, Butch Morgan. Morgan appeared spick and span in clean skivvy shirt and khaki trousers, his red mustache carefully combed. He stood smartly at attention while Halsey effusively praised his cooking. As the admiral went on and on, Butch looked increasingly uncomfortable and began to twist his skivvy shirt and toe the ground. I knew something was coming from him but I wasn't sure what. Finally Halsey stopped for breath, an opportunity Butch exploited with, "Aw . . . , . . . , . . . , Admiral."

I dismissed him as the group dissolved into laughter. The story quickly spread through the fleet and even reached Washington. The next morning Halsey decorated some of my officers and men before I escorted him to the airfield. At the plane he turned and with eyes twinkling said, "Vandegrift, don't you do a thing to that cook."

Once Jeschke squared away his 8th Marines I renewed

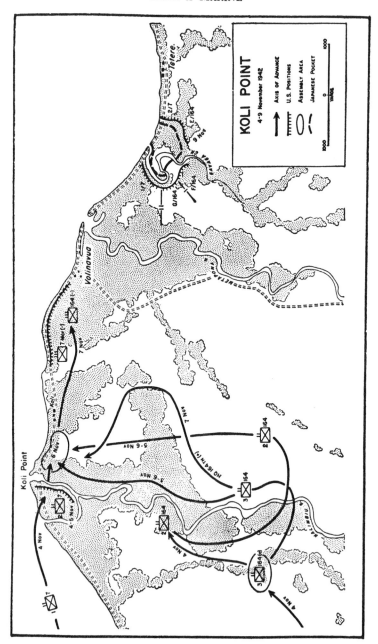

the western operation toward Poha. Again weather, green troops and a well-entrenched enemy combined to slow the push. On November 11 Halsey informed me of a large enemy fleet sailing from Truk presumably to join other units concentrated in forward areas—another attack forming against us. Two heavy air raids on this day partially confirmed his warning. With great reluctance I called off the western action.

Early the next morning Turner's transports delivered the 182d Infantry, another reinforced regiment of the Americal Division. This movement, covered by task forces under Admirals Callaghan and Scott, proceeded smoothly enough. But even as the troops were hurriedly disembarking I was reading a series of alarming intelligence reports.

The Japs seemed determined to disrupt this movement and regain complete control of our seas. To meet the oncoming enemy fleet Turner merged the covering forces into one group under Callaghan. That afternoon enemy air struck his ships besides hitting us on Guadalcanal. The raid over, Callaghan escorted the transports south and then reversed course to meet the enemy. Another task force commanded by Admiral Kinkaid and built around the still partially crippled carrier *Enterprise* was steaming toward us from the south.

Callaghan's cruisers and destroyers met the enemy north of Lunga Point shortly before 2:00 A.M. The battle would have pleased Mars. For nearly an hour we watched naval guns belch orange death with such rapid vehemence that the island seemed to shake beneath us. First light showed dispersed American ships, some of them frantically lowering small boats to pick up swimming survivors from less fortunate ships. Once again our doctors and corpsmen spent the day operating on wounded and burned sailors; once again our aircraft smashed away at Jap ships limping from the action.

We knew it was not over, but an evening flight from carrier *Enterprise* which landed at Henderson Field doomed our hopes for the arrival of Kinkaid's task force. Pilots reported the *Enterprise* still far to the south although Halsey had directed Admiral Lee to steam ahead of the carrier with his battleships, cruisers and destroyers. Unfortunately Lee failed to arrive in time to intercept the night's bombardment, a vicious forty-five minutes that cut Cactus air force nearly in half.

Shortly after dawn one of our search flights located the Japanese fleet about 150 miles to the northwest. A second flight screamed down on the leading ships, knocked out two cruisers with no losses to themselves. In a separate effort *Enterprise* planes struck another task force, sank a cruiser and damaged three others plus a destroyer. More important to me, these planes also found and immediately attacked the main Japanese transport group. We picked up the ball at Henderson Field, a hot action continuing without respite throughout the afternoon. We lost five planes but sank a heavy cruiser, seven transports and damaged several other capital ships and transports.

Darkness passed the ball to Lee whose van destroyers engaged the enemy before midnight. Soon the heavy thunder of battleship guns drowned out the lighter destroyer fire, again a fantastic spectacle which offered no clue as to victor or vanquished until the dawn showed the enemy gone. But the same dawn revealed a sight now sickeningly familiar to the tired crews of the small boats and to the doctors who inherited their salvage.

The dawn also revealed four enemy transports beached west of Tassafaronga, choice targets worked over throughout the day by our planes and by del Valle's long-range artillery.

If I have given coherence to this battle narrative, it is from knowledge after the facts. Throughout these days and nights our radios received (and sent) a good many messages that furnished us only a partial picture of the combined action. Although on November 15 we did not yet know the extent of our losses, we knew that we had won. Even while our first planes were taking off I sent the following dispatch to Halsey with information copies to all interested commands:

We believe the enemy has suffered a crushing defeat— We thank Lee for his sturdy effort of last night—We thank Kincaid for his intervention yesterday—Our own aircraft has been grand in its relentless pounding of the foe—Those efforts we appreciate but our greatest homage goes to Scott, Callaghan and their men who with magnificent courage against seemingly hopeless odds drove back the first hostile stroke and made success possible—

To them the men of Cactus lift their battered helmets in deepest admiration.

A few hours after releasing this message I learned that Admiral Scott, Admiral Callaghan and over 700 officers and men of the Navy gave their lives in the action that helped save our own.

The costly victory brought warm messages from old and loyal friends.

From Admiral McCain:

The time has come—For Halsey, Fitch, Harmon, Vandegrift—Three rousing cheers.

From Halsey:

To the superb officers and men on land, on sea, in the air and under the sea who have performed such magnificent deeds for our country in the past few days—You have written your names in golden letters on the pages of history and won the undying gratitude of your countrymen—My pride in you is beyond expression—No honor for you would be too great—Magnificently done—God bless each and every one of you—To the glorious dead—hail heroes—rest with God.

A short time later I heard from an old friend, Admiral Stark, serving in London:

I do not have to tell you what I think of the Marine Corps. I have been on the record too much in the last few years before Congress and elsewhere.

Perhaps no greater tribute could be paid to you than that the officers and men under you are living up to the finest traditions of the United States Marine Corps.

May continued success and achievement be with you. The stakes are high in the particular hot spot in which you were launched.

My best wishes and best of luck to all.

The pleasure brought by these and other messages was greatly reduced by the announcement of John A. Lejeune's passing. I understand that prior to his final failing he was very proud of our accomplishments. Well should he have been since it was his fine hand that guided so many of us toward amphibious fruition.

On November 16 I received a long-awaited letter from Kelly Turner. After giving details of the recent naval action he went on:

> This afternoon a dispatch came from Commander South Pacific Force [Halsey] asking when we could provide transports for sending the rest of the American Division up there, and to begin moving out some of the Marine regiments. My reply was that the *Hunter Liggett* can begin loading now, and the *President Jackson, President Adams,* and the *Crescent City* can begin loading on the twentieth; with the recommendation that the Eighteenth Construction Battalion go along to act as stevedores and chauffeurs. If this is approved, you should be able to begin evacuating Marines by about the 26th. I hope that you can make plans to leave all of your heavy equipment, motor vehicles, tents, etc., up there, in hopes of getting your units re-equipped when you come out.

General Harmon next reported the imminent arrival on Guadalcanal of General Patch, who commanded the Americal Division. All this was propitious enough but left a number of questions hanging in the air. I wrote Arch Howard, chief of staff to Barney Vogel who commanded the newly formed 1st Marine Amphibious Corps in Noumea:

> If the First Division is to commence its evacuation on that date [November 26], I would certainly like to know it at the earliest possible moment. I would like to know where we are going, for if we return to Wellington, we have a setup already there. If it is to be Auckland or some other new place, certain staff officers should precede the first contingent and make necessary arrangements.
> The question of what to leave or not to leave here should of course, I think, be by General Vogel's direction. It would, of course, greatly facilitate the evacuation if all heavy equipment could be left. As you have seen by our dispatch, the Amphibious Tractors are shot; however, they have paid for themselves one hundred times over.

Our truck transportation, that which we have here, has taken a grueling punishment running cross-country and over improvised roads to such an extent that it is practically worn out. Our canvas is in fair shape. A good bit of it is of the new type which both this Division and the Second Division should have as it blends in with the country and is not visible from the air. I certainly do not want to leave green canvas here and get khaki canvas in exchange. It is bulky and requires time for loading.

Engineering equipment is another question that worries me. Every piece of engineering equipment that is now on this island should remain. God knows it is little enough as it is to do a Herculean job of building roads, bridges, dispersal pits, etc. On the other hand, we must be assured of replacement. After we are out of here, and we have more time, I will submit to General Vogel some recommendations *re* additional engineer equipment such as portable bridges, which any unit must have in projecting themselves forward in this type of territory.

Meanwhile the war continued.

With the enemy checked I wanted to consolidate my position secure in the knowledge of his whereabouts. Calling in Evans Carlson I asked him to extend his patrol to include the Mt. Austen area, mopping up where he could and destroying some bothersome enemy artillery if possible.

Carlson took back with him an Australian guide, a number of native scouts, and the redoubtable Sergeant Major Vouza who, recovered from his ghastly wounds and proudly wearing the Silver Star, demanded to return to duty. Operating in the southern area for the rest of November, Carlson's patrol, which we supplied by airdrop, accomplished everything I hoped for by the time it returned to the perimeter in early December.

Simultaneous with calling in Carlson I gave Ed Sebree the better part of two Army regiments, Jeschke's 8th Marines and Cates' now very tired 1st Marines for a reserve and asked him to push west. The operation started quite smoothly but soon ran into an enemy who reacted quickly and in strength. On November 23 I halted it, deciding to hold what I had. I was facing a reshuffling of units preparatory to our leaving the island and was also concerned by intelligence reports of another Jap fleet build-up. As it turned out the enemy's naval attempt was met by Admiral Wright's task force which on November 30 took a terrible beating in fighting the enemy ships.

Our time was now growing short. We devoted it to readying the units for transfer. On December 3 I reported to General Vogel:

In order to actuate this move [General Patch assuming command of the island] we have had members of his staff sections with members of our staff sections ever since your departure. In addition, so that the turnover could be in an orderly fashion, we had his Quartermaster take over all commissaries as of the thirtieth of November. Also, his Motor Transport people are now functioning in charge of motor transportation. This, of course, leaves certain of our service troops available to move whenever there is a ship available for their movement—the Army having the proper force and being perfectly capable to carry on. In addition to the above, and in my mind of far greater importance, is the fact that we now have the necessary troops to initiate a push to the westward. I feel that as long as the Americal troops are fresh troops they should initiate the action. I further feel that if there is to be a turnover in command in the near future, it is only fair to the responsible commander that the plans for this action should be made by him and his technical staff, and that he should have the final say relative to the contemplated action, and that the command not be shifted in the midst of it. As you know, we have pushed out and have, I think, a sufficient area to protect the field.

We now enter into the third and final phase of mopping up the Japs that are here, building and developing this into a base. Again, I would like to suggest that the Commander who is to carry this through to completion be the Commander to initiate it. I believe you know me well enough to know that I am not trying to get out of any duty for myself and my staff, but I do think that in fairness to those who are to carry on the command should change very shortly after the departure of the Fifth Regiment.

By dispatch I learned that on December 9 the 5th Marines would embark with other units going out in increments of a few days' interval. On December 7 I issued my final division letter on Guadalcanal, one in which I tried to summarize our accomplishments in these long, brutal months:

In relinquishing command in the Cactus Area I hope that in some small measure I can convey to you my feeling of pride in your magnificent accomplishments and my thanks for the unbounded loyalty, limitless self-sacrifice and high courage which have made those accomplishments possible. To the soldiers and Marines who have faced the enemy in the fierceness of night and combat; to the Cactus pilots, Army, Navy, and Marine, whose unbelieveable achievements have made the name "Guadalcanal" a synonym for death and disaster in the language of our enemy; to those who have labored and sweated within the lines at all manner of prodigious and vital tasks; to the men of the torpedo boat command slashing at the enemy in night sorties; to our small band of devoted allies who have contributed so vastly in proportion to their numbers; to the surface forces of the Navy associated with us in signal triumphs of their own, I say that at all times you have faced without flinching the worst that the enemy could do to us and have thrown back the best that he could send against us. It may well be that this modest operation begun four months ago today has, through your efforts, been successful in thwarting the larger aims of our enemy in the Pacific. The fight for the Solomons is not yet won but "tide what may" I know that you, as brave men and men of good will, will hold your heads high and prevail in the future as you have in the past.

Two days later in an informal ceremony I passed command of Guadalcanal to General Patch. That day men of the 5th Marines embarked, some so weak they could scarcely climb the cargo nets draped over the sides of the fat transports. Two days later I walked to our small cemetery called Flanders Field to take my own farewell of the almost 700 officers and men of my command who died in this operation. I looked in silence on the rude crosses that bespoke valiant deeds by great men. The words of Robert E. Lee came to mind:

What a cruel thing is war; to separate and destroy families and friends, and mar the purest joys and happiness

God has granted us in this world; to fill our hearts with hatred instead of love for our neighbors, and to devastate the fair face of the beautiful world.

XVI

Australian Interlude

A JCS dispatch of November 29 settled our immediate future: 25th Army Div is assigned SoPac Area and will proceed White Poppy [Noumea]—1st MarDiv is to be relieved without delay, and assigned to SoWesPac Area and will proceed to Australia for rehabilitation and employment— The purpose of this transfer is to provide an amphibious division for the future formation of an amphibious force to carry out amphibious operations under the commander SoWesPac Area [General Douglas MacArthur]—Halsey arrange with MacArthur details of transfer of 1st MarDiv.

Halsey did not protest the JCS ukase but in a dispatch to MacArthur he questioned the choice of Brisbane for our rehabilitation:

> Medical survey First MarDiv indicates seventy-five per cent latent or active malaria rate—Consider minimum rehabilitation time three months and possibly six months— Information here indicates climate and conditions Brisbane entirely unsuitable rehabilitation this division—Earnestly recommend location vicinity Sydney or farther south— Major General Vandegrift due arrive Brisbane twelfth via airplane—Fifth Marines due arrive on twelfth.

From Guadalcanal several of my staff and I flew to Noumea for a conference with Halsey. After reviewing his correspondence with MacArthur, he told me, "I don't know what you're going to find over there, but if I can do anything for you don't hesitate to let me know."

With that he called in his large staff and delivered an effusive speech on behalf of the 1st Marine Division, concluding with several complimentary remarks concerning

205

its commander. My staff later accused me of muttering Butch Morgan's classic reply to Halsey, but this was not true.

After a brief but pleasant rest in Noumea we flew to Brisbane. During the trip I noticed Bill Twining doodling on an envelope and asked him what he was doing.

"I thought we should have a distinctive shoulder patch for the 1st Division," he replied. He showed me the rough design of what a few weeks later became our official patch: a shield of blue holding the red figure 1 and the five stars of the Southern Cross superimposed on it. The word "Guadalcanal" ran vertically down the numeral.

MacArthur's representatives met us and escorted us to our new camp. I soon reported to General Vogel in Noumea:

> The camp site is not one I would have picked for recreation and rehabilitation of an outfit who needed just that and not combat training. It is forty-five miles from town with limited amount of transportation. The grounds are well suited for camping as the soil is sandy and well drained. The camp consists of company messhalls and galleys, which are adequate, pit type latrines, shower houses with cold water only.

After inspecting the camp I flew to Port Moresby to report to General MacArthur, who gave me a most cordial and hospitable reception. So as not to interfere with our administration or training, he placed us directly under his command as part of his general reserve. He made many complimentary remarks about the Guadalcanal campaign in which he showed intense interest.

He also briefed me on Eichelberger's current operation against Buna in New Guinea, next on his plans to take Lae and Salamaua as steppingstones to the northwest. Although I could not see the 1st Marine Division logically participating in such operations I said nothing, content in knowing we could not move for a minimum three months during which a great deal could happen in the higher command circles.

In a later talk with him I questioned the Brisbane camp area. MacArthur obviously wanted us to stay there, but said if I insisted he would send us to Sydney. Since no camp site was immediately available in the Sydney area, he felt that any hasty move would simply cause confusion.

Upon my return to the division I was impressed with the earnest efforts of the Army to bed us down and do everything possible toward our comfort. I was also assured by an Army surgeon that the area was nonmalarial, an important point because of our high incidence of this fever. We seemed set for a reasonably pleasant and profitable stay as I reported to General Vogel on December 20:

> We are making arrangements to send men on leave for ten days, having a train that will hold five hundred of them . . . which will depart daily for Sydney. . . . My present scheme is as follows: Leave and liberty, together with re-equipping and reclothing until the whole of the Division that so desires has an opportunity to get ten days' leave. This, of course, will finish in stages commensurate with time of arrival of the advance units. After that, disciplinary and hardening drills and exercises. The terrain here is good for training, and the mountainous roads with practically no traffic are excellent for hardening up the men. Our plan is to hike battalions from their camp sites to the beach, where they will stay for about four days, other battalions arriving as the one there leaves. This will cover a distance of thirty-four miles each way. There are good bivouac areas en route, also good recreational facilities for that number of men at the beach selected.

This plan blew up on the following day when my division surgeon, Warwick Brown, declared us to be smack in the center of an anopheline mosquito area—the same malaria-bearing breed we encountered on Guadalcanal. According to Warwick, the troops would infect the mosquitoes which in turn would reinfect the troops, a vicious circle which offered no local solution. A surgeon of the Army staff, Colonel Petters, confirmed Brown's fears, adding that the original Army survey erred in its findings. Sir Raphael Cilento, director of the Queensland Health Service who apparently was not originally consulted, fully backed Brown's statement in a letter in which he also expressed concern for the health of the civil population.

On December 23 I wrote MacArthur these facts and concluded:

It is requested that the question of locating a camp for the rehabilitation of the First Marine Division be reconsidered, and it is urgently recommended that the Division be moved to a nonmalarious area so that the Division personnel will not continue to reinfect itself, and may the sooner be brought to a state of health warranting it again being assigned to combat missions.

Two days later, with over 500 serious malaria cases overflowing our hospitals, MacArthur authorized his local medics to confer with us as to a new location. I was ready for this and immediately sent a team to Sydney with orders to travel on to Melbourne if necessary to find the right place.

My officers recommended the Melbourne area. On January 1 MacArthur authorized our transfer but added:

No transportation facilities are available in the Southwest Pacific Area to effect the move which will have to be carried out by shipping made available from the South Pacific area . . . the already overburdened railroad facilities of Australia cannot cope with such a movement without jeopardizing operations upon which our forces are now engaged.

Recalling Halsey's earlier offer to me, I now asked him for help. I knew how he was hurting for ships, but I was not surprised at his instant reply: he was arranging for all further troops coming from Guadalcanal to disembark in Melbourne and was sending the *West Point* to move the Marines now in the Brisbane camp to Melbourne.

By January 15 I was reporting to Vogel from a camp outside Melbourne:

Our several camp sites are well located on ground that is well drained; they are both close to small towns and to areas in which we can train. They are only some thirty-five miles from the city and are connected with it by both bus and rail transportation. We are the only large number of troops here, and the facilities are therefore not overtaxed. The Red Cross and other such similar units are delighted to have some material upon which to work. The officials, both military and civil, have been most cordial and helpful. The Army Base Depot, particularly

Colonel Galway, have done everything possible to make us comfortable and to help out.

We could not have been in better hands. Having had little contact with military units, the people of Melbourne opened their hearts and homes to us. Melbourne is a perfectly beautiful city enhanced by a cool climate—all that it had to offer was offered to us. In addition the Army maintained a nearby base hospital staffed with medical units from Cleveland, Ohio, a splendid group of professionals who made our return to health their primary concern.

These doctors really proved a godsend. When I was standing on the docks to watch the first contingents of Sims' 7th Marines disembark, a British colonel remarked, "I was in charge of a base in the Middle East and saw thousands of men come through on the way to rest areas. None appeared as tired and worn as your men." The commanding officer of the Cleveland unit said to me a little later, "Had I room I would suggest we send this whole regiment to the hospital. Lord knows they look as if they need it."

Shortly after we settled in Melbourne, General Holcomb ordered me and Jerry Thomas back to Washington for conferences. Before leaving I flew to Port Moresby to pay a courtesy call on General MacArthur. I was certain that I had annoyed him in the process of getting the division transferred to Melbourne, so I was agreeably surprised when he greeted me with a smile and outstretched hand.

"Vandegrift, what are you going back to the States for? To become President?"

I looked him in the eye. "General, I thought maybe you would know why I was going back."

He recoiled slightly, then recovered. "No," he said, "you were dead right in taking your division to Melbourne."

At the Washington airport General Holcomb warned me to expect little rest during the next few weeks. The American people, he explained, from the President to the average citizen, were awfully proud of their Guadalcanal Marines and very hungry for details of the campaign—I would be dogged by the press and speaking schedules.

The next morning I appeared before the press in his office, answered what questions I could, and was hustled over to the JCS consisting of Admirals Leahy and King and Generals Marshall and Arnold.

These gentlemen asked me to review the Guadalcanal campaign. They next posed numerous questions, some of them predicated on reports from the South Pacific, from both Halsey and MacArthur's bailiwicks. In no particular order I made a number of points which I later submitted in memorandum. I offer them simply to show what we learned from Guadalcanal and what my own thinking was in these still early days of the war:

The Japanese soldier: tenacious, asks no quarter and expects none, has so far in the war died rather than surrender; we can expect this in the future. He is no better at jungle fighting than we—when he attacks it costs him eight or nine to one, when we attack it costs us one and a half to one. We should not under-estimate him but we should not make something of him that he is not—"invincible." He will not be a pushover but ship for ship and gun for gun I know that our people are superior.

Present Pacific strategy: I do not believe that the strategy of pushing in each finger from the end is the way to accomplish the result desired. I think it would be far better to cut him off at the wrist, in other words, I think it would be unfortunate to have innumerable Bunas [an operation recently completed by the Army in New Guinea]. I would like to say here, as I have said before, that the only reason I can see for taking these islands is either to take an airfield away from the Japanese, thus denying it to them and acquiring it for our own use in projecting our air and surface craft forward, or seizing an island on which there is not an airfield for the same purpose. I cannot agree it is necessary to occupy every foot of ground between Henderson Field, New Guinea and Japan proper in order to defeat Japan. For example, I believe that so long as you reduce the enemy forces on Guadalcanal to such a state of impotency that they cannot endanger the field, the fact that there are a few Japanese imbedded in jungle hideouts is of no consequence.

Air: Japanese employment of air strength, like their employment of ground strength, is unsound. Attrition of planes and pilots must already have hurt them. I don't believe that we can conquer by air, but believe that it will be forward projection of air and surface vessels with sufficient well-trained ground troops to hold or seize the positions that we need which will be the answer. We have learned a lot from the air operations, and I believe one of the main things we have learned is that horizontal bombing unless in enough strength to drop a large pattern, which generally is uneconomical, is useless against ships that are underway. I believe that in the defense of airdromes in areas where we do not have absolute control of the sea that the employment of dive bombers should be stressed both by the Army and ourselves.

Training: too much stress cannot be laid on squad, platoon, company, and battalion training. The basic training should be so conducted that the ground soldier is familiar with woods and looks on them as a friend rather than an enemy. Night noises should become as common to him as the sights he sees in the day and no less disconcerting. We should condition our men by difficult cross-country hikes and accustom them to living on iron rations such as rice, bacon, coffee for periods of time while going through the jungle. The Japanese is no more able to live off the country in the strict sense of the word than we. As a matter of fact, on Guadalcanal groups of Japanese who had been isolated from their parent organization completely deteriorated and were a pushover for our men.

In this connection in the South Pacific theater, one of our greatest problems is malaria. Such is the perniciousness of this disease that we will have to plan to replace the fighting units and send them back to nonmalarious country for rehabilitation. I feel that units should be evacuated after a given length of time to a cooler climate and built up, and that these rehabilitation areas should have as much thought given to them as training camps in the vicinity of a theater of operations for staging-in processes.

Mr. James Forrestal, the Undersecretary of the Navy, asked me similarly to address the Secretary's conference. Bristling with vitality he absorbed these and other details and began at once to ponder suitable changes. At his instigation I soon began a whirlwind round of speeches to such institutions as the Army War College, Marine Corps Schools, Army training camps, Mr. Magnuson's House Naval Affairs

Subcommittee, civil organizations such as the Union League Club in Chicago and the Cleveland Advertising Club, and to numerous groups of defense workers. In each speech I tried to tell one phase or another of the Guadalcanal fighting, tried to assure the audience that the Marines were getting the best possible treatment both in and out of battle, that they were dedicated to a long struggle but felt confident of final victory.

I wanted very much to tell these things to the families of my men and was delighted when the *March of Time* invited me to make a nationwide broadcast on January 28. Here I stressed the treatment we tried to provide the troops. I spoke of plasma and sulfa drugs, of the Navy's splendid and courageous work in evacuating wounded and bringing in food and medical supplies, of the Army's superb hospital in our present location. I thought this was important to fathers and mothers, wives and sweethearts—just as it was to the men themselves.

On February 4 an invitation to the White House interrupted this schedule. My family and I were ushered into President Roosevelt's office. I had known the President, who with his usual charm made us feel completely at ease. With my wife and son looking on he read a citation and placed the Medal of Honor around my neck. I quote part of the citation because the national gratitude applied as much to my command as to myself:

> With the adverse factors of weather, rain and disease making his task a difficult and hazardous undertaking, and with his command eventually including sea, land and air forces of the Army, Navy and Marine Corps, Major General Vandegrift achieved marked success in commanding the initial landings of the United States Forces in the Solomon Islands and in their subsequent occupation.
>
> His tenacity, courage and resourcefulness prevailed against a strong, determined and experienced enemy, and the gallant fighting spirit of the men under his inspiring leadership enabled them to withstand aerial, land and sea bombardment to surmount all obstacles and leave a disorganized and ravaged enemy.
>
> This dangerous but vital mission, accomplished at the constant risk of his life, resulted in securing a valuable base for further operations of our forces against the

enemy, and its successful completion reflects great credit upon Major General Vandegrift, his command and the United States Naval Service.

I returned to a vigorous lecture schedule, an interesting experience which greatly heartened me because of the attitude of the general public. The reader might remember this period, a time of astronomical shipping losses in the Atlantic which placed the outcome of the war in considerable doubt. Despite a certain gloom I found no spirit of defeatism and a tremendous pride and interest in what we already had accomplished in the Pacific. By dispatch I shared my experience with my command:

I have received a most cordial reception here. Everyone has evinced the greatest interest in our work. What was done at Guadalcanal by all Americans there receives the highest praise. As your commander I receive all this in your name. I know only too well that this praise is meant for you and that you are deserving of everything that is said about you. I recount in public and in private the heroic deeds that you have done. I have told them how you stood at the Tenaru and battled for fifteen hours until your enemy was completely annihilated. I have told them of the battle of Edson's Ridge where 400 brave raiders and parachutists stood from midnight until daybreak and slugged it out against an enemy four times their strength —and how that enemy retreated at dawn leaving the ground covered with their dead. I have told them of the battles of October, of how the bar at the Matanikau was littered with tanks destroyed by gunners who could not fire until they were only a few yards away; of the massed attacks against our jungle lines where things were touch and go for hours, but no man gave way. I told them of the superb work of our artillery and antiaircraft where men stood to their guns for days and days without relief. I have told them of the ten battles of the Matanikau and how in each of them you took heavy toll of a hard-fighting, well-equipped enemy. I have told them of the magnificent work of our airmen who wreaked such havoc on enemy land, sea and air forces; of how on that September day I stood and watched our last four Grummans rise to meet twenty-six bombers covered by an equal number of Zeros, and of my joy at the battle's end when those four gallant lads returned safely to earth.

And these folks here at home have heard from me of the hours, days and weeks of sweat and toil on beaches handling stock, and in the jungles cutting lines and seeking out the enemy. They know also that having given fully of your strength and courage you are now resting in a hospitable land and that having rested and healed their sick and wounded, the men of Guadalcanal will be again ready for whatever this war may bring.

We flew back by commercial airplane, stopping a day or two in Pearl Harbor where Admiral Nimitz caught us up on events in the Pacific. We flew on by Pan American Clipper, a unique service long since obsolete. Each morning early the plane departed in order to make a landfall before dark. About 4:30 P.M. we reached some island, swam, dined and slept before starting off the next morning—time consuming but a restful way to travel. I passed the long hours of flight by discussing socialism with a New Zealand diplomat and pioneer socialist, Walter Nash, who one day would serve as prime minister of his country. At the end of the trip he said, "Vandegrift, I surely have enjoyed this flight. For three days we have discussed socialism. I firmly believe I am right and I know you believe you are right. So we have gotten absolutely nowhere."

In Noumea we called on Admiral Halsey and General Vogel. Halsey generously sent us to Brisbane in his plane. From there I telephoned General MacArthur to report in and to tell him something of my trip. Again he was most cordial. He congratulated me on my decoration and told me that General Krueger, commanding Sixth Army to which my division was now attached, was more than satisfied with Bill Rupertus' progress in my absence. I reached Melbourne at the end of March. Because of Bill's fine work I could write General Holcomb a couple of days later:

We have now started our amphibious training and our first phase will be completed in the next few days. . . . We are getting our equipment in a very satisfactory manner, and I hope before long we will be completely equipped again.

Civilian friends have often asked how one goes about rebuilding a shot-up division. In the case of the 1st Division the problem was to square away the men, rest them by recreation and restore them to health. Recreation did not stop with wine, women and song. While the troops naturally liked the gracious young ladies of Melbourne, a good many of them were not overly intent on tanking up on beer. Assuming this would be the case, the people of Melbourne stocked their beautiful Cricket Club with large quantities of beer and very little milk prior to turning it over to the Marines. The rich, creamy milk disappeared in about fifteen minutes— they later worked hard keeping sufficient quantities available. The Australian army quartermaster told me he had never seen men drink so much milk.

Once the troops were rested and partially restored to health, we returned them to their pride, first by disciplinary drills—the old close order drill—and then by short hikes getting longer and longer, working into small unit training and progressing to amphibious training where we stood upon my return.

General Walter Krueger flew down to witness our early amphibious exercises. A soldier of the old school, Krueger was a real Spartan, sparing of praise. I was more than pleased when he made several compliments on the appearance and attitude of officers and men and the appearance of our camp sites which he inspected with a highly trained, critical eye. Naturally he had to find fault with something. His time came when I took him to my combined quarters and CP, a perfectly beautiful country house belonging to the American representative of the McCormick Harvester Company. Looking over the ivy-covered walls and the pleasant interior, Krueger growled, "Well, Vandegrift, you certainly are doing very well by yourself here."

I promptly answered, "I certainly am, sir. You are older than I am, General, and of course you are senior. But five dollars will get you twenty-five that you haven't been as uncomfortable for so much of your career as I have. I don't need to practice it. I can take it when it comes, but when there is no need I don't want either me or my men to be miserable."

Much to my relief he laughed. The next time I visited his

headquarters I noticed he had installed rugs and overstuffed furniture in his own quarters.

Unit training progressed rapidly. On April 14 I reported to General Holcomb:

> I have just come in from two days out in the training area and am indeed very much pleased with the way things are going. There is a noticeable difference in combat discipline in the training now over that which we had at New River and our exercises in the Chesapeake. Our night landings are made without noise, without verbal orders and without the rattle of equipment. One of our landings was made against the headland at one o'clock in the morning most successfully. One of the Australian generals, when I showed him the place of landing the night before, insisted that it could not be done.

I remember this particular landing well since in going down one of the cargo nets I nearly broke my leg. Like most of the troops I was slowly getting back into shape, but I was still underweight and slightly weak. In the same report to General Holcomb I wrote:

> Our sickness still remains a major problem as we have some four thousand sick, three thousand of whom are malarial. I made an inspection of the hospital last week and was greatly pleased with the way the men are being cared for. In talking to the commanding officer, he feels that very shortly we should have a decided drop in our malaria patients. . . . We are getting along very well with our re-equipping and will soon be fully equipped. Our motor transport is in far better shape than it was when we left the States . . . our people in the supply section here have redesigned the water tank so that more than one man can get water at a time. In fact, there are twelve spigots and a major spigot for stock pots. That was one of the crying needs on Guadalcanal—the inability to re-water a battalion in a rapid manner.

Two weeks later I wrote Deacon Upshur in San Francisco:

> The Division is now getting rapidly back on its feet, and when I tell you that the last three battalions that came

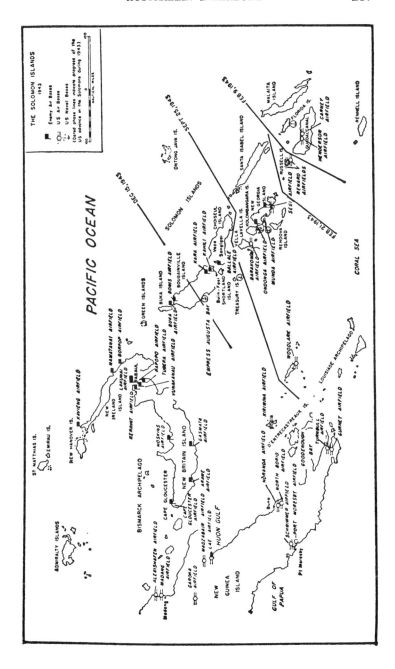

in from the training areas hiked thirty-two miles a day ...
for two days, you will see that they are well along physically.

I divided my time between the field and headquarters.
Admiral Halsey and his staff visited us as did other prominent
persons including Nelson Johnson, my old friend from
China days now our ambassador to Australia. Nelson brought
his lovely wife and children down for a day. In Peking
I had made his little boy an honorary corporal of Marines.
I now promoted him to sergeant and to keep peace in the
family made his daughter a corporal.

Throughout this period General Holcomb supplied me with
the details of his office, quite often asking my concurrence
with long-term officer assignments before he made them. He
still intended to retire at the end of 1943 and was trying
to figure out the best way to work me in, assuming the President appointed me the next Commandant. Knowing I preferred
to remain in the Pacific until the last possible moment, the
Commandant in a change of slate on July 1 brought Barney
Vogel back to the States and gave me command of the I
Corps in Noumea.

The division now stood in excellent shape with replacements trained and equipped sufficiently for regimental level
exercises. I held no qualms in turning command of this
splendid outfit over to Bill Rupertus who had been through
so much with me.

As a surprise the division staff and commanders appeared
at the airport to say good-by while the division band played
the division tune, "Waltzing Matilda," and the "Marine Corps
Hymn"—a wonderful but very sad farewell to this glorious
body of men.

XVII

Assault at Bougainville

I FOUND New Caledonia a beautiful island of long, white sand beaches. The temperature of its days varied from 70 to 85 degrees while trade winds cooled the nights. In 1943 its capital city of Noumea resembled a West Indies town—ramshackle in a pleasantly unpainted way with galleries encircling the second stories of residences and louvered doorways flanked by brilliantly blooming flowers.

It was not so pretty diplomatically since the Vichy governor general resented or pretended to resent the presence of American forces. I got along with him because I saw him only on rare social occasions.

As corps commander I perforce became concerned with the over-all Pacific situation. All the time we were fighting on Guadalcanal, MacArthur's forces including Australians were fighting on New Guinea, a one-time priority area for the enemy but reduced by Guadalcanal to a secondary effort.

In December, 1942, the Australians took Gona; in early January, 1943, MacArthur's units captured Buna and later Sanananda to remove the enemy threat to Port Moresby. Then in March the battle of the Bismarck Sea stopped a reinforcing enemy surface force. An Australian force already occupied Wau, the idea being to advance from there on Lae and Salamaua, and later to Finschhafen—the operation which MacArthur briefed me on in Port Moresby.

At this point MacArthur planned to move the 1st Marine Division across the wide strait to the island of New Britain from where he would work his way to the bastion of Rabaul. These operations, current and planned, stood in consonance with his over-all strategy of reaching Japan via the Philippines (see the front endpaper map).

But now operations in Nimitz' theater showed signs of running away from MacArthur's strategy. The Guadalcanal

campaign originally complemented this strategy of reaching
Rabaul through the central Solomons, at the same time re-
lieving the immediate threat to Port Moresby. In reality
it kicked off a drive up the central Solomons that ultimately
worked itself into Nimitz' own strategy, which was steadily
reverting to prewar naval planning—a strike through the Central Pacific in order to reach Japan. This was precisely the
strategy predicted and planned by Pete Ellis over two decades earlier.

To neutralize Japanese air attacks from Munda on New
Georgia Island and from another little island called Kolombangara, Halsey had some months previously pushed a small
Marine raider force to Pavuvu and an Army regimental combat team to Banika, two adjoining dots called the Russell
Islands about 65 miles northwest of Guadalcanal. Supported by airfields there and on Guadalcanal, Halsey pushed
forward to Munda, an operation primarily under Army command although utilizing Marine forces, mainly raiders and
defense battalions.

At the end of June, 1943, Army troops landed relatively
unopposed on the off-island of Rendova. A few days later
Marine raiders and Army units landed at night at Rice Anchorage on the northern end of New Georgia. Here Harry
Liversedge's 1st Marine Raider Regiment, with Sam Griffith
commanding the 1st Battalion and Mickey Curran the 4th Battalion, made a difficult forced march to cut the trail between
major Jap garrisons. This operation, complete with rapid
air and naval actions, was in full bloom when I came to Noumea.

My command consisted of the 3d Marine Division, about
to sail from New Zealand for Guadalcanal (secured since
February), and a number of air, raider, defense battalion
and other independent units. Charlie Barrett, one of the most
original thinkers in the Corps and a pioneer in amphibious
operations, commanded this division with Hal Turnage, one of
my oldest friends, serving as his ADC. In Australia, Bill
Rupertus commanded my old division, Lem Shepherd being
his ADC. Bill came under the operational control of General MacArthur but I retained administrative control. I also
held administrative control of the 2d Marine Division commanded by Julian Smith, whose ADC was Leo ("Dutch")
Hermle. Presently training in New Zealand this division re-

mained under operational control of Nimitz, who had earmarked it to land on Tarawa, a small atoll in the Gilbert Islands.

Satisfying the wants of these various commanders meant a careful juggling of replacement troops, senior officers, new equipment and available supply. My biggest problem concerned supply, a field in which the Navy at this point did not exactly excel. We lacked even a standard operating procedure, yet our arsenal of weapons and equipment daily expanded. The M-1 rifle already had replaced the old Springfield, the LCVP and LCM were replacing the Higgins boats used at Guadalcanal, and the older Alligators were giving way to the Water Buffalo.

To smooth out the supply function I moved Cece Long in as supply service commander. To help him turn out a standard operating procedure I "borrowed" Fred Wieseman from Bill Rupertus. Fred had performed splendid service in the D-4 section of the 1st Division ever since New River days; I wanted his keen mind to go to work on this immense problem which was not going to be solved for a good many months.

Part of my job in Noumea consisted in briefing frequent important visitors. One was Mrs. Roosevelt, who had tried unsuccessfully to visit us on Guadalcanal. She now turned up sporting a letter from the President to Halsey and me—she would go to the island provided we could take satisfactory security precautions, which we did.

Eleanor Roosevelt was a remarkable woman, seemingly tireless during her frequent peregrinations. When Halsey and I met her in Noumea we proposed to take her to the Red Cross center where she could comfortably rest from her long flight. No, indeed—she insisted on going directly to the nearest hospital. She spent the bulk of her time in New Caledonia visiting our sick and wounded, talking to them by the hundreds. In each case she took the man's home address and upon her return to America wrote his family.

Although the Munda operation progressed satisfactorily, its capture would not entirely reduce the New Georgia defenses. Halsey decided to follow it by bypassing Kolombangara and landing on the Vella Lavella and Arundel islands to the north.

The cleaning out of this area corresponded in a sense to what MacArthur was trying to do in the southwest. As he would soon face the New Britain campaign, we eventually would face the Bougainville campaign which soon became my major problem.

To take Bougainville I was given Charlie Barrett's 3d Marine Division, an Army division (at first Lawton Collins' 25th later changed to Bob Beightler's 37th), Alan Shapley's Provisional Raider Regiment, Brute Krulak's 2d Marine Parachute Battalion, Ed Forney's 3d Marine Defense Battalion and Brigadier Row's 8th New Zealand Brigade Group.

The *raison d'être* of the Bougainville operation was the Japanese airfield complex which we originally planned to strike directly. As reconnaissance reports and further intelligence filtered in, this proposition looked less and less attractive since we believed the bulk of an estimated 35,000 troops to be concentrated around the southern airfields.

We could not hope to gain strategic surprise. I believed we would forfeit tactical surprise by landing in the south. In an attempt to repeat the Guadalcanal success by hitting where the enemy wasn't, we finally chose an area called Empress Augusta Bay, about halfway up the western coast of this 130-mile long island. We planned to land on beaches or what would have to pass for beaches running northwest from Cape Torokina. If we could get our forces securely ashore there we thought to hold against whatever Japanese troops worked their way from across the island at Kieta, about 30 miles distant, or up from the southern end of the island. Meanwhile we would have to rely on aircraft from carriers and the Solomon bases to protect us until constructing an airfield.

Once Halsey accepted our basic plan we proceeded to refine it. My own position became slightly complicated. I had been given my third star in late July and was expecting to leave for the States in the near future—a fact theoretically known only to Bull Halsey, Jerry Thomas and Charlie Barrett but one I suspected was known generally throughout the area. Barrett would succeed me as corps commander, which meant that all planning had to be done in the closest co-operation with him and his staff on Guadalcanal, also the headquarters of Rear Admiral Wilkinson, who had replaced Kelly Turner.

Toward the end of July my staff and I began to spend an increasing amount of time on the island, about a six-hour hop by PBY from Noumea. When I first returned I thought of Rip Van Winkle awakening from his long sleep. I wrote Bill Rupertus:

Went up to Cactus the other day and you wouldn't know the place—gravel roads running in every direction, more planes than we ever knew existed on about seven different airfields. The only thing normal was the dust, which was suffocating, and the false alarm air alert at about daylight in the morning.

Rear Admiral Wilkinson, whom I had not earlier known, impressed me as a first-rate naval officer bent on doing the best possible job. I wanted no command confusion familiar to Guadalcanal days, so I told him I proposed to operate in accordance with FTP-167 and advised him to become familiar with it if he wasn't already. From that time on we encountered few difficulties.

On a later visit I found him staging out the Vella Lavella operation, the prelude to Bougainville. He kindly invited Jerry, Charlie Barrett and me to join him in his flagship, an interesting experience I later reported to General Holcomb:

I had never seen a small boat movement, consisting entirely of APDs and LCIs and was interested to see it. It went off well, was well planned and executed. There was no ground opposition, but our friends, the Japanese, reacted promptly with their air. Our fighters did a splendid job of intercepting or I may not have been so cheerful about the story. Only six got through, three of which evidently recognized the flagship and dived at it. I had a grandstand seat (and I can assure you it was a *seat,* because I was sitting on the deck) as I was on the signal bridge. One dropped just fifty feet off the number two turret on the port side, and another one one hundred feet off the quarter on the starboard side. I am saving a shirt as a souvenir which is completely covered with black marks from the powder stains of the spray laden from the powder blast—a little too close for comfort. Wilkinson's orders were simple, brief and explicit—so explicit in fact that no order except the original one had to be issued during the operation. As I said before, this was an unopposed landing, but nevertheless it speaks well of his ability.

He dropped me off at Munda as I wanted to stop and say "hello" to Pat Mulcahy who, with his airmen, has done a marvelous job at that place, as have also Scheyer and his defense battalion, and the tanks from his battalion and the Tenth [Defense Battalion]. His working with light tanks amongst the bunkers of that place was really remarkable, and we can be justly proud of them.

Admiral Halsey wasn't too pleased with my Vella Lavella excursion. Back in Noumea he gave me hell and told me not to go on any further operations where I didn't belong.

I spent the rest of August coping with various administrative problems besides working on the Bougainville planning. I was greatly saddened at this time to hear of Deacon Upshur's accidental death in a plane crash. Deacon was an instructor of mine in 1909. Through the years of campaigns abroad and duty at home I had come to respect his tremendous integrity and to value our close friendship.

Also in August the Commandant relayed President Roosevelt's orders for me to make a tour of all Marine Corps activities in the Pacific before reporting to Washington. Early the next month I left on an inspection trip with Jerry Thomas, whom I was taking back with me. We stopped at Woodlark Island to see some of our people and then went on to General MacArthur's headquarters, which was just receiving the first reports of the Lae operation.

MacArthur welcomed me warmly, brought me up to date on his show, and told me how pleased he was with Bill Rupertus and the 1st Division. Upon seeing me off he put an arm around my shoulder and said, "Vandegrift, I'm sorry to see you going back home. If you stayed here with me I would be only too glad for you to command one of my corps."

I flew on to spend a couple of days with General Krueger and next to see Bill Rupertus and my old division, then staging at Milne Bay and Goodenough Island for the Cape Gloucester landing. The division looked simply wonderful—I was sure Bill would carry out the forthcoming operation with distinction.

Back in Noumea I turned command of the I Corps over to Charlie Barrett in an informal ceremony. Jerry and I then flew to New Zealand to see Julian Smith and the 2d Marine Division. Bad weather forced us to land on Norfolk Island, a curious, indescribably beautiful place where the mutineers of the famous ship *Bounty* had been jailed. The thatched roofs and carefully trimmed hedges surrounding the houses reminded me of an English village. To repay the warm hospitality of the governor and the New Zealand fighter squadrons I sent them some badly needed rations from Auckland.

I was very much interested in Julian Smith's plans for the Tarawa landing and very much impressed with his security measures to safeguard those plans. For some reason Julian was delayed on the way to the plans section, so I went on by myself, of course in full uniform. A very earnest young corporal stopped me and asked to see a special pass which I did not possess. Politely but firmly he refused me entrance, three stars or no. I told him, "You are right. Those are your orders and you stick to them." Julian appeared quite upset when he found me waiting on a bench.

I received a thorough briefing on this operation, which posed an entirely different tactical problem than either earlier landings or the forthcoming Bougainville show. In the Central Pacific the jungles of the South and Southwest Pacific give way to coral atolls. Varying considerably in size and shape, these amount to a barrier reef surrounding a lagoon. They rarely rise more than ten feet above sea level, which for our purpose meant ideal airfields.

Tarawa atoll belonged to the Gilbert Islands, originally British owned but for fifteen months occupied by the Japanese. In the atoll the island of Betio, defended by an estimated 4,000 enemy, formed part of a complex completed by Makin Island to the north, the same place earlier raided by Carlson's raiders, and a smaller island called Apemama to the southeast (see map Chapter XVIII).

The JCS assigned the task of taking this territory to Nimitz whose amphibious task force commander was our old friend, Kelly Turner. By now the Marines had created another corps, the Vth Amphibious Corps commanded by Holland Smith with Bobbie Erskine his chief of staff at headquarters in Pearl Harbor.

Holland was given two divisions for the Tarawa assault: Julian Smith's 2d Marine Division and Ralph Smith's 27th Army Division. The Army was to take Makin Island, defended by an estimated 800 enemy including laborers. Julian was to take Betio, his secondary objective being Apemama.

Available intelligence placed the bulk of Japanese defenses on the seaward sides of Betio, which meant a direct over-the-beach assault. To try to reduce the obvious casualties of this course, Julian decided to bring the assault troops into the lagoon north of the island and land on either side of a jutting finger pier. Since coral was known to obstruct the various landing areas, he went further and decided to use the amphibian tractor for an assault vehicle as opposed to its former primary role of a supply carrier. Julian planned to send the first three waves ashore in his 75 available amphibian tractors followed by normal landing craft. To reduce casualties further he counted on preliminary naval air bombardment from the Ellice Islands to the south and on naval gunfire from surface ships. In the event, an admiral when speaking of the naval gunfire plan was said to have made the classic statement, "We do not intend to neutralize this island, we do not intend to destroy it. Gentlemen, we will obliterate it."

More than pleased with what we saw in New Zealand, we flew on to the Fijis, an interesting flight because the batteries on our PBY went out, which would have been disastrous had we made a water landing. At Suva in the Fijis I was a guest of Sir Philip Mitchell, commissioner of the South Sea Islands, who had visited me earlier on Guadalcanal. He was hosting some Marine air units who would play a prominent role in the Tarawa show. I was delighted at their general appearance and attitude.

We stopped next in the Samoa Group where Charlie Price commanded a large rear echelon. My chief concern here centered on a reported outbreak of elephantiasis, or "moo-moo," a wretched glandular disease that can prove fatal. Charlie's doctors assured me the disease was under control and was not liable to break loose. The rest of his command seemed to be in excellent shape although, as he pointed out, too many of the Marines had been too long in garrison there.

Charlie had been a close friend of mine for years and told many amusing stories of his experiences in this area. On one occasion while inspecting a small island he was ceremoniously presented to its king, a plump Samoan very interested in international affairs. Charlie delighted him by pulling out a world map and briefing him on various military operations. Inspecting the map closely the king said, "That is a beautiful map. But where is Samoa?" Charlie pointed to the appropriate flyspeck. "Humph," said the king, "who ever made *that* map?"

From Samoa we island-hopped to Hawaii, stopping to see each Marine air unit and defense battalion along the way. Upon reaching Pearl Harbor I flew to Midway, inspected its courageous garrison and returned to a major shock: a dispatch stating that on October 14 Charlie Barrett had suffered a fall and died. Nimitz next received a dispatch from Halsey asking me to return to Noumea to take over corps command since Roy Geiger could not get there in time for Bougainville, scheduled for November 1.

Jerry and I left early the next morning on the long flight back. I found Noumea a depressing place—Charlie Barrett had been one of my oldest and best friends. But war will not stand still for sentiment. We buried him the next day and turned to for the Bougainville operation. His staff and commanders were as deeply grieved as I and it took a little doing to return them to the necessary perspective. Fortunately Houston Noble, Charlie's chief of staff, took over and, as I wrote General Holcomb, "in five days did a stupendous amount of work with his staff on plans and orders."

I made Noble assistant corps commander and Jerry Thomas my chief of staff. When Geiger arrived I planned to make him assistant corps commander with Noble chief of staff so that Jerry and I could be relieved shortly after the landing.

My major worry centered on a change of allotted shipping due to a shortage caused by the forthcoming Tarawa landing. Instead of bringing the entire 3d Division to the target as I originally planned, only two-thirds would go in initially. The 21st Marines and other supporting units including the Army's 37th Division—my corps reserve—were to arrive by shuttle over a three-week period.

This spelled a serious dissipation of strength at a time when the Japanese were certain to react quickly and furiously to the landing. I had been far too impressed by the Japanese habit of piecemeal commitment on Guadalcanal— a major failure—to even hear of such a proposition. When Wilkinson's staff failed to respect our complaint, I went to Halsey. He finally saw the point and ordered the transports

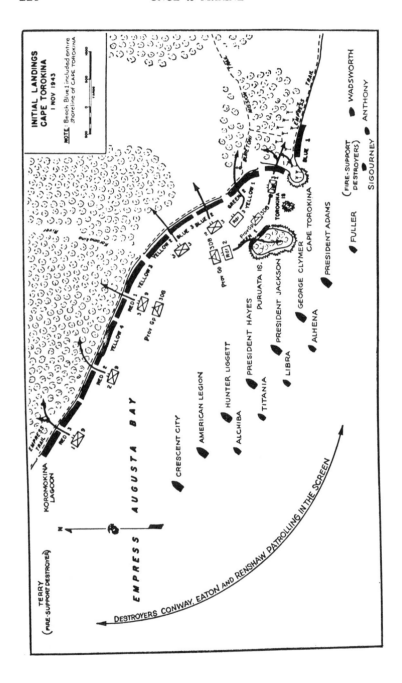

to return to Guadalcanal immediately after the initial landings to bring up the remaining troops.

Four hours before D-day Row's New Zeland brigade struck
the Treasury Islands, about 65 miles southeast of target, in
order to distract the enemy and to guard our line of communication. Three days later the first echelon of the division
sailed from Guadalcanal. Subsequent events transpired on
schedule. The parachutists conducted a diversionary landing
on the small island of Choiscul where their commander,
Brute Krulak, though wounded, stayed to take his objective.
Aside from trouble with heavy surf on a couple of the
beaches and considerably heavy enemy opposition, the main
landing went off in splendid shape, division command moving
ashore late in the morning. Simultaneously the raiders landed
on Puruata Island, securing it the same day.

Just before Turnage moved his CP ashore an enemy air
raid succeeded in pushing a few planes through the marvelous cover provided by our planes. I was standing on
the bridge with Admiral Wilkinson and his Marine planner,
Henry Linscott. The latter frowned at the heavens. "I hope
those are bombers and not torpedo planes."

"What the hell difference does that make?" I asked.

"The way I figure it, the bombers can hit you and you
won't sink, but if a torpedo hits you you're gone."

I remembered then that he had been on the *McCawley*
when she was torpedoed and understood his reasoning.

When we recovered from the evasive action taken during
the air raid I went ashore to check with Hal Turnage. I found
him his usual calm self, very pleased with the landing and
the progress of his troops pushing inland to primary objectives through jungle worse than we had found on Guadalcanal.

Hal asked me to spend the night, but not wishing to breathe
down his neck I returned to Wilkinson's flagship. It was a
wise choice. Wilkinson, worried by the threat of further air
raids, wished to take four still partially loaded transports
back to Guadalcanal to pick up the next contingents. I argued vigorously against this. I remembered only too well
what the sight of those disappearing transports meant to
us on Guadalcanal. I would have taken this one all the way
to Halsey if necessary, but Wilkinson changed his mind and
put to sea for the night.

Early that afternoon we had learned of a force of Japanese

cruisers and destroyers sailing toward us from Rabaul. Standing out to meet them was Rear Admiral Tip Merrill's Task Force 39. The fleets collided about 3:00 A.M., a violent action costing the Japanese a cruiser and several destroyers while our forces escaped without losing a ship. We returned to anchorage the following morning, finished unloading in the afternoon, and steamed back to Guadalcanal.

On November 4 I reported to General Holcomb:

> I have just returned from the Bougainville operation, which went off beautifully and was one of the best examples of co-ordinated amphibious effort that I have seen so far. The timing was perfect. The air, both fighter and bombardment, was superior . . . the landing went off smoothly, the air, surface and ground co-ordinating as a well-running team. The Third Marine Division that made the assault landing were green troops in their first engagement. Their morale was high; they did not flinch under the spattering of machine gun fire on the approach to the beach, pushed in rapidly and accomplished their mission in a very expeditious and excellent manner. . . .
>
> So far, after four days, things are going as planned. I have gotten Admiral Halsey and Wilkinson to speed up the embarkation of the Army Division, and the first combat team of that element is loading today. The whole division will be in, things going well, by the seventeenth. I plan to leave here after the second combat team of the Thirty-seventh Division is boated in transports and has shoved off. Geiger will go up in a couple of days, so that he can make his own plans and grow up with the defensive installations. Needless to say all of these things meet with the approval of COMSOPAC [Halsey], and he agrees on the times mentioned. My present plan, therefore, is to leave here on the eleventh.

I cannot overstate my satisfaction with the initial phases of this operation which demonstrated how much we had progressed in both means and techniques since the Guadalcanal landing fifteen months earlier. Obviously our training programs were sound and were paying off. On Bougainville, besides providing excellent cover and prelanding bombardment, our airmen exercised the first of the real close air support tactics that were to become such an integral part of Fleet Marine Force doctrine.

The spirit of the ground troops continued to amaze me. Fighting mud and rain in addition to a furious enemy, they lived through weeks of hell without letting down. As on Guadalcanal, humor never deserted them. One story concerned an officer who noticed a helmet floating on a large puddle of rich muck. Suddenly it raised to reveal the dripping face of a Marine sergeant.

"Hello," said the officer, "you're in pretty deep."

"Deeper than you think, sir," said the sergeant. "I'm on top of a bulldozer."

On November 9, satisfied that the operation was running smoothly, I turned First Corps command over to Roy Geiger. Two days later Jerry Thomas and I left for the States.

XVIII

I Inherit the Marine Corps

SOON AFTER my arrival in America newspaper headlines screamed the news of the Tarawa assault to the nation. Thrilled by the audacity of the landing, the American people forgot that such a landing perforce costs lives. Our release of casualty figures quickly changed national pride to indignant gloom. A variety of factors, chiefly a hidden reef which prevented landing boats from reaching the beaches and an incredibly well dug-in and powerful enemy, exacted a heavy toll: well over 3,000 casualties in just over three days.

Most journalists did not realize that they had observed the first successful true amphibious assault of all time. At Tarawa we validated the principle of the amphibious assault, a tactic proclaimed impossible by many military experts. Of course it was costly—we all knew it would be, for war is costly. But hereafter the enemy could never know where or when we would strike. Hereafter no matter the strength of his bastion the enemy could never feel secure. This was the real lesson of Tarawa, this the public did not immediately realize.

I did not learn the details of the operation until I reached Washington early in December. By then the Commandant could tell me of the excellent work of such officers as Merritt Edson (who won a spot promotion to brigadier general), Dave Shoup and Lieutenant Hawkins (who won Medals of Honor), and of the hidden reef which stopped the landing craft and forced Marines to disembark and wade ashore unprotected from entrenched enemy fire. Years later Dave Shoup described to me how he and his young runner waded hand in hand through bloodstained water; just as they reached the fire-swept beach a bullet caught the boy and killed him. We knew by now that close air support had not

232

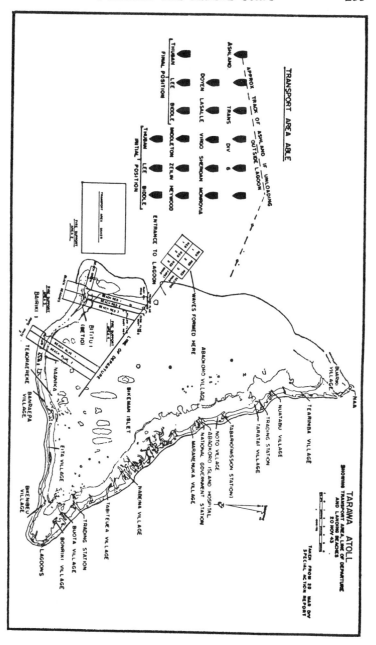

worked well, and that naval gunfire rather than obliterating the island seemed to have made little difference.

And no wonder. One report described a dugout constructed of six feet of reinforced concrete overlaid with two feet of sand, then two layers of crisscrossed iron rails, three more feet of sand, two rows of coconut logs topped by a final six feet of sand. This dougout withstood direct hits from 2,000-pound bombs. To neutralize its occupants, Seabees took it apart layer by layer, drilled a hole in the concrete and fired a flame thrower through it.

I studied the reports more carefully because in Noumea Roy Geiger was looking already to his next operation, the assault of Guam, and I wanted to exact the most out of Tarawa. I wrote Holland Smith:

The people in your area will immediately have available to them the lessons to be learned from that show [Tarawa] as will also Harry Schmidt's outfit [4th Marine Division] who had observers there. . . . Could you have someone make a summary of the salient facts brought out by this show, as, for example, use or non-use of Alligator boats, and their effectiveness, gunfire, bombing, etc., and let me have it at an early date so that it can be gotten to Roy, as his planning will start almost immediately.

Holland replied:

We are now making up a summary of the salient facts established by the Gilberts show and we are forwarding you a copy in the near future. I have already requested Edson to send a copy of all orders issued by the Second Division to Roy Geiger. . . . There is one definite point that I wish to stress: Where the hydrographical features are similar to the Gilberts only Alligators can land. Naval gunfire for the destruction of coast defense guns is a function of the Navy, but when the landing begins, the Landing Force Commander should have "the say" as to where, when, and what kind of fire he needs. When you receive my final report you will note things that must be corrected if we are to avoid disaster in the future. Only a military man with a background of experience and education can run the show on the beach and we must never surrender that thought.

On the basis of Holland's summary and other information we worked out a number of changes which resulted in a reorganization of the Marine division. We placed this into effect early the next year.

We continued to receive considerable criticism of the casualties suffered at Tarawa. I found myself at odds with the official naval policy of downplaying what some persons seemed to believe a disaster. I felt that the American public should be told the truth—that victory in war, just as victory in peace, sometimes has to be costly. When a censor wished to hold up photographs of dead Marines on the Tarawa beaches I refused to consider it. In my opinion the sooner the American people realized the sort of war we were fighting the better it would be all the way around. On December 15 old Senator Walsh telephoned me his concern over the national reaction. The senator was a good friend of the Marine Corps, and I welcomed the opportunity to spell out the problem in a letter to him:

A landing attack is recognized by all military experts as being the most difficult and costly of all forms of attack. Losses at Tarawa were heavy, and losses will be heavy in future attacks of this nature.

One must distinguish between the attack against a large land mass, such as Guadalcanal, Bougainville, Sicily or Italy, and the attack against a small island such as Tarawa. In the former case, the defender, not knowing where the landing attack will strike, and not being strong enough to defend heavily all likely landing beaches, is forced to leave the landing beaches comparatively lightly defended in order to concentrate the bulk of his forces in some central location or locations from where it can be moved against the attacker, once the location of the main landing attack has been definitely determined. By rapid movement of his main force, the defender attempts to secure local superiority at the point of landing prior to the attacker being able to develop large forces ashore.

Conversely, the attacker, having the initiative, is able to select the point of landing, and will, other things being equal, select a location which is least heavily defended. If he has achieved surprise, he can expect no serious resistance initially, and in turn endeavors to land rapidly and develop large forces ashore before he is struck by the defender's main forces.

In the case of a heavily defended small island such as Tarawa, the defender can readily diagnose the point of attack, and due to the small distances involved, can readily concentrate his forces against any landing attempt, and concentrate practically all the fire of his artillery against the attack without being forced to the time-consuming effort of displacing his artillery forward. Hence, the defender can afford to dispose initially the bulk of his forces along the beaches where he can pour concentrated fire against the attacker at the moment when the attacking forces are most vulnerable, namely, at the moment when, comparatively helpless and exposed, the attacking troops are approaching the beach in small craft and debarking therefrom.

The attacker attempts to "soften" resistance by naval gunfire and aerial bombardment. Where the defenses are very strongly constructed, as at Tarawa, the gunfire and aerial bombardment have only partial effect. Many of the hostile installations will remain operative and fire from them must be faced.

A coral island, such as Tarawa, in addition to its natural strength because of its small size, presents, because of the surrounding coral, natural defensive strength. The attackers are forced to disembark from landing craft some distance offshore and wade in against the hostile fire. Losses will be heavy. There are no foxholes offshore. All evidence on hand leads to the conviction that the attack on Tarawa was well planned and skillfully executed. No one regrets the losses in such an 'attack more than does the Marine Corps itself. No one realizes more than does the Marine Corps that there is no royal road to Tokyo. We must steel our people to the same realization.

Senator Walsh replied:

I received your letter of December 15 explaining the losses of Tarawa and I presented copies of it to members of my Committee [Naval Affairs] and released it to the press. It should lead to the minimizing of the criticism that has been made in some quarters without foundation.

I spent most of December at General Holcomb's elbow

being read into the numerous problems of his office. Fortunately prewar duty at Headquarters prepared me to handle some of them. General Holcomb also had been most cooperative in keeping me informed of his major policy and personnel decisions during the past year or more. As a result I quite rapidly oriented myself, benefiting also from the Secretary of the Navy's daily conference. After my Pacific duty this struck me as a strange kind of life. I wrote to Roy Geiger:

> Things are about as hectic as you told me I would find them; and many times have I longed, even in this brief space of time, for the peaceful calm of a bombing raid on Bougainville.

On January 1, 1944, General Holcomb and I together with our families went over to Secretary Knox's office. After reading General Holcomb's retirement orders, including promotion to four stars, he read my appointment as Commandant of the Marine Corps.

General Holcomb and I hastened to the Commandant's House and there the Marine Corps Band serenaded us. Traditionally called a surprise, this pleasant ceremony involved the band's playing a couple of tunes. I then thanked them and invited them inside for the hot rum and sandwiches which we just happened to have on hand for a hundred men.

Back at Headquarters General Holcomb took his leave. When I accompanied him to the door he placed a hand on my shoulder and smiled. "Vandegrift, when I go out this door I am placing twenty years on your shoulders and taking them off mine. You won't relize it at first but you will finally learn what I mean." He nodded as if to confirm his thinking and continued, "You have a good many friends in the Corps. I only hope that when you turn your job over to a successor you have the same number. The Commandant does not make many new friends if he does his job well."

I knew whereof he spoke, for any commander suffers similarly. I remembered an evening in Cuba back in the early thirties during some maneuver. Several of us dined with General Lyman, who· afterward introduced the subject of retirement. He asked me where I planned to retire and I told him Charlottesville, Virginia.

"Why there?" he demanded. "You should live in some place like La Jolla where you will be close to your service friends."

"You are fortunate in having so many friends," I told him. "If upon retirement I have ten real friends I shall consider myself very lucky."

I forgot about the incident until upon my return from the Pacific I dropped in to see him in the San Diego naval hospital. I found him ill and lonely. Reminding me of the evening's conversation in Cuba he said sadly, "How right you were in your estimate of the number of friends a man has after retirement."

I inherited a Marine Corps of 390,000 officers and men.

Bill Rupertus' 1st Marine Division had just landed at Cape Gloucester and was fighting in terrain reported to be a nightmarish mixture of Guadalcanal and Bougainville, where rain fell as high as 16 inches per day.

Julian Smith's 2d Division, having taken Tarawa, was back in Hawaii refitting.

Hal Turnage's 3d Division was still fighting in the agonizing jungles of Bougainville.

Harry Schmidt's 4th Division, in which my son commanded the Special Weapons Battalion, was shipping out from San Diego.

Keller Rockey was at Camp Pendleton, California, putting together a new 5th Division.

Four air wings, independent units and supply depots dotted the Pacific. Simultaneously we maintained detachments aboard ships and on naval stations besides furnishing officers and men for courier duty, other security details and OSS assignments.

As Commandant I was responsible for the administration, training and readiness of these forces to Secretary of the Navy Colonel Knox and to Admiral Ernest King, commander in chief of the United States fleet. I had known Knox for years and dealt quite amiably with him. Poor health increasingly caused him to turn the job over to James Forrestal, one of the smartest men in our government. Forrestal's integrity was unquestionable, his easy grasp of the most complex problems almost unbelievable. I don't remember our ever exchanging a cross word in the many years of our close relationship—I know I respected him as I respected few men in this world.

Ernest King was something else again. Although I had met him in prewar years, neither I nor many people ever knew him. His formidable reputation—juniors liked to say he shaved with a blowtorch—raised him to almost demigod status in the eyes of some of his subordinates. Probably because the Marine Corps boasted its unique brand of toughness I wasn't much concerned about his reputation. Upon paying my first call on him as Commandant I did think we should understand each other, so before taking my leave I said, "Admiral, I want to tell you what I have always told seniors when reporting for duty. If one of your decisions is in my opinion going to affect the Marine Corps adversely, I shall feel it my duty to explain our position on the subject, no matter how disagreeable this may be. If you disagree, I expect to keep right on explaining until such time as you make a final decision. If I do not agree with that, I will try to work with it anyway. I say this, sir, because if you want a rubber stamp you can go to the nearest Kresge store and buy one for twenty-five cents."

King stared at me a moment, then abruptly nodded his head—a characteristic gesture. In the event, I worked more closely with his deputy chief, Admiral Horne, his chief of staff, Admiral Edwards, and his planner, Admiral Savvy Cooke. As will be seen, on a few matters I was forced to go to him and I generally won my point.

In my own Headquarters I pulled Dewitt Peck out of plans and policies and made him assistant to the Commandant. Lou Woods served as assistant commandant for air. W. P. T. Hill headed the quartermaster department and Littleton Waller, Jr., the personnel department. I filled the empty plans and policies billet with Jerry Thomas, whom I spot-promoted to brigadier general. I wrote Holland Smith:

> I imagine this will create quite a bit of talk by officers who believe in seniority promotions, but that leaves me absolutely cold, and I do not belive I could find a better person for that job, irrespective of rank, than Thomas;

and the rank is necessary in order to transact the business.

Holland replied:

I am glad that you spot-promoted Jerry Thomas, because I feel that he is one of the most outstanding officers in the Corps. I am a firm believer in the theory that officers should be promoted on merit, rather than on seniority; and I am glad that you have the courage of your convictions along this line.

The operations currently underway plus those scheduled combined to furnish enormous personnel and supply problems. We had to find the people to bring our veteran units up to strength and to provide replacements for the anticipated casualties. We also had to activate new units if we were to fulfill our tasks—and this was very difficult in view of our personnel ceiling.

Only by maximum operating efficiency could we hope to accomplish what lay ahead. I could not tolerate inefficient officer performance, no matter my personal feelings for the individual. Like the other services, we suffered a few cases of older officers trying to live on past reputations—a failing also familiar to the day of General Ulysses S. Grant. On one occasion Grant expressed contempt for a certain officer.

"But, sir," an aide protested, "he has been through ten campaigns."

Grant replied, "So has that mule yonder but he's still a jackass."

I made my position clear in a letter of January 4 to Holland Smith:

I have nothing but the utmost sympathy for officers who have studied and trained themselves for command in the theater of operations and do not get the opportunity to show what they can do. On the other hand, I do not believe that there is any place on the active list of the Marine Corps for an officer who, with years of experience and study, is given an opportunity in the combat zone and fails. I do not class physical failure in this category, because that is something we cannot control. I do not be-

lieve that this type of officer will command the respect
of his junior officers and men back here in the States, because I can assure you the reason for his coming back
gets widely publicized through the service. I think it
is better that they retire. . . . I intend to order——before
a retiring board immediately if I can legally do it, which
I think I can; and I intend to take the necessary steps to
relieve the Marine Corps of the services of——. I intend
to do that in each case of officers reported not fit for combat duty through failure other than physical, because if
they are not fit for combat duty in time of war, I can
see no reason for them.

There was another side to this coin, one which I treated in
a letter of January 19 to Harry Pickett:

[I] have adopted it as my policy of action from the day
I took over, sending dispatches to officers in the field requiring that reasons be given for the detachment of officers. I have seen so much in the Marine Corps of officers
and men being shuffled from one commanding officer to
another because the officer deciding the transfer did not
want to go on record as requesting it. Personally I think
that is wrong, both to the Marine Corps and to the
officer concerned. If it is a question of health . . . a
brief resumé of the facts of days lost, the nature of ailment, etc. could be included; and this office could then,
with all propriety, request the Surgeon General to order
the officers concerned before a retiring board, which I certainly most assuredly will do in the case of any officer
who is habitually sick to such an extent that it hampers
his work. In cases of professional failure I firmly believe
it should be made a part of an officer's record so that
this Headquarters may have some guide as to what senior
officers think of other officers, which will materially affect
their assignment to duty; and later, when and if selection goes back into effect, their promotion.

To solve the manifold problems of present and future I
wanted the closest possible relationship between Headquarters and the field commands. Whenever necessary I promised
to send staff officers from Headquarters to the field; I also
urged my commanders to either come to the States themselves or send staff officers back to confer on vital matters.

This arrangement worked very well. For example, after the Cape Gloucester campaign Bill Rupertus and his chief of staff, John Selden, flew to Washington. Besides furnishing us with valuable firsthand information on the fighting, Bill explained in detail a thorny personnel problem. A good many of his people would shortly have been serving more than twenty-four months overseas. His new rehabilitation camp on the island of Pavuvu in the Russells was not conducive to high morale—in fact it was extremely primitive and uncomfortable. With his help we worked out a plan whereby 260 of his officers and 4,500 enlisted were rotated home. We also planned to send out sufficient replacements for another major rotation after the next campaign.

One thing certain: to fulfill such obligations luxuries had to go. General Holcomb already had scratched our incursions into the barrage balloon and glider fields. I now took what was left of the raiders and parachutists and made them into a new 4th Marine Regiment in honor of the 4th Marines who went down on Bataan. I further disbanded such ancillary organizations as the secret beach-jumpers and put their people into the new 5th Division forming at Camp Pendleton. Keller Rockey also received a large number of combat veterans who had been recuperating from malaria and elephantiasis at Klamath Falls, Oregon.

With two independent regiments in training on Guadalcanal, the logical course in my mind was to add another regiment and make a 6th Marine Division. This would give us two complete amphibious corps, providing we could persuade MacArthur to release operational control of the 1st Division. Anticipating this move, I sent Jerry Thomas on a tour of posts and stations to blast out any excess personnel he might find. Before long nearly everyone in the Marine Corps became privy to my personnel policy: "There are only three kinds of Marines: those who are overseas, those who have been overseas, and those who are going overseas."

I did not immediately broach my plans to King since I knew that General Holcomb had won permission to establish the 5th Division practically over General Marshall's dead body. On that occasion Marshall tried unsuccessfully to extract a promise from King that if we were allowed the 5th Division we would not activate another single unit for the war's duration.

Marshall's attitude foreshadowed a problem which increasingly claimed my time: interservice rivalry with all its disruptive ramifications to the war effort.

In 1942 President Roosevelt turned the question of service manpower ceilings over to the general direction of the JCS. In 1943 Army members of a JCS committee charged with studying the question began to object to the increasing size of the Marine Corps. As near as I could figure, their objections rested on what they liked to call "a duplication of effort" on the part of the Marines vis-à-vis the Army. These objections undoubtedly arose in part because the Army greatly feared that it was going to lose control of its Air Corps and foresaw the day when its former exalted position in the American defense picture might very well diminish.

That such jealousy could arise at a time when America was facing her greatest crisis in national history infuriated me. I frankly did not care who did what job so long as the job was accomplished. The Marines had performed two important early tasks, the emergency reinforcement of Iceland and the invasion of the Solomon Islands, only because we were sufficiently ready to move out. On Guadalcanal no one would have more welcomed early relief by the Army than I. We were not relieved earlier on Guadalcanal because the Army could not furnish a division to relieve us. Rather than usurping the Army's job, we performed it as well as our own.

The course of the war already had confirmed our prewar belief that Marines should assault with the Army following to fight the sustained land warfare effort. In everything from organization to arms, equipment, experience and philosophy the two services stood distinctly tailored for those roles. Decades of expeditionary service plus intense study and experiments in amphibious war stood behind the Marine concept of moving out fast and striking hard. We reasoned that acceptance of early casualties meant lighter casualties in the long run. The Army did not.

The conceptual difference unfortunately proved more than academic. It was shown at Makin Island in the Gilberts operation when Holland Smith grew dissatisfied with the progress of Ralph Smith's 27th Division. In early December, 1943, Bill Rupertus informed me of planning difficulties for the Cape Gloucester campaign—difficulties surmounted only by the personal intervention of General MacArthur, who decided to let Bill run his landing the way he thought best.

Pacific strategy further complicated the situation to the Army's disadvantage. By early 1944 President Roosevelt supported King's strategy of advancing across the Central Pacific to take either Truk or land in China prior to turning north on Japan. Although the JCS subscribed to it, opinion was not at all unanimous, particularly that of General Marshall and to a lesser extent General Arnold. This seemingly did not bother King, who blithely planned to invade the Marshall Islands and then the Marianas.

It did bother the Army. Having put its strategical eggs in Douglas MacArthur's basket—that is, approaching Japan by the Robin Hood's barn of the Philippines—the Army high command found itself increasingly on the outside looking in in the Central Pacific. Beginning in 1943 it attempted to subordinate the Marine command in Pearl Harbor. In early 1944 Admiral King showed me a memorandum by a ranking Army officer in Hawaii who suggested that Marine Corps officers were not professionally capable of commanding corps. In vew of this officer's own record of command, his charges were particularly fantastic but they did show the hard feeling that existed in certain quarters. To this we wrote a strong and blunt reply, but at the same time I cautioned Holland Smith to be on his guard in dealing with those Army officers who seemed to be hypersensitive relative to any of their plans or any of our criticisms. I concluded:

> We have, in the Pacific and at home, the absolute confidence of the Navy High Command in the Marines' ability to accept that which they are told to do, and it is highly important that all of us act so that we do not lose it.

This letter reached Holland shortly before the Marshalls operation. A group of vastly spread coral atolls, the Marshalls protected the front and northern flank of the Japanese base at Truk as well as flanking an approach to Japan proper. Of 32 separate atolls covering some 650 miles of ocean, the Japanese had fortified 6. We decided to assault two of them, Kwajalein and Roi-Namur.

For the two-pronged operation Holland divided his forces into a Northern Landing Group, composed of Harry Schmidt's

4th Marine Division plus a defense battalion, which was to take Roi-Namur. He gave command of the Southern Landing Force to Major General C. H. Corlett, whose splendid Army 7th Infantry Division and two defense battalions were to take Kwajalein.

Following heavy prelanding bombardments by surface, air and artillery (landed on neighboring islands), the two forces struck on January 31. The Marines took Roi-Namur in two days; Kwajalein fell two days later (see end-paper map).

I was greatly pleased at the improvement in various techniques displayed by these landings. Although Schmidt encountered some difficulties in the Roi-Namur landing he was able to report:

> So many people did well that it would be difficult to single out anyone for outstanding work. All the Regimental Commanders did well. Hart had the toughest job. Cumming had the most arduous . . . Underhill had general charge of Phase One. I am very fond of him and admire his ability and character. He will make a fine division commander and is ready and fully qualified for promotion . . . the Navy did a grand job in this show. They have found a formula for saving lives in situations that you have no choice as to where to attack.

Holland held one more trick up his sleeve. Convinced back in Pearl Harbor he would not need to land his corps reserve he quietly drew up an operations order to land it on Eniwetok. After the task force sailed he showed it to Kelly Turner who, although surprised, approved it with a few alterations. Hard on the above landings the 22d Marines and the Army's 106th Infantry less one battalion struck this vital atoll—a force almost identical to that specified by Pete Ellis more than twenty years earlier.

Rear Admiral Hill later wrote me:

> The Eniwetok Operation turned into a most interesting and quite difficult job due to the fact that we found that considerable reinforcements had arrived there shortly before we did. This threw a difficult burden on [Brigadier General T. E.] Watson, as with only five landing teams available, and having to use three landing teams on each

of the three major assaults in a period of five days, there
was considerable reshuffling of forces required as you can
well imagine.

Watson handled this whole affair in a manner which
was a credit to you and the Marine Corps. He knows his
weapons, and has outstanding qualities of leadership,
determination, and guts.

It has been my pleasure to recommend him, in official
correspondence, for promotion to the grade of Major General, and I am dropping you this line just to let you know
about him and that this official letter will reach you in
due course of time. It was a real privilege to have him
along in the Eniwetok Operation, and I will certainly be
looking forward to the day when he may be along as a
Division Commander on an even tougher assignment.

In closing I wish also to add a word of praise for Colonel
J. T. Walker and the Twenty-Second Marines. They did a
wonderful job and deserve all the praise which can be
bestowed upon them.

We followed this victory with Bill Rupertus' successful conclusion of the Cape Gloucester campaign. In early February
he informed me:

> We have learned much, especially [from] our errors
> from Guadalcanal, and I feel sure that we have profited
> by them in this operation. It has been one of the smooth-
> est, most co-ordinated operations that it has been my ex-
> perience to participate in, even including our peacetime
> exercises.

He then passed on the most disturbing news of General Krueger's plan to re-equip the 1st Division at Gloucester for
an operation six months hence. This defied every notion
of proper rehabilitation with which I was familiar. I was
further disturbed two weeks later when Bill wrote of Krueger and MacArthur's plans to use the 1st Division in shore-
to-shore operations including the assault of Rabaul.

The correct solution for this and other problems, I believed,
amounted to establishing a single Marine Corps command
in the Pacific. I envisaged this as a Fleet Marine Force commanded by Holland Smith with two corps of three divisions

each. As an ancillary I wanted a single supply service fed primarily through our depot of supply in San Francisco.

In a conference with Admiral King I reminded him that he had lent the 1st Division to MacArthur solely for amphibious assaults. I recognized the difficult situation since MacArthur had personally told me in Port Moresby that he would relinquish control of the division "only over my dead body." I showed Rupertus' letter to King and Mr. Knox, both of whom promised to try to get the 1st Division returned to Navy control. I also emphasized the importance of a single Marine command and my plans to establish it.

My desire increased in March when a JCS directive canceled the landings against Kavieng and Rabaul, and ordered the Marianas operation designed to capture Saipan, Tinian and Guam.

This dictated a change in our air organization. In early 1944 we boasted four air wings with another forming—a total of over 100,000 Marines including some 10,000 pilots. Primarily because of a lack of carriers the bulk of our overseas aviation units remained in southern and southwestern rear areas concerned primarily in keeping bypassed islands neutralized and in bombing Rabaul. These missions included some very hot actions—it was down there, for example, that Greg Boyington rose to prominence—but little was being done to bring Marine air into direct support of Marine ground actions.

With Lou Woods and Jerry Thomas I worked out a plan now submitted to Admiral King. By eliminating fifteen squadrons we wanted to increase the size of our remaining squadrons and put air groups aboard the newly developed escort carriers to furnish direct air support for the forthcoming amphibious assaults. I further wanted to consolidate all Marine aviation into a single command—Aircraft, Fleet Marine Force Pacific.

King eventually saw the logic of our plans and finally approved them. We began reorganizing the next summer.

XIX

Problems of a Commandant: I

IN LATER years people frequently asked me what I did as Commandant. I always told them of the *New Yorker* cartoon which as I recall showed a medieval monarch standing grandly draped in sables atop his castle ramparts. Next to him stood a harridan of a queen obviously harassing him. His words formed the caption: "What do I do all day? Why, I *reign,* that's what I do."

My job is perhaps best described by a typical day, if such ever existed. I was at my office by eight o'clock. For an hour I read dispatches and whatever correspondence time allowed. At nine I attended the Secretary of the Navy's conference. This meeting was held in the Navy Building and usually included Colonel Knox, principal subordinates such as Mr. Forrestal, various civilian and naval heads of departments, and occasional important guests. The Secretary presided over the conference, primarily a staff meeting to air major difficulties and assign action to appropriate divisions.

After the conference I attended a naval intelligence briefing which posted me on the latest military developments. I then returned to the office, worked on dispatches and correspondence, ate luncheon at Headquarters, and spent the afternoon working with subordinates and receiving visitors. Around six I went home, usually with a briefcase full of unfinished work.

Home, the Commandant's house on Eighth and I Streets in Washington, is unique in the armed forces. As part of the Marine Barracks complex it is flanked by other houses or quarters assigned in my time to the assistant to the Commandant, the assistant commandant for air, the quartermaster general and the commanding officer of the Barracks. Adjoining these houses are bachelor officer quarters, then, finally, the troop quarters and various ancillary buildings.

The Commandant's house is one of the show places of Washington. You enter through a high-ceilinged hall with a powder room and fireplace on the right and a large dining room on the left. This hall melds into a cross-hall leading on the left to two large drawing rooms with chandeliers equal to those at Versailles. The south side of the drawing rooms gives way to a wide tiled porch which overlooks the enclosed parade ground of the Barracks. The other side leads to a stairway. A second story features a large apartment on one end, two bedrooms with baths on the other; a third floor holds another living room, three bedrooms and baths. To run the house I was authorized two Marine orderlies, one of them Sergeant Smith who had been with me since 1941, four Navy messmen and a gardener.

I explain this because I accomplished a large part of my job in this house. Official Washington often operates in a behind-the-scenes manner. By the time most legislation reaches the House or Senate its fate has already been established by men talking it over at parties or other informal meetings.

We entertained frequently and at considerable personal expense. A typical guest list of those years read: Secretary of the Treasury and Mrs. Fred Vinson, the Secretary of the Navy and Mrs. James Forrestal, Senator Leverett Saltonstall, Representative Clare Boothe Luce, Admiral and Mrs. Marc Mitscher, Admiral and Mrs. J. O. Richardson, Major General and Mrs. A. H. Turnage. I suppose that most of my guests got tired of hearing me talk about the Marine Corps, which was the primary reason they were invited to my house. Once at a banquet someone caught me offguard by asking my hobby. I replied, "The same as my business—the Marine Corps."

I found that in the quiet of the drawing room, with a fire burning and the body refreshed by a good dinner, I could often reason more effectively with various admirals and legislators than in a crowded office with telephones and aides interrupting every few seconds. I would hesitate to say how much gain accrued to the Marine Corps from entertainment in the Commandant's house, but it was a lot.

One aspect of the job called for frequent appearances at various Congressional hearings. General Holcomb always maintained splendid relations on the Hill and from my prewar service with him I thought I knew why. I tried to keep a finger on every aspect of the Corps; one of my first orders was to prepare a book broken down into those categories that congressmen worried about, particularly at budget time. I tried to inculcate our legislators with the belief that, having nothing to hide, whatever I said would be as accurate as I could make it; if I did not know the answer I would try to find it for them. I worked very closely with Senator, Walsh, who headed the Senate Naval Affairs Committee, and with Mr. Carl Vinson, who headed the House Naval Affairs Committee. In my opinion these two gentlemen ranked among our top legislators. I did everything within my power to gain their trust and confidence and before I had finished I think I did so.

I found most congressmen quite reasonable with a genuine desire to understand. Shortly after taking office I was called to testify on a request of ours for additional clothing appropriations. The Pacific war was already spelling Gargantuan requirements. In fiscal year 1943 we used 1,500,000 pairs of field shoes; we needed 2,225,000 for the next year. In 1943 we used 1,295,000 dungaree jackets and 1,691,000 dungaree trousers; for 1944 we needed, 2,000,000 and 2,500,000 respectively.

One congressman wondered why we could not salvage more clothing. I explained the unusual conditions of jungle warfare, pointing out that a man scarcely wore anything that could be salvaged after a few weeks. Fortunately I had a film of the Bougainville operation to prove my point. They were very impressed and granted the appropriation.

This was intended as a realistic approach and, I learned, was accepted as such. Later when the stakes were very high it would pay off.

Besides Congress, I often appeared before segments of the American public. I had always believed that Americans were proud of the Marine Corps, and I now did what I could to keep them proud, to keep them our friends. I was gratified at the congratulatory messages received when I became Commandant, for these came not only from friends within the Corps, and other services but from hundreds of civilians whom I had never met. I answered these and other well-meaning letters, sent signed photographs and autographs as requested, and kept my office telephones as open as possible— a time-consuming business but one that brought rewards.

My aides formed an integral part of this task. I retained three: Paul Drake, Bud Schwenke and Buddy Masters. They looked after the administration of my office and house besides running the Marine Band tours. Their tasks did not stop with housekeeping duties. They often worked closely with my military secretary, Colonel Joe Burger. They monitored all correspondence and I frequently used one or more of them to investigate and report on particular problems. Together with our Woman Marine secretary, Mary Chiuli, they relieved me of an enormous burden besides providing a good many light moments.

Each of the aides wanted to return overseas and each pestered me for orders whenever opportunity arose. I rotated them when I could; for example, in 1945 I brought Jeff Fields back from the Pacific to become my senior aide. Buddy Masters proved particularly obstreperous in this respect. Although he was a veteran of extremely hazardous service with the Chinese underground, he feared that the war would end before he could command a battalion. In the spring of 1945 he grew increasingly restless. When the office was empty during a lunch hour one day he took a bag of Iwo Jima sand which someone thoughtfully had sent me and poured it around his desk. I noticed it upon my return and asked him what it was. He said, "General, that's the sand of Iwo Jima which is probably the closest I'll get to combat so long as I have to stay here as an aide."

"I'll send you out in due time," I told him. "Now you go get a broom and clean up that mess."

My aides also helped me write speeches and one of them usually accompanied me on out-of-town speaking engagements of which, thanks to Mr. Forrestal who insisted on my frequent appearances, there was never a lack.

I was no natural speaker and my first press conferences and speeches came hard. In San Francisco on my way back to the Pacific in 1943 one reporter wrote:

As he posed with his chief of staff, Colonel Gerald C. Thomas, and General Upshur, the visiting General appeared distinctly ill at ease. His fingers drummed nervously on a chair back, he blinked at the popping flashes of the bulbs and when asked to smile tried his darnedest, but only got as far as a tremor of his lips.

Time and practice repaired some of my initial uncertainty. I found capable guidance from two axioms. One was furnished by Robert E. Lee: "Truth and manliness are two qualities that will carry you through this world much better than policy, or tact, or expediency, or any other word ever devised to conceal or stupefy a deviation from a straight line."

The other was a remark attributed to Henry Clay. As the story goes, General Alexander Smyth, a tedious speaker in Congress, observed, "You, sir, speak for the present generation: but I speak for posterity."

"Yes," replied Mr. Clay, "and you seem resolved to speak until the arrival of your audience."

I used the traditional gambit of a hopefully amusing story as introduction to a speech, but I tried always to use a Marine story. Two remain my favorites. At a war bond rally I told the audience of a Marine sergeant explaining the benefits of a foxhole to a newcomer. "It isn't everybody," said the sergeant, "who gets to see where his taxes are going."

I told a group of very rich and powerful New York industrialists that as a soldier trying to sell war bonds to the financial and industrial leaders of the nation I felt like the new Marine recruit stationed at the gate of a highly secret activity. He was to admit only automobiles carrying a special tag. One day he stopped the car of a ranking admiral and asked to see the tag. Ignoring him the admiral curtly ordered his driver to go on. The Marine sentry said, "Pardon me sir, but I'm new at this. Who do I shoot—you or the driver?"

Sometimes my slant backfired. I once accepted an invitation to speak in Hartford, Connecticut—I thought to a group of war veterans. The audience turned out to consist of civilian workers, so I perforce gave an extemporaneous performance. The next morning the local paper ran my prepared speech—I have always imagined the interesting scene between the editor who listened to my talk and the reporter who was supposed to have been listening.

Unlike Smedley Butler, I never did feel comfortable speaking extemporaneously. I normally used a prepared speech. Since my eyesight was steadily deteriorating, my aides printed the speech on medium-sized cards in very large print. I then studied the speech carefully, using the time on the plane or train.

On one occasion after the war I was invited to speak in

Miami. I took Buddy Masters with me. Buddy was a very relaxed man—he was normally asleep by the time we were airborne. I told him he was either a man of immaculate character who had no problems or worries or else he was the world's biggest blackguard who just didn't give a damn. Anyway, while Buddy slept until we landed in Miami, I worked on my speech.

That night the first blows of an impending hurricane suddenly blackened the dining room where I was to perform. Buddy hustled up some candles but I still could not read the words. I gave the speech as I remembered it. Buddy told me it was nearly verbatim and said it was one of the best I had ever given.

I worked hard on these speeches because I wanted the American public to realize that we were not an inhuman machine but rather individuals trying to do the best job we could under the circumstances. I think the message got across, and I think the Corps made many friends thereby.

Quite inadvertently I made a very good friend because of one speech. This was Admiral Lewis Strauss, who asked me to address his New York synagogue. Noting his silence on the train I asked if something was wrong. "Yes, there is," he said. "At the station your aide told me that young Archer was due home today. I know he was wounded on Iwo Jima and I know how badly you must have wanted to meet him in Washington." Lewis never forgot that.

In addition to speaking invitations I welcomed any recognition of our effort. In February, 1944, I gratefully accepted an honorary Doctor of Laws degree from Brown University. I accepted a similar degree from Colgate University early in March. On each occasion I tried to tell the audience the importance of what the students had been doing to what we in the Corps were trying to do. Everett Case, the learned and gracious president of Colgate, later wrote to me:

> While my two sons, age eight and four, were duly impressed by hearing their father and the Commandant of the Marine Corps, they were even more excited—if the truth be told—over hearing the Marine Band. They already knew the Marine Hymn by heart, but now they

are more convinced than ever that there is no greater
piece of music.

In these early months problems hurled themselves on the
hours. I even found myself in a major crisis concerning the
fair sex.

When General Holcomb authorized the Women Marines I
was in the Pacific. The story goes that when he signed the
necessary paper the portrait of the crusty old Commandant,
Archibald Henderson, crashed to the floor of the Commandant's house. I was not alone in critically eyeing the addition,
nor did I change my mind until making an inspection trip of
the west coast prior to coming to Washington.

I was astonished to find these young women occupying 202
different jobs ranging from grease monkeys to talkers in aircraft towers. Everywhere I inspected, senior male officers
enthusiastically endorsed their work.

Having thus opened my eyes I was distressed when their
splendid commanding officer, Lieutenant Colonel Ruth Streeter,
reported rumors of my intention to disband them. To squelch
this I arranged for Mrs. Roosevelt to take a review on the
anniversary of their founding. It was probably the coldest day
in the history of Washington but that gracious lady stood it
out. Later in the Fort Myer drill hall she gave them a heartening talk. I followed Mrs. Roosevelt and told them that in a
few months they would reach their authorized 18,000
strength—in other words, they would soon be responsible for
putting a complete Marine division in the field.

One crisis replaced another. I now learned of a naval attempt to acquire our San Diego recruit depot, the argument
being that we had sufficient land at both Camp Elliott and
Camp Pendleton. The Navy had wanted this property for
some years since it sat adjacent to their naval training center and held some excellent buildings and family quarters.

I opposed any such transfer. I believed it essential to have
our recruit training physically separated from organizational
training. Our recruit depots ran on a unique concept that a
man was not a Marine until he graduated. Only then could
he wear the globe-and-anchor emblem or dress blues, and
until he earned these privileges he would remain isolated
from organizational Marines.

Tradition also entered. Marines had built the San Diego

base from nothing. I told Admiral Horne, deputy chief of naval operations, "You are going to have a terrible revulsion of feeling from Marines if you let your people grab that depot. The area was salt flats when we acquired it. Marine officers and men and their families worked with wheelbarrows building it to a base. I was there myself when Smedley Butler started the tree program."

Admiral Horne received my argument sympathetically but the project snowballed in spite of him. In February Mr. Knox called a conference on it, but by then I was prepared. Realizing that after the war we would have to yield some of our west coast land I decided to yield now if forced.

Sure enough the Navy representatives told their heart-rending story about lack of space. Turning pointedly to me, Mr. Knox allowed something must be done. I told him I wished to be fair. Realizing the pitiful plight of the Navy I wanted to offer them Camp Elliott, which easily held 12,000 men. The Navy representatives nearly died. They wanted Camp Elliott like they wanted a barren island. Mr. Knox, however, beamed and told them to accept such a generous offer gratefully. Events justified my logic—the Marine Corps still holds the San Diego and Pendleton bases.

Shortly after this crisis the bubbling pot of interservice rivalry, which contributed only to the enemy's cause, finally boiled over into Congress. The House of Representatives appointed a committee headed by Mr. Woodrum to explore an armed forces merger.

A less opportune time could not have been chosen to raise this divisive issue. Nevertheless, commencing in 1943 the War Department had begun generating strong pressures for the merger of the armed forces into "a single Department of War." Simultaneously Army and Army Air Corps public information agencies opened a campaign to condition public and Congressional opinion to the theme of merger. As one ranking admiral told me, "We are worrying about winning the war while the Army is attempting to win the postwar."

In May, 1944, the committee invited me to testify regarding the place of the Marine Corps in the armed forces. Knowing the hazy, sometimes emotional thinking among segments of Congress on this vital question, I deliberately framed my statement in simple terms. I first defined the problem:

> As we understand it, the problem now under consideration is to determine what system of organization of all the armed services will ensure the most efficient employment of the country's military resources in peace and in war.

I briefly discussed the types of major tasks given to the armed forces. Defining one of these as a projection of sea power, I tried to show the integral relationship between the Navy and the Marine Corps in performing this task. I did not want these gentlemen to think of this as a concept unique in my mind, so beginning with the ancient Greeks I sketched the development of amphibious warfare up to the present. To drive home the advantage of combat readiness I bluntly told them:

> Prompt availability for overseas operations and speed of employment therein are characteristics of a Marine Corps integrally a part of its Navy. This applies not only to major warfare but to minor expeditions, such as have frequently occurred in the past. Lives and money were often saved, both to the United States and to the countries assisted, by the prompt availability of a subordinate naval land element. The initial American occupation of Iceland, in the summer of 1941, provides the latest example. The required force of Marines was assembled, equipped and transported in a very short time. No delay was caused by interservice consultation nor by the submission of differences of opinion for solution by higher authority. The Navy issued the orders, and the Marines went to Iceland. It was as simple and effective as that.

After further illustrating this point with the Guadalcanal-Tulagi landings, I came to a major portion of my testimony:

> As the war developed, the need for amphibious troops became greater and greater in order that we might project our operations overseas, rather than to fight a defensive battle on our own shores. The Marine Corps was expanded to many times its original size. To date,

every Marine division that has completed its training, and most of our trained defense battalions, have already engaged in combat with the enemy. I know of no other military organization which has had such a high percentage of its combat units engaged in active operations.

I tried to explain the fantastic tactical demands levied by the amphibious assault and why we were able to meet them so effectively. To emphasize my statements I even penetrated the curtain of the future—as it turned out quite accurately:

Amphibious operations are highly specialized. Amid all the other requirements for employment of the peacetime forces, under conditions of shortage of funds and personnel, only a specialized organization, closely integrated with the Navy, can be expected to continue efficient training and development in that type of operation after the war. In time of peace, the Fleet Marine Force would continue to be a laboratory for field tests of new equipment and for development of ideas on amphibious tactics, technique and material. In the event of another war requiring early employment of amphibious forces, the necessary striking force would be at hand, organized, equipped and trained.

After defending America's conduct of the war to date, I qualified my views:

With the entire record of this war available to us after its termination, we should study and plan, we should clarify obscure incidents, and we should keep our minds open in the interim, to ensure the best organization when we adopt it. Otherwise, we may adopt one prematurely that would later appear less desirable, when all the facts are at hand as a basis of judgment. By opening up and continuing discussion of these matters, we believe this committee is performing an invaluable service in collecting data, directing attention to the problems involved, and ensuring careful scrutiny of all the questions at issue in their solution.

That the committee seemed favorably impressed soon developed from questions, an undreamed bonus. For example:

> MR. ANDREWS: What is the representation of the Marine Corps in the Joint Chiefs of Staff?
>
> VANDEGRIFT: We have no representation, sir. We are a subordinate part of the Navy, and as a part of the Navy, we are represented by a Navy representative.
>
> MR. ANDREWS: Are there no Marine Corps officers in the subsections of the Joint Chiefs of Staff?
>
> VANDEGRIFT: There are Marine Corps officers in the Navy division of the subsections.
>
> MR. MAAS: If we abolished the Marine Corps in any proposed consolidation, the land forces would have to assign to the Navy a duplicate of what the Marine Corps is anyway. Nothing would be saved?
>
> VANDEGRIFT: Yes, sir. It would not be as good for the outfit loaned or for the person who gets them.
>
> MR. MILLER: Under our present policy, can Marine Corps officers with amphibious experience be used for the training of Army troops?
>
> VANDEGRIFT: Yes, sir. Prior to and during this war . . . the Marine Corps First Corps and the Marine Corps Second Corps, as it was at the time, trained four Army divisions.

Several committee members and other congressmen later complimented me on the "foresight" of this testimony. I told one of them, a close friend: "It's only a matter of degree from the old days in Haiti when the Senate commission visited my district. I had nothing to hide then, I have nothing to hide now. Any logical examination of these issues should surely preserve the Marine Corps and all it stands for in our history."

Although President Roosevelt caused the Woodrum hearings to discontinue—they were jeopardizing service harmony —I was old enough to know that the pot would keep boiling. From this time on I never took my eyes from the brew.

XX

Problems of a Commandant: II

WE WERE moving well by the spring of 1944. Our fleets and amphibious divisions were blooded, experienced units which we believed could take anything. King already had told them to take the Marianas, specifically Saipan, Tinian and Guam. The capture of these islands would cut Truk off from the Japanese homeland besides giving us airbases within range of Tokyo and naval bases to support further operations in any direction including the China coast. In King's mind the Marianas were the key to the Central Pacific—I agreed with him (see endpaper map).

The operation was assigned to a Joint Expeditionary Force under Kelly Turner's command. Holland Smith commanded the Expeditionary Troops consisting of his own V Amphibious Corps and Roy Geiger's III Amphibious Corps. V Corps, comprising Tommy Watson's 2d Division, Harry Schmidt's 4th Division and Ralph Smith's 27th Army Division was to take Saipan and Tinian. Geiger's III Corps, composed of Hal Turnage's 3d Division, Lem Shepherd's 1st Provisional Marine Brigade, and Andrew Bruce's 77th Army Division would strike Guam.

Initial planning for Saipan looked good. Against an estimated 19,000 enemy defending a mountainous and wooded island about 12 miles long and 5 miles wide we proposed to send a total force of over 75,000 troops.

On June 15 the two Marine divisions struck the western beaches of Saipan. Against incredibly difficult resistance they pushed inland, their casualties heavy.

Two days after the landing, fleet intelligence reported a large Japanese task force steaming down from the north. Admiral Spruance quickly canceled the Guam operation scheduled for June 18, pushed the rest of the 27th Division ashore, moved his transports south and steamed his

259

fighting fleet to meet the enemy. The action resulted in the famous "Marianas Turkey Shoot" which destroyed nearly 350 enemy planes and sank three enemy aircraft carriers.

Hard fighting continued on Saipan. On June 22, both Marine divisions being badly mauled, Holland brought up Ralph Smith's 27th Division, heretofore mopping up the area south of the landing. Holland moved this division into the center of a line flanked by the 2d Division on the left and the 4th Division on the right.

So far everything proceeded smoothly, if grimly. The day after the 27th Division captured the southern airfield its commander was asked in a recorded interview what he thought of the working arrangement between the Marines and the Army. Ralph Smith replied:

> I am glad you have given me that lead because it seems to me this is an appropriate point to emphasize the perfect teamwork that has existed between the Navy, the Marines, and the Army. It irritates me a little to read these stories back home because a soldier and a Marine get in a fight in a saloon that the relations between services are at cross-purposes. Nothing could be further from the truth out here in the field. In this landing, we came in behind the Marines. Because of the conditions under which we are landing, we had very little of our supplies ashore. Ever since we landed, we have been using largely water, rations and ammunition that the Marines have helped us get ashore and furnished to us. Some of our casualties have been evacuated to Marine hospital ships [sic]. We are now getting our own supply installations ashore that Admiral Blandy has been able to get in for us during the last two days, but for the first part of the operation we were entirely dependent upon the Marines. And I want to take this opportunity to stress the very cordial feeling that exists between the outfits. One of the 165th's [Army regiment] officers remarked to me this morning that Saipan has sealed the blood brotherhood between the services.

On June 22 Holland Smith reported to me:

> The fighting has been terrific and our casualties to date are over 6,000. Total dead are approximately 100 officers and 600 enlisted men, not including missing.

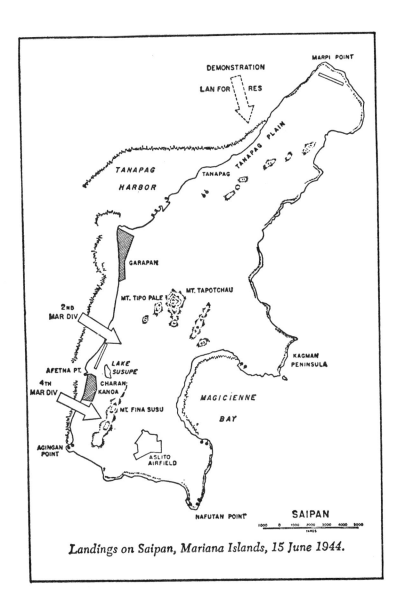

Landings on Saipan, Mariana Islands, 15 June 1944.

Mortar fire on D day was the most terrific thing I have
ever seen. Naval gunfire drove the Japs off the beach and
they withdrew to approximately 500-1,000 yards, and
went to work with their mortars. The artillery from the
foothills was pretty tough. As soon as we got some of
our artillery ashore, the air located the mortars and artillery and a great number were put out. . . .

Our artillery, including Corps [heavy artillery], is doing
a magnificent job. Air support has been superb. Naval
gunfire on call has been excellent. The pup planes [ob-
servation planes] have done an outstanding job, but have
had many operational casualties. . . .

The shore and beach parties have been working night
and day for 7 days. Yesterday we handled on the beach
9,000 tons. We are going to capture this island, but I
predict over 10,000 casualties. The terrain is ideal for
defense and, as you know, the Japs are masters at this
game. So far I feel that we have not encountered the
bulk of the enemy forces. . . .

The 2d and 4th [Marine Divisions] have lived up to
our Marine traditions. You will be proud of their achievements. The 27th [Army Division] has done all that we
asked, but has not yet had a real fight. . . .

The Japs were waiting for us but their greatest strength
was in the north. As we progress to the north, their lines
will be shortened and the going will become tougher . . .
tomorrow will probably be the toughest day, and I expect
to pass Ralph Smith through Harry [Schmidt's 4th Divi-
sion]. . . .

To describe what next happened I will use hindsight, not
because it offers anyone an advantage but merely to prevent
repeating myself. These events have been cited in detail in
any number of standard references on the Saipan campaign.

With three divisions on line Holland began pushing north.
Ralph Smith's division, after delaying its attack for almost
an hour, struck heavy resistance, made but slight progress
in overcoming it, and ended the day dangerously to the rear
of the attacking Marine divisions. Ralph Smith's poor progress seriously disturbed Holland. That afternoon he went
to the Senior Army officer on Saipan, Major General Sander-
ford Jarman, expressed his concern and asked Jarman to
speak to Ralph Smith. Jarman later wrote:

I talked to General [Ralph] Smith and explained the situation as I saw it and that I felt from reports from the Corps Commander that his division was not carrying its full share. He immediately replied that such was true; that he was in no way satisfied with what his regimental commanders had done during the day . . . and stated that if he didn't take his division forward tomorrow he should be relieved.

When the Army attack again bogged down on the following day, Holland conferred with Admirals Spruance and Turner and with their approval relieved Ralph Smith of his command. Jarman replaced him and later reported:

Based on my observations of the 27th Division for a few days, I have noted certain things that give me some concern. They are, first, a lack of offensive spirit on the part of the troops. A battalion will run into one machine gun and be held up for several hours. When they get any kind of minor resistance they immediately open up with everything they have that can fire in the general direction from which they are being fired upon. Second, at night if a patrol comes in around their bivouac area they immediately telephone in and state they are under a counterattack and want to fall back to some other position. Third, I found that troops would work all day to capture well-earned terrain and at night would fall back a distance varying from 400 to 800 and sometimes 1,000 yards to organize a perimeter of defense.

Subsequent events unfortunately validated Jarman's observations. Neither he nor his successor, Major General Griner, could repair the division's lack of esprit and training so essential in fighting this type of war. Later in the campaign two of its battalions were terribly mauled because they failed to tie in properly against a banzai attack, although Holland Smith personally warned them of this possibility. Worse, by falling back they uncovered a supporting battalion of the 10th Marine Artillery Regiment, which forced our gunners to fire 105s with fuses cut to muzzle-burst—the shells exploded 50 feet to their front.

Leaving out the 27th's performance, any commander traditionally and by law holds the right to relieve any subordinate—right or wrong, peace or war. I relieved commanders in Haiti, I relieved them on Guadalcanal. Throughout the war commanders relieved subordinates, normally with no commotion. It isn't pleasant because it may mean that the commander judged wrongly to start with: but it happened numerous times in both the Pacific and European theaters, and it will happen as long as men go into battle.

This relief stemmed from nothing personal. Holland thought very well of Ralph Smith, as did I. Ralph had been my neighbor in Washington before the war and I liked him. But under the same field conditions Holland would have relieved a Marine officer and so would I.

Holland's action amounted to a command decision. It should have been treated as such. It probably would have been except for the senior Army commander in Pearl Harbor. Lieutenant General Richardson unfortunately chose to make a *cause célèbre* out of the event. Without consulting Nimitz he appointed a board of Army officers to investigate the case. He himself flew to Saipan, ignored Holland, visited the 27th Division, reviewed the troops and distributed medals.

When he did call on the Marine commander, in the presence of witnesses he berated him and insulted his command. He was playing with dynamite—as anyone who knew Holland can testify—but Spruance, aware of the ugly situation, had pledged Holland to suffer in silence. When Richardson pulled the same stunt on Kelly Turner, who labored under no such pledge, Turner reportedly gave him back his own.

The matter could have ended there but unfortunately someone leaked the story to a San Francisco newspaper. A subsequent and highly prejudicial story indicted Holland and the Marine Corps, an ironical twist since about the same time the casualty figures came in. The operation cost 2,000 Marines and 250 Army soldiers killed, 6,000 Marines and 1,000 Army soldiers wounded.

Furious at this obviously unfair attack, I told the Secretary of the Navy and Admiral King that I stood completely behind Holland. King did, too, but thought that in the best interest of fighting the war we should adopt a "no comment" policy. Logic forced me to agree, anyway for the time being, but I privately wrote Holland:

Let me say right here that I think you showed more

forbearance than I could possibly have shown under similar circumstances.

Toward the end of the Saipan campaign my long-awaited reorganization of the Pacific command took place. This made Holland commanding general of the new Fleet Marine Force Pacific. Harry Schmidt moved up to V Corps command; Cliff Cates, who had done a fine job running Marine Corps Schools, took over the 4th Division slated to spearhead a landing against the neighboring island of Tinian.

In planning the Tinian assault, Cates assumed correctly that the Japs expected us to land in the south around Tinian Town. Instead, he recommended risking a landing across the narrow, improbable northern beaches.

Planes, ships and artillery on Saipan pounded the target until July 24 when a separate landing force feinted in the south. Spearheaded by a pitifully small assault force—the narrow beaches would allow no more—the 4th Division smashed in from the north, a most successful tactical surprise that cost 15 killed and some 200 wounded. Turner gave Schmidt two weeks to take this island—Schmidt presented it to him in nine days.

The feat particularly impressed the Secretary of the Navy, who released this statement:

The attack on Tinian is being made by the same troops that conquered Saipan. After 24 days of the meanest kind of fighting through cane fields and caves, followed by 10 days of so-called rest, these men are in shape to conduct a second major assault. This is an outstanding military achievement.

Cates later wrote me:

I believe the battle of Tinian will be an example of a model operation. (Please excuse my lack of modesty.) Its execution was almost perfect although we certainly did not follow the book solution when we landed two divisions on beaches less than 200 yards wide. I impressed on my boys that the quicker we got the job done the quicker we would get a rest, so they almost ran a foot race down the island. Of course, the resistance didn't compare with Saipan, nor the operation as a whole, but, considering the reduced strengths of our units (some battalions less than 400), it couldn't have been better.

Three days before landing on Tinian we struck Guam. The delay occasioned by the Jap naval threat proved a blessing since it allowed 17 days of prelanding naval and

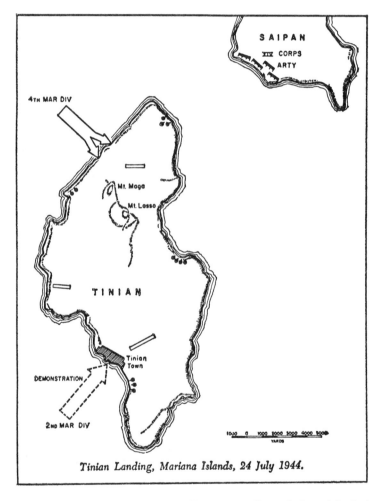

Tinian Landing, Mariana Islands, 24 July 1944.

air bombardment, a joint effort co-ordinated by Admiral "Close-in" Conolly, a real master. Despite our preparation the three-pronged assault suffered severe casualties but held on until artillery and Army reserve landed. Subsequently Shepherd's brigade and General Bruce's 77th Army Division worked north to the Orote Peninsula while Turnage's 3d Division pushed east. To Conolly's everlasting credit the troops, engaged in some of the most difficult fighting in the Pacific war, continued to receive superb naval gunfire support. Some ships fired as high as a thousand tons of shells a day.

These actions plus the Saipan command controversy increased my desire to visit the Pacific, a trip finally possible in late July. With several of my staff I reached Honolulu on August 8. I found Nimitz in excellent spirit and quite optimistic about his war. Being eminently realistic, however, he readily saw the need for a sixth division of Marines and at my request so wrote Admiral King.

After several days of conferences Nimitz invited me to fly to Guam with him. We touched down on Eniwetok and Saipan. Eniwetok impressed me by its extreme nakedness, which called for the most open assault; Saipan by its extreme density, which called for the most ferocious fighting after costly assault across confined beaches.

The island of Guam was just about secured when we arrived. For three days Geiger and Turnage briefed me on the appalling battle, one still being fought in the north. Guam's heavy forests and precipitous cliffs have to be seen to be believed—its size and density are such that sporadic resistance continued until the end of 1945, indeed two Japanese soldiers almost unbelievably held out until 1960.

Nimitz having returned to Pearl Harbor, I borrowed a twin-engine plane from Roy Geiger and flew to Tinian and there met my son, Archer, just getting ready to leave the island with his unit. We had seen very little of each other since 1942, so with the blessing of Harry Schmidt I named him a temporary aide for my Pacific tour. He had been wounded on Saipan, and besides he would be back in Hawaii ahead of his division.

On Saipan I spent a couple of days with Tommy Watson, who so brilliantly led the 2d Division through that campaign. Tommy was bursting with pride in his people and told me

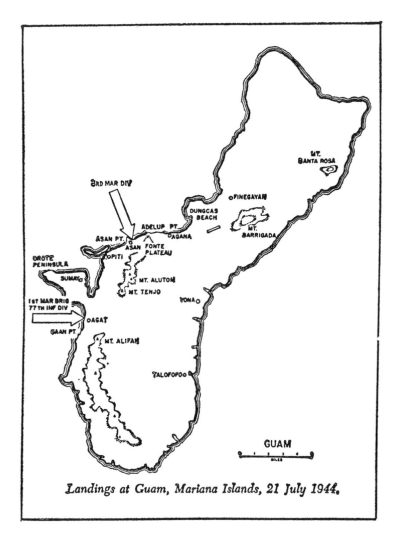

Landings at Guam, Mariana Islands, 21 July 1944.

many stories of their incredibly brave actions. One concerned
a radio operator lying face down in a field under enemy fire.
Each time a group of mortar shells exploded he called back
to his CP, "Hold it, there's a little interference here."

We flew on to Guadalcanal, now an enormous supply base
scarcely recognizable to a former inhabitant, then to Bougainville for conferences with General Mitchell, commanding

Marine aviation in this vast area. I emphasized to Mitchell and his commanders how highly we regarded the achievements of their pilots to date and how we were trying hard to transfer some squadrons aboard escort carriers for future campaigns.

By small plane I flew to Banika, inspected a supply unit, and continued on to Pavuvu where the plane landed on a dirt road in lieu of an airstrip. I found Bill Rupertus on crutches, his ankle fractured by a fall during a recent landing maneuver. He was in excellent spirit and proudly showed me the camp which the 1st Division had hacked out of mud and coconut trees, the prominent features of this wretched island which swarmed with huge rats and slimy land crabs.

Bill and his ADC, O. P. Smith, were busily planning for their next landing: Peleliu Island in the Palau Group. The JCS, influenced by MacArthur's desires, chose this objective for several reasons. MacArthur was heading for the Philippines—simultaneous to our landing on Peleliu his units would land on Morotai Island, the southeastern end of the Philippine complex. With its two large airfields Peleliu flanked the lines of communication to the Philippines. In enemy hands this spelled murder for MacArthur's advance; in our hands it would not only cover his right flank but would provide air support for his later landings at Mindanao and Leyte, targets beyond the range of fighter planes on Saipan. As a further gain its capture would neutralize the neighboring islands of Babelthuap and Koror to the north and would complete the encirclement of Truk, now lying almost helpless in the rear.

A small island about 6 miles long and 2 miles wide at the widest portion, Peleliu featured a spine running most of its north-south length. Bill gave considerable thought to landing in the north but finally decided to hit the southwestern beaches, which were wider and would lead to more rapid capture of the vital airfield. The plan seemed reasonable to me but we both knew, considering the estimated 10,000 enemy compressed on this small rock, that it was going to be another bloody one.

We island-hopped back across the Pacific to Honolulu. There someone told Nimitz of our reaching an island with only a slight reserve of gasoline in our tank. After giving me the devil for traveling around the Pacific in a twin-engine plane,

he asked King to provide me with a suitable command plane.
King agreed.

I returned to Washington tired but very pleased by my
talks and observations. Besides the various units, I had
visited as many aid stations, field hospitals and base hospitals as time allowed. I was certain our wounded were receiving the best medical attention in the world, a fact I continued
to stress in my many speeches of this time. On September
5 I wrote General Holcomb:

> I had a most enjoyable and profitable trip in that I
> covered 22,000 miles in 18 days, saw all the force, corps
> and division commanders and practically all the regi-
> mental and battalion commanders in the field.

I was also able to report:

> I have just received approval from the Commander in
> Chief of the formation of the Sixth Division. A dispatch
> to that effect will go out this afternoon. Lem Shepherd's
> name is now before the Senate to be a major general and
> he will have that unit. I have at last gotten authority to
> have a Fleet Marine Force Pacific . . . This will give us
> two corps of three divisions each with an extra reinforced
> regiment, which will be formed later. . . . Another thing
> we have done, which I pinch myself now and then to see if
> I am still awake, we have gotten both Nimitz and King
> to approve a division of the larger CVEs [aircraft car-
> riers] for use of Marines. That will give us four carriers
> with a carrier group of Marines aboard, and I can assure
> you that took some days of hard talking.

In this relatively quiet period I brought Holland Smith back
for a well-deserved rest in the States. With Saipan still
fresh in mind newspapermen converged on his arrival in
California. Although he handled the questions adroitly, one
photographer caught him scowling—a picture naturally cap-
tioned with a tie-in to Ralph Smith. *Time* magazine now added
fuel to the fire by running a story of the Saipan controversy
highly favorable to the Marines. Once again King ordered a
"no comment" policy and the issue finally quieted. I also
brought back Roy Geiger and Lem Shepherd for short
periods. I sent Louis Woods out in exchange for Field Harris.

I would have preferred similarly to rotate all top officers but simply did not have enough of them to permit it.

News from the field remained excellent. Cliff Cates informed me:

> The Saipan-Tinian operations are past history and we are now shaking down and getting some rest prior to starting a strenuous training program. Although we had fairly heavy casualties, and very tough going, the morale of the men couldn't be better. Even their physical condition is excellent, which is an agreeable surprise to me. The sick rate is low and their general condition is much better than I had expected. It is far different from the 1st [Marine Division] when they left Guadalcanal.

On August 24 Hal Turnage reported from Guam:

> The situation here continues well in hand. The mopping-up process produces good results; since all organized resistance ceased on 10 August, to date approximately 2,000 Nips have been run down and killed by patrols. To date 3d MarDiv has 7,706 notches on its guns— known enemy killed. I believe a conservative estimate of the known and unknown enemy killed by this division would be at least 9,000. Our bulldozer burial details are still actively employed.

I hastened to try to make the worth of these operations known to the public by speaking whenever possible. It seemed to me that Americans were entitled to learn as much as we could tell them of the conduct of these campaigns and the reason for heavy casualties. Besides speaking frequently, I never refused the call of a gold-star mother and I paid close attention to incoming correspondence on this sad subject, answering each letter as it arrived. Sometimes this was unusually difficult, as my letter to the mother of a boy killed on Guam indicates:

> On my return from the Pacific, I received and read your very wonderful letter which I appreciate more than words can tell. I knew, of course, that your son had been killed and had been worrying about it as I remembered it was I who got him into the Marine Corps and got him

sent to the combat zone when by all rules of the game he should have been doing something else.

Yes, you are right, the Marine Corps has suffered a loss equal to that of yours, and the country also has suffered a loss in that had he been spared, his work in chemistry would have done much for the country. I feel relieved to know that he was killed doing what he wanted to do, serving his country in one of the finest divisions that we have; that he was killed in taking from the Japanese the first piece of American territory that has been regained.

In my mind this time-consuming task was vital to humanity and was clearly a task for every officer whose men died or were wounded for him, the Corps and country. I wrote one of my division commanders on the subject:

It [the writing of such letters] may seem rather trivial, but it is just the not doing of such trivialities that has tended to give the Marine Corps a name for callousness as shown by the letter I am enclosing with this. About a month ago, I was down in Atlanta and I saw a Mr. —— whose son was killed in Guam. . . . I talked to him for about thirty minutes and he is the first parent who has lost someone that I was unable to show that the Marine Corps was not callous to the death of their people. He was very courteous but was firmly convinced that whereas I thought he would be informed and that the commanding officer of his son would write him nevertheless it would not happen. I am also enclosing with this a copy of a memorandum that was sent out by air mail requesting that the commanding officer of [this man] write a letter to the father and mother. Will you please see personally that this is done and right away. If it is not a practice in [your division] for the commanding officers of the lower units such as companies and battalions to write such letters, I think it is a good idea that it be started. . . . This is not something one cares to get out an order about but it is something that the junior unit commanders should in all decency want to do.

I could not have felt more strongly about this subject. One day an aide, Buddy Masters, came to me. "General," he said, "I'm worried about your eyesight which is getting worse. You read all day here in the office and then you take a couple of hundred Purple Heart certificates home, sign them at night and read some more. I have found a way to ease this."

"How?"

"The other day over at Navy I saw a new machine bought for the Secretary. It writes his signature automatically, and it only costs a few hundred dollars."

"Save the money," I told him. "If those boys can get wounded, I can find time to sign my name on their Purple Hearts."

XXI

Victory

THE 1st Division assaulted Peleliu on September 15, 1944, one of the least publicized and most difficult World War II campaigns. For a month these Marines defied a defiant enemy, a tortuous terrain, and to cap it all a climate as vagarious as anything yet encountered. Masterfully conducted, the enemy's defense was as rigorous at the end as at the beginning. A sign found in a dugout translated to: "Defense to the death. We will build a barrier across the Pacific with our bodies."

I followed the action closely from daily briefings and from reports by Bill Rupertus. On October 18 he wrote:

> This terrain which we had to finally pocket the remaining Japs in was the worst I have ever seen. . . .
> Today I called for a company of Marines from one of the battalions to do a small mopping-up job. The Company designated by the Battalion Commander, Major Hurst, now consists of about 80 enlisted. However, when the word got around about the job that this Company was to do, 200 men answered roll call when this Company was lined up. These 200 men were permitted to do this mopping-up job. When you have men like this there can never be any doubt in anyone's mind as to the outcome of any task you may assign them.

I replied immediately:

> Let me congratulate you and the Division on the perfectly splendid work that you are doing in your present operation. Of course it is nothing new for the First [Marine Division] to do excellent work because they have done so right along but this is one of the hardest jobs that

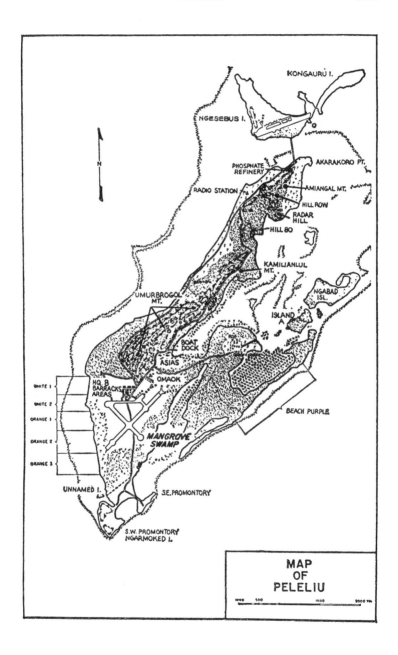

KONGAURU I.

NGESEBUS I.

PHOSPHATE
REFINERY

AKARAKORO PT.

RADIO STATION

AMIANGAL MT.

HILL ROW

RADAR
HILL

HILL 80

KAMILIANLUL
MT.

UMURBROGOL
MT.

NGABAD
ISL.

ISLAND
A

BOAT
DOCK

ASIAS

OMAOK

WHITE 1

WHITE 2

ORANGE 1

ORANGE 2

ORANGE 3

HQ. 8
BARRACKS
AREAS

BEACH PURPLE

MANGROVE
SWAMP

UNNAMED I.

S.E. PROMONTORY

S.W. PROMONTORY
NGARMOKED I.

MAP
OF
PELELIU

1000   500   1000   2000 Yd.

they have had handed them and I want you and them to know that we back here appreciate it. Of course I will say this officially a little later on when the action is over but I want to say it personally to you at this time.

Meanwhile we planned ahead.

It is important for the reader to understand our position vis-à-vis the JCS. Although I did not sit in this august body which made the decisions we carried out, several Marine officers did represent me at Navy planning levels under the JCS. This ensured us a flow of information on projected operations and also permitted us a limited voice in their selection.

I personally am not one for Monday morning quarter-backing. Although some of the JCS strategy has been questioned by latter-day experts, I feel today as I felt when coming off Guadalcanal in 1942: our strategy perhaps was not perfect because no strategy ever is, but I thought we were doing the best job in the circumstances.

Critical readers should keep in mind that we and our leaders undoubtedly could have done a better job had Congress as the voice of the people met prewar appropriations requests. That they did not is simply one of the many "dead cats" of American history. I see no reason to labor the failure brought on by the pathetic fallacy of isolationism, but it does help to explain some of our early so-called mistakes.

At this time the JCS chose Iwo Jima for an early 1945 target. This was a difficult decision. Intelligence described Iwo as a barren rock of volcanic ash defended by a strong force with prepared defenses superior to those being encountered on Peleliu.

The decision to take this island resulted from integrated service thinking. Primarily the Army Air Corps wanted it. Curt LeMay's heavy bombers were currently striking Japan and particularly Tokyo from the recently acquired Saipan and Tinian airfields. Radar located on Iwo Jima warned Tokyo of approaching B-29s and fighters based on Iwo attacked the returning bombers. We also needed an interim field for aircraft damaged over target, many of which were going down at sea.

The JCS also decided to take Okinawa later in the year—a choice which did not surprise me. Not long after my return from the Pacific, Jerry Thomas brought in one of our Pentagon planners who provided me with the welcome news of the Formosa invasion finally being scratched. I wanted nothing to do with landing on Formosa, which would have absorbed nearly every Marine and soldier in the Pacific. With MacArthur in the process of taking the Philippines the JCS lost interest in Formosa. As yet, our planner said, nothing had replaced it.

In the ensuing discussion Jerry pointed out the advantage of projecting our air onto the Chinese mainland. When I agreed, the two officers laid a map on my desk. Jerry said, "I have measured the operational range of our aircraft on these calipers."

He placed one arm of the calipers on the central Chinese coast and drew an arc through the Pacific. The line crossed Okinawa. With my approval our officer suggested this target to his co-planners. So far as I know this was the origin of the Okinawan campaign—slightly ironical since Nimitz, despite a good many arguments to the contary, gave top command of the operation to the Army.

Army or no, we were participating up to our necks in both campaigns, which were to tax our personnel and supply resources to the utmost. That autumn I presented these figures at budgetary hearings:

ITEM	ISSUED 1943	NEEDED 1944
Medium tanks	250	553
Amphibian tractors (*cargo*)	856	2,777
Amphibian tractors (*armored*)	184	562
81mm mortars	314	650
Bazookas	985	3,390
Jeeps	2,198	3,154
2½-ton trucks	2,166	3,328
Pyramidal tents	77,022	120,000

The landings of spring, summer and autumn already had caused grave personnel difficulties as did the attrition of time. During Lem Shepherd's brief visit to the States, he asked if it were possible to send home the 1,500 troops in the 22d Marines who had served nearly thirty months in the Pacific. In a letter of October 16 to Holland Smith I pointed out that the Corps had reached its peak strength with slim chance of a further personnel increase—all future operations must be accomplished with our present numbers. Our only salvation lay in rotation, which meant veterans going out a second time. We had to bring Shepherd's 1,500 men and many more, particularly from the 1st Division, home for a rest. The alternative, which I would not consider, was disbanding the 1st Division.

On October 19 I informed Harry Schmidt:

> Things here are going along about as usual, our main effort now being to get replacements out to you and the others in the Pacific. In order to do this, we must get the long-timers back; we must pare down all unnecessary personnel so that we can maintain a rotation. We cannot get any additional men and we have got to fight this war out with the number we now have. The question of what type of men we have rests a great deal with the commanders in the Pacific for if they do not allow the ones who have been there longest and who are tired to come back, in my opinion the war effort as far as the Marine Corps goes is going to be hurt quite a bit.

I decided now to bring Bill Rupertus home, his command going to the 1st Division's Guadalcanal artillery commander, the redoubtable Pedro del Valle. Bill was already tired when I saw him in the Pacific, and I let him stay on only because of the personal request of Admiral Halsey. I knew the Peleliu campaign must nearly have exhausted him. He of course did not see things my way, but quieted down a little when I gave him command of the Marine Corps Schools heretofore run under my direct aegis. As usual he turned all of his immense energy and talent to the new job, but only shortly after taking over at Quantico his heart acted up and he was sent to the Bethesda Naval Hospital.

Another important change sent General Underhill to Pearl Harbor to serve as force inspector for Holland Smith's large command. Ever since Haiti days I had been a bear on inspection. This was my first step in setting up a new Corps-wide system as soon as possible.

Although I did not anticipate a swift end to the war, I thought we now held victory in our grasp. So did Admiral

King, who conceived the quaint idea of reorganizing the Department of the Navy, a plan I studied with raised eyebrows. The Marine Corps existed as a separate establishment within the Department of the Navy unlike the various naval bureaus. I had no intention of being absorbed by the chief of naval operations.

Voicing my fears to Jerry Thomas, I asked him quietly to investigate the proposal and keep an eye on it. I asked him further to work up a postwar personnel plan which I felt should be put into law immediately after the war if not before. With three-fourths of our operating forces in the Pacific, I did not think we would immediately demobilize and I further foresaw a larger postwar Marine Corps whose officer cadre would have to come from reserve officers now in uniform. Subsequent study caused us to suggest a Corps of 8,000 officers and 100,000 men. When we discussed our plan with naval officers and remarked that they should come up with a similar working figure, we were met with uncomprehending stares—an oversight which, as will be seen, cost the Navy dearly.

The hydra-headed monster of administration sometimes weighed heavily on my nerves. In early 1945, when a senior officer asked me to approve some unofficial reliefs of subordinates, I replied:

> I thought I had made it definitely clear to the Fleet Marine Force Pacific and to each division commander that I did not approve, nor would I tolerate, the relief of officers from divisions, nor the relief of officers from the Pacific Ocean areas on personal letters or personal reports not backed up by official action. I know General [Holland] Smith is cognizant of this and has told me both verbally and in writing that he agrees and approves of this action.

> It is not necessary for a division commander . . . to have evidence which would convict before a General Court Martial to relieve an officer for inefficiency. All it requires is the moral courage to go on record as stating that this or that officer, in the opinion of the division commander or higher command, is not competently exercising command over his unit and in the opinion of the division commander is not competent or efficient to hold the job he now has.

I suspect I was a little tired now, as were most of us. I saw evident fatigue in President Roosevelt's face when in late December we persuaded him to inspect the New River base called Camp Lejeune. He loved excursions of this nature. Inevitably his spirits rose when he left Washington. On this occasion he told me he still thought the base should have been located elsewhere. Privately he told Ross McIntire how proud we should be of this base. Ross said he had never seen the President more enthusiastic about any camp.

I saw the President again in January when I dined at the White House. As was the custom we retired into a drawing room where he sat on a divan, motioning various guests to come over for a word or two. He relaxed easier than most men, but there was no missing the fatigued and drawn face. On this occasion he chatted about his trip to Haiti when he was Undersecretary of the Navy and recalled my having accompanied him around my district. He told me how much he enjoyed the experience and his pleasure in being escorted by the "Horse Marines"—he referred to a squadron of mounted gendarmes.

A month later I sat in Congress to hear the President's report on the Yalta conference. For the first time he did not arise to speak, but apologized for the weight of his leg braces and remained seated. This was the last time I saw him alive.

Admiral Nimitz directed Holland Smith to command the Expeditionary Forces for the Iwo Jima assault scheduled for February 19, 1945. These consisted of Harry Schmidt's V Corps composed of Bobbie Erskine's 3d Division, Cliff Cates' 4th Division, and Keller Rockey's new 5th Division.

Neither Holland nor I cared for the initial command arrangement which superimposed Holland and his staff on Schmidt and his staff. We saw Iwo Jima a corps task which Schmidt should handle without anyone looking over his shoulder. Holland presented our arguments to Nimitz without avail.

Iwo Jima obviously was going to be tough. A small island remote from anywhere, an estimated 23,000 enemy manned a labyrinth of underground emplacements said to be the work of years. No other islands lent themselves for feint attacks, which meant showing our hand by long-range

preliminary bombardment. To counter the sacrifice of tactical surprise we wanted particularly heavy prelanding bombardment. On January 12 a letter from Holland aroused
my qualms:

As you know, I have nothing to do with the great strategy in the Pacific, and only express myself when called
upon for a statement. I believe that the operation [Iwo
Jima] is not worth the casualties we will suffer. On two

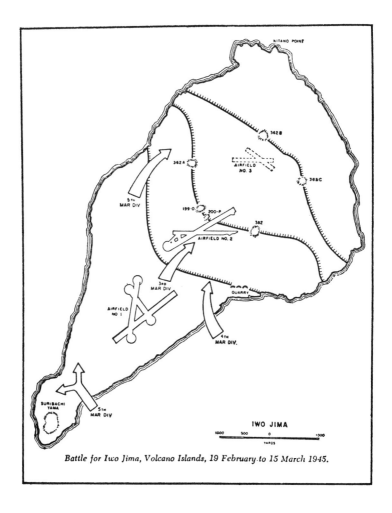

Battle for Iwo Jima, Volcano Islands, 19 February to 15 March 1945.

separate occasions I protested that naval gunfire is in-
sufficient, with the result that it has been increased to
some extent, but not enough, in my opinion, to suffice. I
can only go so far.

We have done all we could do to get ready . . . and
I believe it will be successful, but the thought of the
probable casualties causes me extreme unhappiness . . .
would to God that something might happen to cancel the
operation altogether.

The "something" earnestly desired by Holland was familiar to but a few of us. It was the atomic bomb. It was not
quite ready and no one knew if it would ever be ready and
even then if it would work.

Until the time it worked we had to prosecute the war with
the means on hand. I could not agree with Holland's doubts.
Air Corps losses in men and planes returning from Tokyo
raids were mounting alarmingly and would mount as the
bombing effort continued. To naval planners and to King in
Washington I repeated Holland's complaints and asked for
all possible support. King assured me Nimitz was doing the
best with what he had. I am convinced this was true.

The Marines landed on February 19, 1945. Soon after
the first waves scrambled ashore the stunned enemy recovered. More than once in those early days his savage, fanatic
resistance placed the issue in doubt. That it was resolved in
our favor was due to a fighting spirit unexcelled in the
history of warfare. Those Marines held on while companies
were reduced to platoons and platoons to squads in strength.
They not only held but they inched north. They killed all who
stood in their way.

Although I was prepared to defend our casualties in this
epic struggle, I was pleased when Mr. Royall, the Assistant
Secretary of War, called to congratulate the Marine Corps
on its pending victory. General Marshall, he informed me,
had asked his planners if they thought the Iwo Jima operation was necessary and if so would the Army have landed
under a similar plan. The planners replied: yes, the operation was necessary; yes, the Army would have landed similarly.

On March 6, with heavy fighting embracing the island, I
wrote Holland Smith:

Captain Lademan [USN] came over this morning with his fire [naval gunfire] charts and gave us a perfectly splendid presentation of the show from the gunnery end of it. I note that he was very frank in stating that there was not sufficient gunfire prior to D day, that he felt they had learned that deliberate aimed fire at point targets is what is needed rather than concentrations. Of course you and I have known that for some time and have talked about it. I brought the question up some three or four months ago to [Admiral] Savvy Cooke and I have mentioned it to Admiral King. I intend to mention it again in no uncertain terms. It seems to me we have gotten to the stage in this war when the ground commander's recommendation as to what is necessary in the way of gunfire support should be listened to rather than someone else's idea who might perhaps want to expedite the landing. I know that you did everything humanly possible to have this accomplished. Nimitz and Sherman are here and I am going to make the opportunity to talk to them on the same subject, whether it will do any good or not God only knows.

Had a nice talk with the Secretary [Mr. Forrestal, who took over upon Mr. Knox' death] this morning and he is loud in the praise of the Marines. He said that the picture of planting the flag on Mt. Suribachi would keep the Marines in existence for the next five hundred years if nothing else did. He then went on to say how much he had enjoyed being with you and how well everything went. He was particularly profuse in his praise about [General Bobbie] Erskine. . . .

This has been one of the hardest fights in Marine history. I have carefully read all of the operation plans and I have followed very closely the summaries and dispatches and I can see nothing from the Marine Corps angle that was left undone that should have been done or where we needed to change it.

Jim Forrestal witnessed the landing and first days of the Iwo Jima fighting, which he graphically described at the Secretary's conference. Unfortunately events soon placed his prediction of Corps longevity in jeopardy.

Admiral King continued to show the greatest interest in the fighting. Nimitz he assured me, was supporting us to his utmost. As the world knows, it was not enough. In five weeks of the incredible struggle required to take this tiny island we lost 5,300 dead and a great many more wounded. Those who suffered the loss of their loved ones and those who were badly wounded should know that the possession of this hideous island saved many more thousands of lives than it cost. These lives wore a different uniform, that of American airmen, but they were American lives, they were brothers-in-arms.

Public reaction generally supported our fight. The famous Rosenthal picture of the flag raising on Mt. Suribachi stirred millions of human breasts. The postmaster general sometime later informed me that first-day cancellations of the Iwo Jima stamp broke all existing records in the main Washington post office. Telephone calls and letters by the hundreds and thousands bespoke the nation's pride in its Marines. To the few dissidents I tried to explain the gigantic issues at stake. Sometimes I was successful, sometimes not.

A few days after the initial landing I received a call late one night. A frantic woman in Chicago had heard from a friend that her son was wounded—she demanded to know how badly he was wounded as well as his present location.

"I just don't know," I told her. "I don't even know your name."

She told me her name and added, "You must know how my son is, where he is."

"I want to tell you something," I said. "My own son was badly wounded on Iwo Jima. I don't know how badly and I don't know where he is. I know he has been evacuated and is receiving excellent care, and I know the same is true of your son. If you will leave me your telephone number I will have you called the minute we get any information."

Somewhat mollified, she hung up.

I could not blame any mother for worrying or even for trying to assuage worry by abusing me or the Corps. I did resent parental influence particularly when the Marine did not wish it. One case occurred in Australia after the Guadalcanal campaign. The wife of one of my young officers prevailed upon her politically powerful father to have her husband ordered home. General Holcomb asked me to look into the matter. I called the officer in and explained the situation.

"I know my wife is worried," he told me. "So are lots of

other wives and mothers. I not only don't want to go home, but I sincerely ask you not to send me home."

I wrote General Holcomb:

> I could not help but congratulate him on his decision because it was, in my opinion, a very manly thing to do. I am, therefore, not returning him to the States.

At a dinner party shortly before the end of the war I was set upon by a woman saying in a loud voice, "I thought I heard someone congratulating you on the high percentage of Marines serving overseas."

I allowed as how we were proud of this particular record.

"My son isn't overseas. He is down at Camp Lejeune and is miserable. I don't see why he can't get overseas."

I learned the young Marine's name. Thinking I was doing a favor, the next day I arranged his overseas orders. A week later, the war having ended, his irate father called me at my office—would I cancel his son's orders. The boy wished to marry and, according to the father, there was no conceivable reason for his going overseas now. I refused to consider changing the orders.

Returning to the Iwo Jima period, Mr. Forrestal did all he could to make the American public realize the value of our sacrifice. He knew what the casualty figures meant to me and to other Marines and on all occasions displayed the utmost compassion at our losses. I later wrote Holland Smith:

> I personally feel that in the whole thirty-seven years of my service in the Marine Corps there has never been a finer Secretary of the Navy or one more keenly interested in the Marine Corps nor more alive to our trials and tribulations.

In late March we declared the island secure. Holland returned to Pearl Harbor from where he wrote me on March 21:

> I returned on Saturday via Guam where I spent two days. Admiral Nimitz and his staff were particularly cordial, and apparently realize what a serious fight we had on Iwo. Before leaving here in January I predicted 20,000 casualties which at that time met almost with derision.

Personal catastrophe added to the burden of these days. Bill Rupertus did not recover from the heart ailment that put him in the Bethesda hospital. Despite the best treatment, his heart continued to misbehave and in late March he faced physical retirement. Since I knew his record would still make him an asset at Quantico I wrote him offering to call him back to active duty from retirement.

Late on March 25 I was at home when Colonel Kilmartin, commanding the Marine Barracks at the Naval Gun Factory, telephoned to report Bill *in extremis*. I hastened to his side. He was dead when I arrived. The next day I received his letter thanking me for and accepting my offer to return to active duty.

Bill's death came as a low blow. After we buried him I wrote General Holcomb:

> The Marine Corps has lost one of its finest officers and I have lost one of my finest friends.

As if to acknowledge the service to the nation rendered by the Marines on Iwo Jima, I was promoted to four-star rank in early April, 1945. This made me the first four-star general on active duty in the history of the Corps. I was more than gratified by the flow of congratulatory messages which seemed to approve of the Corps's finally coming of age.

During the Iwo Jima fighting I had wanted to get to the Pacific, not only to visit the wounded and the troops who were fighting so hard but also to see something of the largest operation yet mounted in the Pacific war—Okinawa, slated for April 1.

Much as I hated to admit it, my presence in the field could have yielded very little. I held the utmost confidence in my commanders or they would not have been there. In Washington, on the other hand, I had my job—at this particular time the perennial, seemingly endless Congressional hearings attendant to the next budget. On April 8 I finally shook free of the capital.

Field Harris, assistant commandant for air, Jerry Thomas and I flew to the west coast, inspected installations in San Diego and San Francisco and proceeded to Honolulu. After conferring with Holland Smith and his staff I flew to the island of Maui to visit the splendid 4th Marine Division just returned from Iwo Jima, its fourth assault.

At the airstrip Cliff Cates silently handed me a dispatch reporting President Roosevelt's death. I was terribly shocked. All of us in Washington knew the President was tired and undoubtedly ill but I never dreamed he was so ill. What indomitable spirit and courage this man mustered in those final weeks and days.

My gloom deepened at the sight of Cliff's diminished division. Every inch the field commander, Cates tried to give me some idea of the fighting on those awful sands. As I talked to him and to many of his officers and men I felt a terrible gratitude made the worse because no word of mine could express it properly and fully.

We flew on to the newly established Guam headquarters of Admiral Nimitz where I inspected Bobbie Erskine's 3d Divison also just recently returned from the Iwo Jima battle. I received a rude shock in Guam. To my consternation Nimitz did not think I should visit Okinawa—my main reason for making the long trip. I thought I knew what was bothering him. It was the Saipan controversy and was probably the main reason Holland Smith was sitting back in Pearl Harbor. In Nimitz' mind, I concluded, a senior Marine general by barging into Okinawa might upset the applecart of command relations. I subtly tried to quiet his fears, but at the same time I let him know I intended to visit my Marines.

He countered with a suggestion to visit Iwo Jima. Recognizing a temporizing attitude and wanting to see the island anyway, I flew up the next day with Jerry and Field Harris. The commanding officer of the Army garrison unit showed us around. He had built a road up to Mt. Suribachi, the elevation on the extreme left from where the enemy poured his lethal shower on the landing Marines. I later wrote General Holcomb:

> I have had the privilege of going to Iwo and standing on Suribachi, and the terrain from there just beggars description. . . . I still don't see how they got ashore and having gotten ashore, I don't see how they stayed there.

A few enemy remained on the northern end of the island. We watched Army troops unseal caves and try to persuade the soldiers to surrender. Those who chose to come forth were treated well. Those who chose to die were accommodated.

Finding the official climate on Guam still temporizing, I left for Saipan to see my good friend Tommy Watson, commanding the 2d Marine Division which formed the Tenth Army reserve for Okinawa. Tommy was most annoyed not to have been landed initially on Okinawa. Still hoping for action he was holding his troops on an alert status, his canvas and other supply remaining aboard the transport force anchored in the harbor. Obviously here was a splendid division not only ready but aching for combat.

Back in Guam Nimitz received me most cordially and invited me to accompany him and his chief of staff, Forrest Sherman, to Okinawa. Space forbade taking more than one of my party, so Field Harris chose to fly south to visit his air units in the Philippines.

Escorted by a dozen fighter planes we left the next morning for Okinawa. During the flight Sherman brought up the subject of service unification. I was surprised to find him so wholeheartedly favoring it and also to find Nimitz in seeming sympathy with many of his statements. I could not believe that either had given much thought to this complex problem, but said nothing.

The trip proved otherwise uneventful until we reached Okinawa, where sirens announced Condition Red. We already knew of the kamikaze, or suicide, tactic recently introduced by the desperate enemy whose half-trained pilots were crashing TNT-filled planes into our ships. Although our own planes and antiaircraft guns claimed a large number of these fanatics, one or more invariably penetrated our screen to reach the mass of transports standing off the island. And now to our horror one of the gray planes screamed from the sky to crash into a cargo ship, a ghastly explosion followed by flame and black smoke. That night the enemy staged a conventional air raid which cost them fifty-four planes.

The kamikaze tactic underlined the strategic importance of the Ryukyu Islands of which Okinawa formed the key. Almost 100,000 enemy defended this vast land mass of some 500 square miles inhabited by half a million civilians. It was the last redoubt before Japan proper, and the enemy seemed as determined to hold it as we were to take it.

The task fell to General Buckner's Tenth Army composed

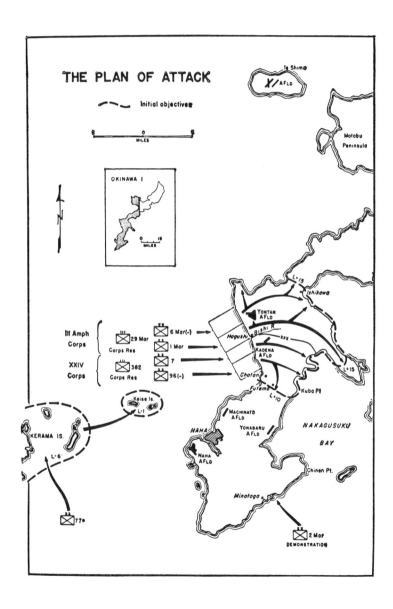

of John Hodge's XXIV Army Corps and Roy Geiger's amphibious corps comprising the 1st, 2d and 6th Marine Divisions. Buckner chose a deceptively simple scheme of assault. On April 1 his combined force struck midway up the western side of the island, an unopposed landing of the Marines on the left and the Army on the right.

Geiger's people pushed in, seized Yontan airfield and headed north. The army seized Kadena airfield and pushed south. By the time we arrived Geiger virtually held the northern two-thirds of the island, Shepherd's 6th Division having taken the bulk of the fighting. But in the south Hodge met increasing resistance; obviously he faced the bulk of the enemy. In a conference at Geiger's CP Buckner voiced his decision to commit the Marines to the south a few days hence.

I did not object to the Marines being committed to the main fight—they were on Okinawa for this purpose. But I did question Buckner's tactical plan. Instead of trying to slug it out with the enemy, Geiger, Thomas and I argued for an amphibious landing in the rear or anyway on the flank of the enemy by Buckner's reserve, the 2d Marine Division on Saipan.

Forrest Sherman, among others, objected to a landing on the far east coast as impractical. We replied that the bay of our choice was the alternate landing area for the original operation, so apparently Buckner had thought it quite practical. Having been shot down on this point, Sherman claimed it would take too long to load out the 2d Division from Saipan. We promised him it could be underway in six hours.

Despite these and other arguments Sherman refused to back us, nor did Buckner seem impressed. I learned later that General Bruce, commanding the 77th Army Division which had fought so well on Guam, proposed a similar plan as did Kelly Turner whose transports were being hurt by the kamikaze tactic.

Unable to intervene further, I visited our ground and air units before departing the island. On my return home I stopped at Camp Kamuela on the large island of Hawaii to visit the 5th Marine Division which had suffered horrible casualties on Iwo Jima. We flew on to San Diego, found the field fogged in and continued on to Albuquerque where we landed with one dead engine and very little fuel for the other.

By the time I reached Washington my worst fears for the Okinawan campaign were being realized. Buckner had pulled the 27th Army Division—that of Saipan "fame"—out of his southern line and had fed in Geiger's corps now trying to push through the heavily defended Shuri Line. Simultaneously kamikaze planes extracted a mounting toll of shipping.

Shortly after my return the war correspondent Homer Bigart wrote in the New York *Herald Tribune:*

> There were two ways of employing the Marine 3d Amphibious Corps after its speedy cleanup of northern Okinawa. It could be landed behind the Japanese lines in the south, or it could add power to the frontal assault on the Shuri line. Our tactics were ultraconservative. Instead of an end run, we persisted in frontal attacks.

With the explosion of this journalistic bomb Admiral King called me to his office. Nimitz, he said, thought I had released this information to Bigart.

"I'm sorry to hear that," I told King. "I regard Nimitz as a personal friend and he should know better than to think I operate like that."

I then showed King the results of an investigation on the affair: not only did Bigart write the article while on Okinawa but Nimitz' own censors in Guam cleared it. Upon learning this, plus a few candid opinions of mine on the tactics being used, King grew quite annoyed and said he would take care of the matter. A day or so later he asked me to discuss it with the well-known columnist David Lawrence. Lawrence's subsequent story began:

> Certain high Navy officers here feel that a major mistake was made in handling the Okinawa campaign. . . . Did the Army officers who handled the campaign adopt a slow course? Were there other landing places that could have been used? Why were the Marine Corps generals who had had far greater experience in handling amphibious operations not given opportunity to carry on another type of campaign that might, perhaps, have meant larger land casualties at the outset, but in the end a quicker all-around result for the armed forces as a whole?

Here in a nutshell was the conceptual difference between Army and Marine thinking earlier discussed. Nimitz realized it as much as any of us. I believe two factors impelled him to let Buckner have his rein: he was probably influenced by certain of his staff officers, notably Sherman, and he wanted at all costs to avoid another Saipan controversy. I have never since discussed it with him—fortunately it failed to impair our friendship which was and remains close.

With the Okinawan campaign ending in June, 1945, we faced a short pause before the grand finale—the invasion of the Japanese homeland. In an all-out effort we had rebuilt the shattered divisions of Iwo Jima which even now were rehearsing the Japanese landing. While the 1st and 6th Divisions similarly reorganized I made a change of command slate.

Realizing the fatigue engendered by Holland Smith's superb performance, I brought him back to the San Diego command. Roy Geiger, who had won a well-deserved third star, moved into Holland's place. I gave Keller Rockey command of III Corps and replaced him in command of the 5th Division with a tough-as-nails artilleryman, Tom Bourke. Geiger responded to his new assignment in a letter of June 26:

> This [Okinawa] has been a hard campaign. The officers and men have simply been marvelous. They have carried on day and night, mud and battle, without a murmur and could have continued had it been necessary. They have carried out every mission assigned by the Tenth Army and have broken through every position of the Japanese defenses which stood in their way in a minimum of time. The Marine Corps can ever be proud of the two divisions which fought on this island. The cost has been high, but the time element was essential and I am sure you will be happy to know that the Marines required no urging to attack, attack, and again attack, until the Japs were completely annihilated. You will never know how I regret leaving the III Corps.

I also succeeded in pushing through a new and in my opinion much-needed department in my own headquarters. On July 4 I wrote Pedro del Valle:

We have never had an Inspector General in the true sense of the word. If you will remember, when General Krueger's team came down to Melbourne [in 1943 to inspect the 1st Marine Division] and when they went back, there wasn't very much they did not know, or that General Krueger did not know. I am establishing in this Headquarters an Inspector General's Department to resemble in no way the old Adjutant and Inspector's Department. It is to be headed by you with two or three colonels and lieutenant colonels on your staff, the inspecting parties to be augmented by specialists from the various sections. The head of the Department comes directly under me and not one of the other departments.

Wanting my hard-working assistant, Dewitt Peck, to have his chance at command, I sent him out to relieve del Valle. I brought Hal Turnage back to replace Peck and Tommy Watson to replace Capers James in the personnel division. I also brought Lem Shepherd home but finally decided to send him out again. He was obviously fit and I did not know of a better division commander in the Corps.

Throughout July we continued to prepare for the invasion of Japan. V-E day released numerous Army divisions for the Pacific war, but we knew only too well what the proposed landing would cost us.

Early in August I invited the Undersecretary of the Navy, Mr. Sullivan, to Cherry Point to inspect a new night fighter of which we were very proud. On the way down he looked at his watch. "Well, it's dropped now," he said. "We will know shortly what has happened."

He referred to the atomic bomb dropped on Hiroshima. We learned of its success in Cherry Point. By the time we returned to Washington a second bomb claimed Nagasaki. The war was over.

XXII

The Battle for Our Survival

THE SUDDEN end of the war raised two immediate challenges: occupation of Japan and northern China and demobilization of the troops.

A JCS directive sent Schmidt's V Corps less one division to the southern Japanese island of Kyushu, an occupation symbolically spearheaded by the 4th Marines. Hunt's 2d Division landed at Nagasaki and Bourke's 5th Division at Sasebo, both combat landings in case the enemy felt inclined to resist. He did not. In a peaceful occupation the Marines disbanded Japanese units, sent the soldiers home and seized and ultimately destroyed their arms, equipment and matériel.

Another JCS directive sent Rockey's III Corps to North China to accept the surrender of the Japanese armies there and help repatriate the troops to Japan. As it turned out, this force was also used to fill the strategic vacuum in support of Chiang Kai-shek who was endeavoring to bring Nationalist forces from the south to neutralize the well-organized Communist forces of Mao Tse-tung operating in the north. Shepherd's 6th Division landed on the Shantung Peninsula with headquarters at Tsingtao. Peck's 1st Division and the 1st Marine Air Wing under "Sheriff" Larkin (soon to be succeeded by Lou Woods) landed at Tientsin, where Rockey placed corps headquarters. He then fanned units out to Peking and Chinwangtao, places only too familiar to me and older Marines.

Meanwhile we were cranking up the machinery of demobilization, an effort greatly hindered by outside pressures from Congress and the American people. These pressures had begun exerting themselves at the end of the European war when the Army demobilized some of its units. A good many Marine families wondered why we could not bring our long-timers home for discharge. To such inquiries I pointed out that we needed every man we had to fight what still looked like a long, tough war.

With the sudden peace a torrential demand descended upon us to bring the boys home, precisely as was the case after World War I.

From the beginning my policy was to demobilize, not disintegrate the Corps. Eighteen months earlier we had drawn up plans for a postwar Corps of 8,000 officers and 100,000 men. Until Congress established this force by law we were helpless to plan in detail, but it did give us something to go on.

Using these figures which would permit a two division-two air wing Fleet Marine Force, we established a point system for demobilization whereby a Marine received a certain number of points for each month of service, additional points for service overseas and for wounds and decorations. To fill the vacancies we planned to disband three divisions beginning with the 4th Division in November followed by the 3d and 5th Divisions during the next two months. As each division phased out, its high point men returned to the States for discharge while its low point men who were generally replacements went out to join units in Japan and China.

On August 16 I outlined this policy in a letter to my commanding generals:

Plans for the demobilization of the Navy and Marine Corps will come to you before this letter. . . . Our demobilization plan is now in the hands of the Navy and as soon as it is approved by them, I will send you a copy of it. Our cutbacks are now in four phases, depending on the stage and state of our occupational forces. We are going to follow the Army system of credits for sending men home, 85 points being the number of credits necessary. We are going to replace those men in the necessary numbers by recruits and trainees who do not have the number of credits necessary and who are presently located in the States. It is highly essential that all echelons in the Pacific take seriously this question of getting men home who rate getting home, not, of course, below the standard set . . . but living up to it both by letter and in spirit because the future of the Marine Corps will de-

pend on our friends throughout the country, and one way
of losing the friends that we have is by being either in-
different or unjust in our methods and ways of demobilization.

I was very concerned with the future officer picture. The
war produced some superb reserve officers, a high proportion
of whom, according to a poll, seemed interested in entering
the regular service. Anticipating their selection, I had some
educators at Princeton set up a test primarily to show a man's
ability to absorb knowledge. I did not intend to make his grade
the *sine qua non* of selection, but I did believe it would be
an aid in selecting young officers who would prove to be good
career officers.

To make a career in the Corps more attractive for them,
I at once began pushing for a retirement bill. I knew this
would hurt some older and senior officers, but I was determined to avoid an accumulation of deadwood which we garnered after World War I and which lasted into the thirties
and even World War II. On August 5 I wrote Holland Smith:

> With the reorganization and lessening of the number
> of officers in the Marine Corps, some officers junior in
> grade will of course be demoted. I do not think, there-
> fore, that officers who cannot do all of their duties should
> be kept in the service and other officers who are capable
> of doing their duties and have done them in combat
> should be required to be demoted so that these other of-
> ficers can be retained on the active list in a part-time
> basis. Knowing you as I do, I am sure you will agree
> with this. It is my present intention to recommend re-
> tirement boards for all officers who cannot do their full
> duty both at sea and in the field. . . .

This was a very hectic time. In the same letter I wrote:

> Sorry to have put off my trip out to see you but with
> things happening the way they are around here, I just
> can't make it right now. Thought I had the 1946 budget
> completely buttoned up and forgotten only to find I now
> have to rejustify the whole thing beginning next Monday
> or Tuesday, because the chief indoor sport that they en-
> gaged in so universally after the last war—reducing all

appropriations to the barest minimum—is appearing again.

I also cautioned all commanding generals:

> We also want to be realistic relative to supplies. We are all prone to have more than we need for fear that at some time we will be caught with less than we need. Your people should have the necessary amount of equipment and supplies to do their current jobs and those planned for them in the future. A large reserve supply should not be maintained and we should use up that which we have in the Pacific before requisitioning more. Unless it is something for the health and protection of the men, new items of equipment will not be approved. We have fought this war with what we had and we can certainly wind it up with that type of article.

On August 17 I again wrote Holland Smith:

> I will not be able to come out to the west coast this month as I had planned, nor will I be able to get out next month. Congress reconvenes on the 4th of September and we are endeavoring to get our personnel bills through at the earliest possible moment so that we will know how many officers we may expect. Otherwise, we will lose a chance of getting a large number of worthwhile reserves who will not remain hanging around indefinitely without the knowledge of whether they will or will not have a chance to be regulars.

My efforts toward this end proved in vain. Here was a situation that demanded rapid and positive action on the part of Congress, which refused to give it. Our time to strike the reserve pool was already running out, as Dewitt Peck noted in a letter of September 10:

> As to applications for regular commissions—I am told by the division staff that these will be very few in numbers from this division. So far as I can see, this is psychologically the wrong time. You have the inevitable post-war let down. The war incentive is gone, and young men think now only of Pa and Ma and Suzan—or rather Suzan and then Ma and Pa. Also so many have never

encountered the grim realities of the civilian competitive economic struggle. They are set to go back and be big civilian executives. Give them a year on the outside and they will be yearning for the Queen's shilling. . . . This is precisely what was in my mind when eighteen months or more earlier I had pleaded for a reserve-to-regular program.

By the end of September the Japanese occupation was well underway and the first units of the 1st Division were arriving in China. Our position in China promised to be tricky, particularly because our foreign policy was unclear at this time. Presumably without influencing internal Chinese affairs, we first of all were to accept the surrender of various Japanese forces in that area and repatriate them to Japan. We also were to open communications and guard the Kailin coal mines which supplied a great deal of fuel to major Chinese cities. To accomplish his mission Rockey placed outposts along the Tientsin-Peking and Tientsin-Chinwangtao rail lines and posted Marine guards on the trains. In early October he sent me a long report:

> Billeting arrangements in Tientsin are, in the main, satisfactory. . . . Practically all of the buildings taken had been used by Japanese troops. All of the barracks after Japanese occupancy were filthy beyond description. The Japs had pulled out practically all the pipes and electrical fixtures, most of the radiators, at least one-third of all windows were broken, many of the window sashes and doors were removed, etc. Repairs to billets and offices, to keep any semblance of warmth in them this winter, will be a problem. . . .
>
> There are about 50,000 Japs in the Tientsin area. We have been authorized to accept the surrender of Japanese troops when Chinese Central Government Forces are not present. The few Chinese representatives of the Central Government Forces now in North China wanted to take all surrenders; however, we compromised, letting them accept the surrender at Peking, which they particularly wanted, and we took the surrender at Tientsin. Shepherd plans to take the surrender at Tsingtao. . . .
>
> Shortly prior to embarkation, we had orders to send one RCT [regimental combat team] of the 6th Division

to Chefoo, which I gathered was upon the request of the Generalissimo [Chiang Kai-shek]. On the 5th, reports were received from the *Louisville,* then at Chefoo, that the town was completely controlled by the Communists; that the Japanese garrison had evacuated; that there were no United Nations POWs [prisoners of war] or American civilian internees in the area, and that the Communists would resist by force the introduction of Central Government troops or administrative officials into the city. Admiral Barbey had come up to attend the surrender ceremony and after talking the matter over with him, I sent a dispatch to the China Theater Headquarters stating that under the circumstances there seemed no apparent reason for American troops at Chefoo and recommended strongly that Chefoo not be occupied at this time. Later Admiral Barbey and I were directed to go to Chefoo to investigate conditions and make recommendations. At Chefoo we found the Communists in control, the city completely dead and apparently terrorized. There were a few Europeans still in the city, mostly Italians and White Russians, who were having a bad time of it. However, in spite of the obviously bad conditions, Admiral Barbey and I both felt that any landing there would be an interference in the internal affairs of China; that it would be bitterly resented by the Communists, and that there would probably be serious repercussions. Although the opposition could not have been very serious, there was apt to be some fighting, sabotage and guerrilla warfare thereafter. Upon our recommendation, the orders for the landing were canceled.

I felt, at the time, that the forcible occupation of Chefoo would have made things much more difficult in the Tientsin-Peking areas. In fact, while the Chefoo negotiations were going on two events occurred which I believe stemmed from the Chefoo incident. First, a reconnaissance party consisting of Engineers, with a rifle company as guard, on the road to Peking was fired upon by Communist troops and three of our men were wounded. Second, the railroad between Tsingtao and Weihsien was interrupted by destruction of bridges. . . . Since it has been announced that we wlll not land in Chefoo, there has been no further trouble. A Communist general called at our Headquarters in Tientsin (in civilian clothes) and apologized for firing on our troops. He, as well as the Chefoo man, expressed the greatest friendship for Americans and stated that it was their sincere hope that the traditional friendship between the Americans and Chinese could be continued.

One BLT [battalion landing team] was landed initially at Chinwangtao, primarily in order to give us a winter port. Another battalion is at Tangshan, between Chinwangtao and Tientsin. The Kailin Mining Authority operates coal mines in that area. The Generalissimo and the China Theater Command are seriously concerned about reopening the mines in order that coal may be delivered to Shanghai this winter, otherwise Shanghai freezes. The same applies to Tientsin and Peking. . . .

The movement of the Chinese Army from the south will be largely by air using the two fields at Peking. Our job in Peking includes the protection and maintenance of the airfields and, particularly, providing gas for this air movement, which amounts to about 70,000 gallons a month that must be moved through Taku. . . .

The general sitaution in North China is very curious indeed. There are around 150,000 Japanese troops in the Peking-Tientsin areas and some 200,000 Japanese civilians. There are also Chinese puppet troops in large but indeterminate numbers. South of Peking, along the railroads to Hankow and to Shanghai, there are hundreds of thousands of Japanese troops. The area, except for the cities and the railroads, is controlled by the Communists. There are also some guerrilla troops who profess adherence to the Central Government. Central Government troops are only beginning to come in. The Japanese troops, except those that are being disarmed, are guarding the cities and communication lines. The Communists make forays against the Japanese and against communication lines. It is impracticable for the Central Government Forces to move troops overland. The Japanese appear willing to surrender and are mainly concerned with getting the thing over with and back home. The Central Government cannot afford to disarm them and thereby turn the area over to the Communists. In effect, the Central Government and the Japanese are co-operating in the maintenance of a semblance of order in North China.

The puppet troops have apparently shifted their allegiance to the Central Government and are being used in conjunction with the Japanese in the larger cities. When the Central Government can get troops in to take over, I suppose they will liquidate those individuals among the puppet troops who have co-operated too freely with the Japanese in the past. We are now in the process at Tientsin of disarming the Japanese completely, except that we are leaving 10 per cent of the rifles with five rounds of ammunition each, in order that they may protect themselves from attacks and help guard the rather considerable amounts of Japanese material until it can be turned over to us and subsequently to the Chinese Army. . . .

There is danger, I believe, in this confused situation of our becoming seriously involved. I believe also that this danger will continue as long as these very large Japanese forces are present in North China. . . . I am hopeful that we can make a start on repatriation early in November. . . .

I should not fail to mention the wholehearted welcome we received upon arrival. Everywhere the streets, riverbanks and railroads were lined with flags and cheering people. For days they greeted units as they passed and they seemed genuinely glad to see us. . . .

After showing this letter to Admiral King I replied:

I want to congratulate you on the fine work that the III Corps is doing; you and it certainly have your hands full and I have utter confidence that you will be able to walk this very strenuous tightrope and come out with colors flying. I am glad that the reception of the Marines was so wholeheartedly welcome at Tientsin and I imagine it was equally so at Peking.

The dispatches we receive here do cause us grave concern as to becoming involved, but your action at Chefoo and subsequent action at other places has certainly given us every reason to believe that if we do get mixed up it will have been forced upon us.

In this crucial postwar period the War Department chose to intensify its armed forces unification program by introducing the so-called Collins Plan. Named for its principal spokesman, J. Lawton Collins, the proposal caused a furor almost unprecedented in capital circles.

Calling for "unification now," the plan proposed a single Secretary of Defense and a single armed forces Chief of Staff. In my mind its various tenets spelled an attempt to replace the traditional authority of Congress in military affairs with that of the President and the proposed Secretary of Defense. Other provisions would have curtailed the role and missions of the Marine Corps to make it little more than an auxiliary police force. In my mind this would represent the first step in the total abolition of the Corps.

At Mr. Forrestal's request Admiral Radford and I each drew up a secret paper embodying our views on the proposed unification. These raised one hell of an uproar in the JCS but we stuck to our guns, then and later. My paper formed the basis of my testimony to the Senate Military Affairs Committee on October 24, 1945. After pointing to the paradox created by our recent victory and the present military instability caused largely by the atomic bomb, I said:

It is in this receptive atmosphere that there is now put forward a plausible and well-timed plea calculated to capture the imagination of our slogan-loving fellow countrymen—"Unified National Defense." No one has explained what it is, none will commit themselves as to its exact implications but its proponents are uniformly insistent that it must be put into effect at once as if to correct some unrevealable and malignant defect existing in the war machine that has so recently gained for our nation the greatest victory in its history.

The first point that I wish to make is that this legislation, which entails such an abrupt and radical departure from established and successful organizational forms, comes at a time when the armed services have not had opportunity to give to the subject the thorough consideration which it deserves. If there are to be wide and drastic changes in the organization for national security, they must be predicated on a factual basis. We have only begun to analyze the lessons of the war and until we have the benefits of an objective study we should refrain from hastily contrived changes in an organization which has served us so well. We should also remember that the actors upon the stage are not the best critics.

My second point is that since the Army and Navy are only the means through which our war making power finds expression, any reorganization of our national security presents problems which are not met by a realignment of those services. As I see it, our victory was not achieved by our uniformed services alone. It was the end result of the application of an aggregate might made up of every spiritual, material and industrial resource of the country and the active participation of the some 80,000,000 of its citizens. This was the nation in arms, the real machinery of total war that imposed our national aims on two hostile continents. This trend toward total war will continue. In another war the ratio of civil to military force may be higher still and, if we take into account the implications of atomic warfare, it may well be that conventional methods of warfare will occupy a secondary role altogether. It follows that no proposal of this nature should be considered until it is broadened to include a survey of methods of integrating the real sources of national strength—science, industry and production to mention but a few. If this were done it would afford an opportunity to examine each of the parts in the light of its relationships to the whole. Without the aid of such a study it is dangerous to attempt any restatement of the position of the armed services with respect to each other or toward national security itself.

For my own part, and based on my own personal observation, I consider that the war was skillfully and successfully conducted and that we should now be examining the record to determine the reasons for success rather than engaging in the use of innuendo to present our victory in the light of failure.

After touching on the main reasons for the successful prosecution of the war and discussing them in the light of proposed unification, I turned directly to the proposal:

In reading the record of the hearings before the Woodrum Committee on the issue of unification I am impressed by the consistent failure to orient the problem as disclosed by the absence of any real perspective on the part of witnesses. The evidence consists of a series of disconnected and circumstantial arguments pertaining to details.

It is largely a recitation of defects. Some are not relevant to the question of unification at all; and many of the others have already been corrected.

Vagueness and generalization are the order of the day. There is enough substance to support a conclusion that a reorganization of each of the services would be beneficial and that better means of interservice co-ordination in certain fields must be found. However, no sound relationship is established between these deficiencies and the proposal for unification. It is merely asserted that unification would or should eliminate duplication, overlap, and other alleged imperfections. Again and again a diagram has been presented depicting the proposed relationship of the services but only at the highest levels. Likewise it is always assumed that unification will provide a solution for every existing problem, but no attempt is made to establish the validity of the assumption itself. . . . In other words, proponents of unification have asked Congress and the people to accept in blind faith something which they themselves do not entirely understand. Thus the architects, bemused by the symmetry of the roof, tell us that in time they hope to see more clearly the form of the walls which must support it.

I continued on to concrete points of the plan which I felt were shibboleths. Would a single armed forces budget bureau dispensing money to each service as it saw fit really solve anything by usurping the traditional right of Congress in voting service appropriations? Would economy actually result by eliminating what was termed duplication? I told the committee:

There was duplication of facilities in the sense of parallel establishments but this is not duplication in the sense of waste. The point not brought out is that the Army and Navy operate in totally different elements and employ a totally different type of warfare. Each must have its own service elements geared to its own particular needs if it is to discharge its functions efficiently. In my own experience there was never enough of anything in the Pacific. All servicing facilities were taxed to the maximum with little evidence of wasteful duplication. I have not heard that the proponents of unification have criticized the Office of Defense Transportation because the Pennsylvania and the New York Central supported the war effort with parallel systems between New York and Chicago.

After examining other alleged panaceas, I turned to the advantages of the present system, making a point which I believe should never be forgotten in this nation:

Perhaps the greatest advantage of the current organization from a national point of view is that it is responsive to the control of Congress and the people. Through its detailed budgetary authority and its investigative power, Congress can effectively control military policy, correct abuses, and direct reform. This is a part of the democratic process of government which insists that effective control of the military remains in the hands of the people. Under the proposed system, the Congress, depending for military advice on a single responsible individual, would soon lose its intimate sense of association with and responsibility for military affairs because in large part it would be dealing not with the services themselves, but with an intervening agency, charged with all matters pertaining to national security. It would hear conclusions, but could not so readily ascertain the facts supporting or refuting them as it can today. Even if its members chose to circumvent the central agency to consult with the branches they would no longer be consulting the heads of independent services and they would not get the same free expression of opinion. Thus the proposal involves a dilution of the civilian control of the military establishment at a time when it has become evident that what is needed is more civilian control than ever before.

I bluntly concluded:

I hope that Congress will consider the real effect and meaning of unification. It means that absolute control of the armed services may, at some time in the future, pass into the hands of a small, highly organized and politically acute group of officers representing only one shade of political opinion. It means that there would then ensue a leveling process under the name of co-ordination in the course of which valuable branches might first be curbed and then be eliminated altogether. For example, the Ma-

rines, the Seabees and our splendid naval air arm may
not be here in another war to render their unique and
priceless services. Free from any element of healthy competition and under the sedative effect of a throttling and
arbitrary regime the remaining services might well
lapse into lethargy. Thus, if war comes again we may
have no one to show the way and set the pace.

The generally favorable reaction of the committee to this
testimony proved heartening as did outside response such
as this letter from an officer who had worked on the unification problem for the Secretary of the Navy:

> I made it a point to hear your statement before the
> Senate Military Affairs Committee and I want to take this
> opportunity to tell you that it was very reassuring to
> hear such a forceful, forthright statement from one who
> has had more actual experience than anyone else in the
> world with so-called triphibious operations.
> In order to give the Air Forces the autonomy which
> they have fought so hard to gain from the Army it would
> certainly be a great mistake to deprive the Navy and Ma-
> rine Corps of the freedom of expression and independent
> development that are so essential for the preservation
> of a modern, efficient means of self-preservation. Your
> statement was most reassuring and, if men of real vis-
> ion and broad judgment weigh the factors impartially, it
> will have a telling effect.

I held no illusions as to the fight ahead. On October 25 I
wrote General Holcomb:

> The Army is back on the job in full force trying to ab-
> sorb the Navy and with it the Marine Corps. Mr. Forres-
> tal, Admiral King and I have appeared before the Mili-
> tary Affairs Committee with our side of the picture . . . a
> statement made by me before the Senate Committee yes-
> terday morning . . . has received very good coverage in
> the newspapers and also over the radio so I hope it will
> do some good in building up throughout the country an
> opposition to the plan.

The unification furor dampened Congressional ardor for

passing vital service legislation. The Senate Naval Affairs Committee did report the forced retirement bill favorably as did the House Naval Affairs Committee the bill establishing permanent naval strength. But this was prelude to law, not law on which we could act As I told a congressman friend, the situation reminded me of a series of resolutions said to have once been passed by a rather backward county grand jury:

> Resolved, that the present jail is insufficient, and that another ought to be built;
> Resolved, that the materials of the old jail be used in constructing the new one:
> Resolved, that the old jail shall not be taken down until the new one is finished.

In the same letter to General Holcomb I wrote:

> The Navy missed the boat completely on getting legislation prepared and passed for a postwar Navy and Marine Corps. As I have mentioned several times in my letters to you, I have for the past eighteen months been endeavoring to get them to initiate legislation relative to the induction of reserve officers into the regular Corps. With the exception of a few last-minute changes made for political reasons, there is very little difference in the regulations which will be enforced than were in the regulations prepared by a board of Marine officers eighteen months ago. The war came to a sudden close and we were placed in the position of a salesman trying to sell a car without knowing how many cylinders it would have or any other specifications. I fear we have lost a good many worthwhile men by not being able to state what the strength of the Marine Corps would be and how we would go about getting the officer personnel.

This was the most frustrating period of my commandancy. At a time when Congress should have been coping with America's position in an obviously unstable world, and at a time when the armed forces should have been concentrating on the challenge of the atomic bomb to future military operations, we wasted vital weeks and months on the unification hearings. And at a time when America's armed forces should have presented a solid show of strength to the torn and bleeding world, the Army and the Air Force indulged in the most vicious infighting to gain their ends, a campaign that in turn claimed the major effort of the Navy and Marine Corps to preserve their integrity. I deeply resented the capital's atmosphere. On November 30 I wrote Holland Smith:

I feel that our Navy friends rested too long on their laurels and the belief that no harm could come to them. It is just within the last few weeks that they seem to realize the fact that Mr. Roosevelt is dead. Things are not particularly encouraging on the question of the merger. Everyone is now working very hard on testimony, etc., and we still hope we can beat it, if not in the Senate then in the House. As I tried to impress them [the Navy] the other day at a conference we have got to forget methods that we have used before because as much as we hate to realize it, this is not the day of when knighthood was in flower and it's more like a street brawl than a tilting joust. . . .

In addition to having to fight for the Navy's and our own survival there are the ever-recurring fights with our friends from across the river [the Navy] to keep them from encroaching. From my talks with Nimitz [who would replace Admiral King as chief of naval operations], I feel greatly encouraged that we will have very much less pressure to become a bureau than we would have had had the present incumbent stayed in.

Next to the unification battle, personnel formed our most pressing problem. In the same letter to Holland I wrote:

One of the hard parts of the job right now is knowing what in the world to do with these returning generals. I have decided to just double them in all the large posts until such time as legislation clears up so that we may have selection boards to determine who of the 82 will remain to be the 40 generals of postwar strength. This, of course, is provided the 100,000 strength of the Marine Corps goes through.

China considerably added to our personnel worries. We had pitched our demobilization scheme on a rapid withdrawal from there, but the dangerous situation vis-à-vis the Communists dictated continuing commitment. With 72,000 troops still due to come home from the Pacific, we had to cut down as far as possible on Pacific garrisons in order to send short-time Marines to China and Japan. I did not want to send draftees out at this time but finally was forced to in order to get the long-timers home.

During these hectic months I wanted the Marine Corps to demobilize as it had fought—with honor. In my testimony to the Senate I had stressed the incredible value to a service of the intangible factor called esprit—a point emphasized by our disciplined troop behavior as compared with Army troop demonstrations around the world. We were patting ourselves on the back when on January 10, 1946, Roy Geiger informed me by dispatch that a hundred Marines had held a demobilization meeting at Camp Catlin in Pearl Harbor. A small group of noncommissioned officers subsequently delivered their petition to Roy Geiger. They chose the wrong man. Roy read the petition, barked them to attention, broke them to privates and had his sergeant major rip off their chevrons. I answered his dispatch immediately:

> I do hope that we will have no more such demonstrations because with all of the 1946 names by which you choose to dress this up, to an old-line Marine it still borders on near mutiny and shows a lack of discipline. . . .
>
> I wish you would write a personal letter to each of your division commanders and tell them they must indoctrinate their regimental, battalion and company officers with the idea that the Marine Corps is a professional soldier group. . . .

On January 18 I wrote my commanding generals:

> I fully realize the conditions under which you men are serving and the great letdown that comes to a fighting force when they are sitting around seemingly doing nothing. As General Geiger said in his orders, Marines do not meet and demonstrate, and as Silverthorn very aptly

put it, Marines come to their officers with everything from family trouble to tummy-aches, and that is as it should be. A lot of our younger officers and non-commissioned officers do not realize this and should be continually reminded and coached to that effect. . . .

I feel, and I am sure you do, that it is a good idea to tell the men and officers whatever we ourselves know, and I hope that you will go to unusual extents to do so. . . . In reference to the demobilization of Marine personnel, we are bringing them back just as rapidly as we can get replacements trained and sent out. That should be pounded home to them.

Although we suffered no further demonstrations in the demobilization of over 400,000 men, we continued to shoot in the dark regarding the future. In early January Congress introduced a unification bill based on the Collins plan. On January 11 I wrote Keller Rockey in China:

I had hoped to be out and pay you a visit long before this but with the merger still boiling and the budget coming up in the next couple of weeks, to say nothing of permanent strength legislation, I don't know when I can get out.

Our nebulous position seemed dangerously out of proportion to our foreign commitments. On January 15 Rockey reported from the China station:

Our most arduous duty is the maintenance of railway communications between Chinwangtao and Peking. We have a directive that 100,000 tons of coal a month be shipped from Chinwangtao to Shanghai. Coal must also move to Tientsin, Peking and Tsingtao in quantities at least sufficient to maintain the public utilities and heat our own barracks. This means that the mines must be kept running and coal trains moving. We use the lines for shipment of supplies. There has been a steady improvement and now trains are running both day and night to the limit of the available rolling stock. Sectors of the railroad are being guarded by Marines, by Chinese troops and by Jap units which are in the process of relief by Chinese.

Another important duty is the repatriation of Japanese. To date we have shipped out about 150,000, about half soldiers, the other half civilians. This project is proceeding satisfactorily. However, future progress will depend upon the rate at which the Chinese relieve Jap troops now in the interior. . . .

The military situation in North China is not good at all. The Central Government controls, with the help of our presence, the cities of Peking, Tientsin and Tsingtao, together with points on the Peking-Chinwangtao railway. They also control, with the help of the Japanese, various rail junctions and cities in the interior. Elsewhere the Communists and bandits are pretty much in charge.

The Chinese Central Government troops now in North China are not strong enough to control the situation even with our presence, nor do I believe that it would be possible for them to do so with such additional armies as could be moved from the south. The only hope in my mind is a settlement such as is now being attempted. To reach such a settlement it will be necessary to give the Communists a large measure of governmental control in these northern provinces, and permit them to keep part of their armies. These problems are difficult of solution.

Our situation at home and abroad was thus altogether bleak in this month of January but fortunately none of us lost our sense of humor nor our confidence in the future. On January 30 Dewitt Peck, commanding the 1st Division in China, wrote to me:

As to instructing the Marines as to "why we are here" I checked to see that quotes on that subject from the press and the Secretary of State and General Wedemeyer appear in the "Stars and Stripes," the "North China Marine" [newspaper], and radio press bulletins distributed to all units, as well as on the local Marine radio broadcasts. As to my trying to interpret the explanations as given by the abovementioned personages, I find myself at a loss. I quote from General Geiger's letter: "Instruct your commanders that further reductions depend upon the *mission* of the Marines in the Pacific and the recruiting rate. Both are *intangibles* and not susceptible to exact determination by future months." The underlining is mine. It won't be the first time the Marines have served under an intangible mission; but how explain an intangible mission?

XXIII

"The Bended Knee is Not a Tradition of Our Corps"

IN FEBRUARY, 1946, President Truman signed into law the involuntary retirement bill which enabled us to select out superfluous officers. Within a month the ax fell on over half of our generals, a drastic action but one I deemed necessary to the future prosperity of the Corps. When presented with the retirement board's findings I summed up my feelings to General Holcomb:

> I am quite sure you'll be surprised at one or two of them [generals selected out] as I was, but the boards having decided, I felt, and so told both the Secretary [of the Navy] and the President, that if one name was taken off the list, he should disapprove the whole board. There will, of course, be heartaches over this, and Lord knows I regret it, but I do think that looking to the future, the Marine Corps will be greatly benefited by the acts of this board.

To one of my oldest friends who was retired I wrote:

> I do not have to tell you how sincerely and deeply sorry I am that this has happened. You are too good a soldier not to realize the position in which I have been placed. I thought the law was a good one and had it passed. I still think it is a good law. We appointed the boards and they have acted in accordance with their considered best judgment. This same thing has happened in the Navy and neither Nimitz nor I felt that it would be to the best interests of the service to interpose ourselves in the procedure in any way. This decision was reached prior to the report of the boards, both Navy and Marine. I want you to know that I have the same feeling now as regards

to your ability as I have always had and if there is anything I can do to help out after you are retired in getting yourself relocated, please let me know.

In April the air cleared further when Mr. Carl Vinson succeeded in pushing through the Navy strength bill. This authorized a Marine Corps of 7,000 officers and 100,000 men, figures we would have to achieve by August 1 since the new budget would support no more. Mr. Forrestal also directed us to release all reserves and draftees by autumn.

I would have welcomed these measures except for our continuing commitment in China where the situation daily grew more muddled. To clarify it President Truman now sent out General Marshall as ambassador at large. From reliable sources I learned that Marshall wished to withdraw the Marines from North China, a desire I heartily favored though scarcely for Marshall's reasons.

Unfortunately Marshall could come up with no Army divisions to replace the Marines nor, according to Rockey, could the Chinese National Army furnish replacement divisions. As Rockey pointed out, our departure would materially influence the whole explosive situation and he doubted whether under these circumstances we would be withdrawn.

Although we stripped other garrisons to the bone we could not continue to sustain the luxury of III Corps in China. Finally in May Roy Geiger worked out a scheme accepted by the Navy to withdraw the Corps, leaving the reinforced 1st Marine Division.

Meanwhile the unification pot kept boiling. Army and Air Corps campaigns placed tremendous pressure on Congress. In some cases the proponents of unification acted within their rights, in some cases not. On March 15, 1946, I was shown a memorandum from one of Nimitz' admirals who wrote the Secretary of the Navy:

On the night of March 14 I attended a dinner given by the Aviation Writers' Association, at which it developed General Spaatz [Army Air Corps] was to give an off the record talk. His talk was of about fifteen minutes' duration and was a bitter tirade against the Navy. It opened with the following remarks:
The United States knows as a result of the recent war

that it must have an air force. The air force that the nation must have if it is to be properly protected, is the Army Air Force. It would be a waste of the taxpayer's money to have two. . . .

Why should we have a Navy at all? The Russians have little or no Navy; the Japanese Navy has been sunk, the navies of the rest of this world are negligible; the Germans never did have much of a Navy. The point I am getting at is who is the big Navy being planned to fight. There are no enemies for it to fight, except apparently the Army Air Force. In this day and age to talk of fighting the next war on oceans is a ridiculous assumption. It will be fought in the air by an air force with the weapons necessary to fight the next. The B-29 is that weapon and the Army Air Force perfected it so that we would be ready to meet all comers in the air. . . . The only reason for us to have a Navy is just because someone else has a Navy and we certainly don't need to waste money that way. . . .

There is only one airplane that can carry the atomic bomb and that is the B-29. If they insist on a carrier, the only carrier that could do the job would be of a size so great that it would have to have a flight deck 6,000 feet long. It takes that to land and take off a B-29.

This and other patent nonsense regrettably swayed certain members of Congress toward the bill, S. 2044. We did our best to hold our own, but the desire for organizational change mounted in Congressional circles. I did not mind reasonable change, indeed I welcomed it, but if the change were to be that provided by S. 2044, then in my mind the demise of the Marine Corps was a logical result. By the time I was invited to testify before the Senate Naval Affairs Committee I had made up my mind to present the sordid facts as I saw them. On May 6, 1946, I opened my testimony:

Last autumn I testified before the Military Affairs Committee on the subject of unification of the Armed Forces. Since that time the real points at issue have been brought into sharp focus, and it is now evident that the entire problem revolves about two fundamental theories which stand squarely at variance. On the one hand is the War Department General Staff theory—implemented in S. 2044. This contends that the complexities of modern warfare justify an extension of political-military control into fields of government which are essentially civilian in character. Standing in direct opposition to this theory is the Navy's belief that these same complexities in modern war indicate a need for broader participation and closer attention by the civilian elements of government, all co-ordinated by an authority with roots in the Congress, rather than in the Pentagon.

I told the senators I held no wish to comment further on the obvious faults, weaknesses and inequities of the proposed merger plan. Instead I wanted to emphasize the specific effect this plan would have on the United States Marine Corps. In my opinion, I said, the War Department was determined "to reduce the Marine Corps to a position of studied military ineffectiveness"—and added that the merger bill "in its present form" made this objective "readily attainable." So as to leave no doubt in their minds of my position I continued:

> For some time I have been aware that the very existence of the Marine Corps stood as a continuing affront to the War Department General Staff, but had hoped that this attitude would end with the recent war as a result of its dramatic demonstration of the complementary and non-conflicting roles of land power, naval power, and air power. But following a careful study of circumstances as they have developed in the past six months I am convinced that my hopes were groundless, that the War Department's intentions regarding the Marines are quite unchanged, and that even in advance of this proposed legislation it is seeking to reduce the sphere of the Marine Corps to ceremonial functions and to the provision of small ineffective combat formations and labor troops for service on the landing beaches. Consequently I now feel increased concern regarding the merger measure, not only because of the ignominious fate which it holds for a valuable corps, but because of the tremendous loss to the nation which it entails.

After explaining why and how the present merger bill would undoubtedly sterilize the Marine Corps, I stressed what the loss in this force-in-readiness would mean to the nation. Its ability to move out fast was amply demonstrated in World War II by both the Iceland and Guadalcanal campaigns, victories that stood in marked contrast to the British fiasco in Norway—the result of having reduced the Royal Marines to an insignificant force after World War I.

I pointed out that in peacetime the Marines also performed a vital mission—prior to 1933 Marines participated in 50 of the 61 landings designed to protect American lives and property abroad; Marine units served in the field for 49 of the last 50 years, and engaged in actual combat in 27 of those years.

During these decades the Marines in conjunction with the Navy provided the nation with a doctrine, techniques and equipment which became the standard pattern of amphibious warfare adopted not only by our own Army but by the armies and navies of eight United Nations. Amphibious operations proved the key to victory in every major theater of war and, in my opinion, formed the most important contribution any American service ever made in the field of purely prospective development of a form of major warfare. In grim contrast the Army failed miserably to develop two specialties that sprang up between the wars: airborne operations and armored warfare. How, then, could they reasonably claim to usurp our unquestioned pre-eminence in still another specialty?

After developing these themes I placed our fate in the hands of my listeners:

The Congress has always been the nation's traditional safeguard against any precipitate action calculated to lead the country into trouble. In its capacity as a balance wheel this Congress has on five occasions since the year 1829 reflected the voice of the people in examining and casting aside a motion which would damage or destroy the United States Marine Corps. In each instance, on the basis of its demonstrated value and usefulness alone, Congress has perpetuated the Marine Corps as a purely American investment in continued security. Now I believe that the cycle has again repeated itself, and that the fate of the Marine Corps lies solely and entirely with the Congress.

In placing its case in your hands the Marine Corps remembers that it was this same Congress which, in

1798, called it into a long and useful service to the nation. The Marine Corps feels that the question of its continued existence is likewise a matter for determination by the Congress and not one to be resolved by departmental legerdemain or a quasi-legislative process enforced by the War Department General Staff.

The Marine Corps, then, believes that it has earned this right—to have its future decided by the legislative body which created it—nothing more. Sentiment is not a valid consideration in determining questions of national security. We have pride in ourselves and in our past but we do not rest our case on any presumed ground of gratitude owing us from the nation. The bended knee is not a tradition of our Corps. If the Marine as a fighting man has not made a case for himself after 170 years of service, he must go. But I think you will agree with me that he has earned the right to depart with dignity and honor, not by subjugation to the status of uselessness and servility planned for him by the War Department.

Widespread publicity achieved all I hoped for this testimony and more. For perhaps the first time the American public realized the threat to the continued existence of their Marines. Many citizens wasted no time in rising to our defense. As one result Congress tabled the proposed bill.

President Truman, who unfortunately held no particular love for the Marines, next intervened with letters to both Army and Navy calling upon them to resolve their differences in a new bill. Conferences and hearings continued throughout spring and summer with the Navy pushing for its newly founded Eberstadt Plan which in my opinion formed a much more reasonable approach to this vital matter. That autumn the President, on the basis of Army and Navy findings, presented 12 points which he wished incorporated into any future bill. One of them called for a spelling out of the role and missions of the Marine Corps as the nation's ready amphibious force.

In October of 1946 I made a delayed inspection trip to the Far East. From the moment we landed at Tientsin, China struck me as a vastly changed country, and a worse one for the change.

Sam Howard, now commanding the 1st Marine Division,

soon confirmed my immediate impressions. Life in the cities, he explained, was nearly at a standstill. Unable to get raw materials or coal, factory after factory had become idle. Foreign firms were hamstrung by a series of complicated regulations that restricted foreign enterprise in favor of the Chinese. Public utilities were rapidly wearing out with no sign of maintenance or replacement—no one, for example, any longer used the telephones in Tientsin. In all the cities, electricity, water and sewage conditions were becoming hopeless. Rivers and harbors were silting up with no attempt to dredge them. Inflation swept the country: to go out for a drink and dinner meant carrying a valise full of currency.

From Tientsin I flew to Peking, where Julian Frisbie, commanding our regiment there, met and escorted me to a suite in the Peking Hotel. Upon opening the door to my rooms I was confronted by a row of bowing and grinning Chinese: my old number one and number two boys, the amah and the rickshaw boy. Somehow they had survived the vicissitudes of the last ten years. I only hope they have survived what followed.

Peking looked as grim as Tientsin. The Japanese had completely wrecked my old house in the compound by tearing down the walls between the officer quarters and making a great barracks of the whole. It was hard to realize how such an ostensibly neat, flower-loving nation could produce such boorish and brutal soldiers.

In Peking I discussed the military situation at length with General Li Tsung-jen who commanded Generalissimo Chiang Kai-shek's headquarters there. Chiang's tactics obviously differed from our own. Where he dispersed some nine divisions throughout this large area, I objected to even small Marine outposts on the railroad lines, preferring instead a concentration of force in the three central city areas. Even worse, though Li did not admit it, was the common knowledge of the corruption and lassitude pervading the National Chinese forces. I held severe misgivings about the entire situation. It seemed to me the Central Government was caught in the grip of paralysis while the Communists were simply biding their time, letting internal rot achieve its full effect.

Although I did not like the setup I was more than pleased at the job being done by the Marines. Their morale was excellent, their supply ample. But despite their obvious readiness for anything, they formed a relatively small force. I held considerable doubts for the future should the Communist armies decide to move in.

Soon after my return from this 21,000-mile trip I wrote General Holcomb:

> As you have no doubt heard, we are undergoing a very drastic economy wave from the Administration. I hope now, this being Election Day, that after today maybe the pressure will let up some.

It seemed to, for a couple of weeks later we passed the Navy's and the Bureau of the Budget's hearings for a Marine Corps of 100,000 in 1948.

Anticipating this strength figure, I made some command changes. Roy Geiger retired on account of age in November. I replaced him with Hal Turnage. I brought Keller Rockey back to become commanding general of Fleet Marine Force Atlantic which consisted of Tommy Watson's 2d Division at Camp Lejeune and Ralph Mitchell's 2d Marine Air Wing at Cherry Point.

We also seemed to be gaining in the merger battle. In the same letter to General Holcomb I noted:

> I don't know how the merger is going to be affected by this shift-over [the Congressional committee chairmen]. A Republican Congress will certainly be less prone to follow the desires of a Democratic President than would be a Democratic Congress. I do feel though that there is going to be some change and if we can settle for the Navy plan (Eberstadt), which personally I feel is an excellent one, I think we will be most fortunate. In any event, as long as the President sticks to his policy of writing in the functions and organization of the Marine Corps as an integral part of the Navy, we will be safe for at least ten years and most anything can happen in that time.

For some inexplicable reason my speaking schedule again grew heavy and I was also asked to accept a number of honorary chairmanships. As usual I accepted those that seemed beneficial to the Marine Corps, such as the Red Cross chairmanship and a membership on the American Battle

Monuments Commission, a position I still hold. I was also pleased to receive honorary degrees early the next year from Columbia and Harvard.

We needed every ear we could gain. Preliminary Congressional hearings in December put the quietus—at least temporarily—on our proposed 100,000 strength. On December 19 I wrote Harry Schmidt:

> We have been through the devil's own time for the past week since you left on rewriting the budget . . . we lost something by it, but in comparison to the Navy, we certainly came out most fortunately.

Two weeks later I reported to Hal Turnage in the Pacific:

> We are busily engaged with the budget as our friend at 1600 [President Truman] lopped 10,000 men off of us, or a general average of 90,000 for 1948. This is going to put a strain on us and we cannot, of course, do the many and various things that we had planned. We are also being reduced by 500 officers which will be a proportionate cut on a percentage basis right down the line. I do not feel too badly about this though and if we can hold this number, both officers and men, I think we will be fortunate. As some of my Navy friends said, it seems that the Marine Corps belonged to the "favored nations" class and our cuts were nothing in comparison with theirs or, as a matter of fact, with what I hear of the Army's.

By early 1947 General Marshall's mission to China had obviously failed. We were now directed to begin retrenching, the idea being ultimately to leave a force at Tsingtao. Tentatively we planned to bring a regimental combat team back to Guam and an understrength brigade to Pendleton.

Despite this up-and-down and sideway existence I remained optimistic. Quantico was a going concern. The minute the war ended we had shifted over to postwar schools including the old time basic school for young lieutenants. Our Administration School and Command and Staff School were fast repairing the neglect of formal education during the war years, and we were sending officers in all ranks to as many other service schools as possible.

This was a necessary preliminary to probing the military curtain of the future. To better understand that future I wanted a definitive study made of our amphibious past. To this end we contracted with two bright Princeton historians, Jeter Isely and Philip Crowl, to begin work on a book published some years later under the title *The U. S. Marines and Amphibious War.*

But what of the future?

I refused to share the atomic hysteria familiar to some ranking officers. The atomic bomb was not yet adapted for tactical employment, nor would this happen soon. Accordingly I did not feel obliged to made a sudden, sharp change in our organizational profile.

I did feel obliged to study the problem in all its complexity. For if we believed the basic mission of the Marine Corps would remain unchanged in an atomic age, we knew that the conditions surrounding this mission would change and change radically. The problem, in my mind, divided itself into three major considerations: how to reorganize the Fleet Marine Force to render its units less vulnerable to atomic warfare and at the same time retain the final assault concentration essential to success; how to decrease our reaction time or, conversely, attain and maintain a preparedness by which a large unit could mount out in hours; how to put atomic weapons of the future to our own best use.

These and other problems I gave to O. P. Smith and Bill Twining at Marine Corps Schools for analysis by special study groups—a procedure almost identical to that of the twenties when we went to work on basic amphibious doctrine. Practically nothing was deemed too fanciful for consideration. We toyed with large troop-carrying airplanes as the assault vehicles of the future, and with troop-carrying submarines, and with helicopters then in their infancy. Eventually we decided upon the helicopter for our major assault vehicle. Years would pass before Quantico developed what became as breath-taking a doctrine as our earlier 1934 effort. But the seed that grew with the years was planted then.

While young Marines braved these baffling and bewildering days, old Marines passed away. Late in January, 1947, Roy Geiger died at the Bethesda Naval Hospital. Roy knew he was ill months before he returned from the Pacific, but he did not tell me. He knew he could do the job given him, and he preferred to remain at his post without yielding to a devastating illness. With his death I lost the last of my 1909 classmates in the Corps.

XXIV

I Step Down

NEGOTIATIONS between the War and Navy Departments resulted in a merger bill being introduced into the House of Representatives toward the end of February, 1947. Although HR 2319 contained most of the President's 12 points, to my annoyance it made no mention of the role and functions of the Marine Corps. Instead, the legislative representatives of the two departments, Admiral Sherman and Lieutenant General Norstad, recommended that the President take care of this in a separate executive order.

This meant that the statement of Marine functions—in effect, the legal working charter for the Corps—would not be spelled out by law according to the will of Congress. Instead, our roles and missions would be subject to change by any hostile President or Secretary of Defense. Knowing that Congress had defeated the attempts of several of our Presidents (Jackson, Theodore Roosevelt, Taft and Hoover) to put the Corps out of business, I could not welcome the thought of our future resting in the staying power of an executive order. I felt that those who so strongly wanted to omit our roles and missions from law were those who possibly intended to 'give the Marines the bum's rush"—as one of my Congressional friends put it during the hearings.

In short, I felt then, and feel now, that to give the President the traditional powers held by Congress stood in dangerous violation of our democratic principles. The statutory protection which only Congress could provide was a vital necessity if the real and intended character of the Corps, not to mention the country, was to be retained. My feelings were recorded in a letter of February 12 to Hal Turnage:

> The merger is still in a nebulous stage, no bill having been sent down to Congress. The Navy sold out to the

Army in not requiring the functions and duties of the several services to be written into law but rather to be included in an executive order. I hope someone in Congress takes exception to this and sees fit to write the executive order into law. If that is done, the Marine Corps will be safe for the time being, and if not, the price of existence will depend on eternal vigilance and the intestinal fortitude of those in control to stick their necks out to see that we are not run over.

Realizing that I was still facing a fight to prevent being "run over," I now formed a special advisory group headed by Jerry Thomas and Merritt Edson. This group included such colonels as Bill Twining and Brute Krulak and such lieutenant colonels as Schatzel, Murray, Shaw, Heinl and Hittle. In the months ahead these officers worked long, hard hours in helping me pursue what sometimes seemed an uphill fight.

We faced another major problem, which I raised in this same letter to Hal Turnage:

Again I have to solicit your help in economies. You will have seen by this morning's paper that the Republican high command is going to cut the budget come hell or high water, which will mean, I am just as sure as I'm sitting here, another monetary cut for the Marine Corps because we have been put on notice that both the Army and the Navy are to take an additional cut over that that the Director of the Budget made. I fully realize that it is hard for the younger officers to get economy-minded since ever since their entry into the service money, that is, government money, has been of no moment, but everyone in the Marine Corps has got to reverse their machinery and attention back to the prewar days and every dollar we spend has got to do two dollars' worth of work. We are going to take a drastic cut in the money appropriated for civil personnel. That being the case, we must figure ways and means of doing with the enlisted personnel what has to be done with the least interruption to morale and training. Responsible and accountable officers must be held strictly responsible for losses incurred and damage done through carelessness to government property. Stringent inspections are called for.

A few weeks later I wrote the results of the budget hearings to Phil Torrey in California:

> We have finished our hearings before the House Sub-Appropriation Committee, Navy, for funds for 1948 and, I think, came out very well. What it will look like when both the Senate and the House finish it, the Lord only knows, but I believe with conditions as they are in the world, they will be rather loath to cut drastically.

I also brought him up to date on the merger bill:

> Things here are moving along at a rather rapid pace. The so-called merger bill has been sent to the armed forces committees of both houses and I feel that some kind of a bill is coming out. This present bill is the least objectionable of any from our standpoint. In fact it is the Eberstadt Plan with one or two minor changes. I feel that if we can get the functions and services of the Marine Corps written into that bill in accordance with our recommendations of last year and the letter that the President sent to two committees of Congress, the Marine Corps interests will be safeguarded. An additional thing I want to get written in if I possibly can is the fact that wherever Army, Navy and Air officers are written in on the combined staff the word "Marine" officers should be written in also, for, as I told the Admiral [Nimitz] and Secretary [Forrestal] the other day, we are not Navy officers and we are just as competent to be on the staff as the officers of any other service. They will both support me on that theory.

This was my theme of the winter and spring. I spilled it willingly to any listening ear. I also concentrated on it in preparing my testimony for Congress. Aware that I perforce was appearing controversial, I took my planned statement to Mr. Forrestal. He read it and remarked, "Archer, this is a very strong statement. I think we had better discuss it with the President."

We went to the White House that afternoon, using the south entrance to avoid the press. The President received us cordially. Forrestal told him his feelings and the President asked to see the statement. I handed it to him, saying, "Mr. President, this comes within your 12 points. I have not deviated from them because I thoroughly believe you have struck on a workable solution."

He replied, "If you have done that, then I don't think there is anything to worry about."

With that he read the statement, his head occasionally nodding. Upon finishing it he looked at me rather sharply. "You don't trust anybody, do you?"

I quickly answered, "Yes, sir, I trust you, but you are not going to be here forever."

He laughed and I continued, "It is very much easier to get an executive order changed than it is an act of Congress. That is why I would like our role and missions spelled out by law, and that is what I have asked for."

To my surprise he said he had no objection and ended the meeting.

On April 16 I wrote Tommy Watson:

> Present indications are that I'll testify before the Armed Services Committee on unification Friday. I imagine I am in for quite a day. I don't know what the outcome of it is going to be, but I am assured by people who ought to know down there that the basic role and missions of the Marine Corps will be written into the law. If we can accomplish that, I think we are completely safe and it will be up to future generations to be as vigilant in maintaining the future Marine Corps as Marines of the past and present have been in maintaining its status quo as of today. I think the Undersecretary of War, Mr. Royall, did us a great service in his testimony of yesterday because it focused very sharply the War Department's interpretation that the Secretary should be authorized to abolish anything that he sees fit.

The interested and sympathetic reception of my testimony left little doubt in my mind that the protective clauses would be added to the final bill. I was further pleased when toward the end of April the Army chief of staff, General Eisenhower, invited me over to his office for a talk about our differences in opinion.

I had known Eisenhower socially for some time. Pleasant as always, he spoke frankly and to the point. The Army, he explained, held considerable fears relative to the Marine

Corps' expansion. These went back to World War I when we received such favorable publicity from the battle of Belleau Wood.

Without going into that, I told him that publicity of the first war perhaps was not always in good taste in the services. At the beginning of World War II both General Holcomb and I did our best to establish conservative public relations. I hoped he agreed this had been the case during the war. He said he did.

He next stated the opinion of a number of senior Army officers concerning our ambition to become a second army. He shared this opinion; he could not understand our aspirations.

"Of course you can't," I told him. "We don't have any." I explained that this was the furthest from our thoughts—we wished to serve only as the amphibious troops of the Navy preferably in naval campaigns.

We discussed this at considerable length. He said, for example, the Marines wanted 240mm howitzers. I vigorously contradicted the statement and other mistaken impressions held by him, and told him I was willing to do nearly anything to rectify Army fears.

I read him point by point what I wanted written into the pending unification bill, stopping after each to ask if he held any objection. He said he did not; he agreed that in one form or another we had been doing these things with one force or another since 1775.

Finally I told him I would state to any Congressional committee that in addition to its duties on board ship and on naval posts and stations the Corps should be organized primarily to perform amphibious tasks. Its organization should not develop to meet the requirements of a protracted campaign on a large land mass, nor should it include arms and matériel such as the 240mm howitzer, heavy engineering equipment necessary to maintain extensive lines of communication inland, and logistic lines for penetration into large land masses.

If I were to so testify, I asked him, would he approve writing into the bill the functions of the Marine Corps. He said he would.

Despite this mild *rapprochement,* the issue still loomed large throughout the country. For some time various citizen groups had been exerting pressures for one side or the other. I thought that in many cases emotion already had inflamed the issues at the expense of understanding. For this reason I resisted all attempts to spread the controversy or to exert influence from outside sources. On May 14 I wrote a retired Marine general what I had been writing to a great many people:

> Personally, I think things are coming along all right. As I have stated in my testimony, I believe in this bill, with reservations protecting the Marine Corps, and I firmly believe those reservations are going to be put in. I may be overly optimistic but that at this time is my sincere guess on the question, and I don't believe that writing letters and things like that to various senators and congressmen would do any good nor is it, I feel, the thing to do. We have made a straightforward statement . . . to both the Senate and House and have answered their questions over a two-hour period in each chamber. I think the statements were received in both houses with a sympathetic ear and again I say I think we are coming along all right.

Not long after this the legislators in both bodies wrote the desired clauses into the bill. In July Senator Harry Byrd, always a friend of mine and of the Corps, asked me whether I preferred the Senate or House version of the bill. I chose the latter because I thought it better defined our position.

That autumn the passage of the National Security Act of 1947 ended the three-year controversy, albeit temporarily. The new law established three departments—Army, Navy, Air—each administered by a secretary subordinate to a Secretary of Defense, Mr. Forrestal, who sat as a member of the President's Cabinet.

In a letter of August 6 I outlined the provisions of this bill and called on all Marine officers to uphold it in every way. What I felt to be a reasonable victory I wrote in the following paragraph:

> The foregoing passage [Marine Corps roles and missions] is of particular importance to all Marines. Although the role of the Marine Corps in the development of the tactics of amphibious warfare and the immediate

readiness of the Corps to apply these tactics have for many years been a part of United States Naval Policy, the fact has never, until this time, been formalized in law. Now, in unmistakable terms, the Congress has recognized the Marine Corps as an important and essential element of the national security structure, and has taken steps to ensure that its special amphibious function will be perpetuated and progressively developed. It is clearly apparent that the intent of this section of the legislation is to preserve both the identity and the function of the Marine Corps as fundamental components of the nation's military strength.

A further legislative detail remained: the Department of the Navy's desired reorganization, a bill then before Congress. This bill, earlier discussed, in essence would have made the chief of naval operations a sort of Navy chief of staff with, I felt, the Commandant of the Marine Corps subordinate to him. I discussed my fears in detail with Admiral Nimitz, who quickly pointed out that the bill in no way applied to the Marine Corps. Aware that a considerable number of people did not understand the subtle mechanism by which the Marine Corps served in the Department of the Navy, I took the matter to the new Secretary of the Navy, Mr. Sullivan. He signed a letter which we jointly prepared and which stated that the law did not apply to the Marines—in short, the Commandant, as tradition dictated, would continue to answer to the Secretary of the Navy.

That was the last crisis of my tour.

In October I mentioned the question of my successor to Mr. Sullivan, since I wanted to announce the name on the Marine Corps birthday, November 10. Sullivan asked me to send him the files of eight general officers I considered eligible for appointment. Sometime later he called me over—he had narrowed the field to Cliff Cates and Lem Shepherd. With my approval he submitted these names to the President.

President Truman invited Sullivan, Cates and Shepherd to the White House. As I later learned, Secretary Sullivan entered his office alone. After emphasizing the equally outstanding records, the President pointed out that Cates was older than Shepherd and slightly senior in grade—accordingly, he would select Cates. Mr. Sullivan asked him to bring the two officers in and tell them his decision.

Mr. Truman complimented the two generals on their superb records in both world wars, then told Cates he was to be the next Commandant. He turned to General Shepherd: "You are younger and will have your chance the next time."

With the announcement of my successor I began cleaning up here and there. I made a few more speeches, a final inspection of the 2d Divison at Camp Lejeune and of the Parris Island recruit depot. At Quantico I rode in a new test-model helicopter and discussed the new tactical thinking with Bill Twining, who promised big things for the amphibious future.

My future would prove less exciting. For some time corporations had been offering me attractive positions, lecture agencies attractive fees, and publishers attractive contracts. I refused these with the excuse of wanting time to think them over.

On the last day of December I accompanied General Cates to the Secretary of the Navy's office where I read my orders to retirement and received an unexpected star on my Distinguished Service Medal. Sullivan swore in Cates and we returned to Headquarters.

I took leave of my staff, the Headquarters Battalion, and the crack Marine Barracks troops who kindly provided an honor guard, and the Marine Band.

I was in two minds about leaving because that is only human if you have served something you love for nearly forty years. In those years I saw my Corps expand for service in World War I. I saw it wither away during the doldrums after. I saw it grow to nearly half a million men in World War II. I had since fought its demise.

I was proud to command some of the finest troops the world has ever seen. My men came from every walk of life, almost every race and creed. Welded together, organized into splendid regiments, divisions and corps, and filled with the esprit traditional to the Marines, these young men who fought in Pacific campaigns from Guadalcanal to Okinawa left a rich heritage for their Corps and for their country. A grateful nation should never forget what they did. To the names of Valley Forge, Lexington, Concord, Gettysburg, Shiloh, San Juan Hill, Belleau Wood, St.-Mihiel and the Argonne they added Guadalcanal, Bougainville, Tarawa, Saipan, Tinian, Guam, Peleliu, Iwo Jima and Okinawa.

These proud names spelled sublime sacrifice. To those who fought so splendidly, to those who fell and to the scarred survivors, I can speak only the immortal words of John: "Greater love hath no man than this, that a man lay down his life for his friends."

Index

ABC-1 conference, 105
Acheson, Dean 89
Administrative School, 321
Advance Base School, 45
Africa, 93
Albemarle County, Va., 24
Albuquerque, N.M., 291
Alice in Wonderland, 175
Alligator landing craft, 93, 221, 234
Amelia Courthouse, Va., 22
American Battle Monuments Commission, 320-21
American Civil War, 21-5, 62-4
American Club, Haiti, 58
American Red Cross, 208, 221, 320
American Revolutionary War, 24
Amphibious Task Force, 112, 118
Amsterdam, N.Y., 21
André, Jules, 49
Andrews, Mr., 258
Annapolis, USS, 38
Ansel, Walter, 77
Antietam, Md., 21
Aola Bay, 190, 194
Aotea Quay, N.Z., 112, 117
APD craft, 223
Apemama Island, 225
Arcadia conference, 105
Archer, Alexander D., 22
Archer, John, 22
Archer, Percy, 52, 53, 54
Archer, Sarah A., 22
Argonne, battle of the, 331-2
Argonne, USS, 184
Arlington National Cemetery, 32, 95
Arlington Navy Annex, 95
Armed Forces, *see* U.S. Armed Forces
Army Air Corps, *see* U.S. Army Air Corps
Army training camps, 211
Army, U.S., *see* U.S. Army
Army War College, 211
Arndt, Charles, 135

Arnold, Henry H., 107, 110, 244
Arthur, John, 190, 194
Arundel Island, 221
Atlanta, Ga., 272
Atlantic Cruiser Squadron, 30
Atlantic Ocean, 213
atomic bomb, 282, 293, 302, 307, 315, 322
Auckland, N.Z., 103, 118, 164, 200, 225
Australia, 18, 101, 107, 112, 113, 205, 218, 284
Australian Army, 215, 219
Australian coastwatchers, 113, 123, 126, 135
Australian Navy, 113, 129-130
Aviation Writers' Association, 314
Axis Powers, 105
Babelthuap, 269
Bailey, Ken, 154, 158, 166, 169
Bailey, Zeke, 64
Balboa, Canal Zone, 38
Baldwin, Hanson, 162-3
Baltimore, Md., 25
Banika, 220, 269
Banta, Shepherd, 157
Barbey, D. E., 299
Barnum and Bailey, 24
Barracks, the, 24
Barrett, Charles, 77, 220, 222, 223, 224, 227
Bas Obispo, Canal Zone, 36
Basilone, John, 187
Bataan, P.I., 131, 242
Bates, Sanford, 75
Batraville, Benoit, 56, 59
Beaufort Bay, Guadalcanal, 165
Beaumont, John, 47
Beckett, John, 64
Beightler, Robert, 222
Belleau Wood, battle of, 328, 331
Bemis, John, 83, 132
Benet-Mercie weapon, 42
Berkeley, R. C., 77
Berkeley, J. P., 182
Besdeck, Hugo, 64
B-17 aircraft, 117, 120, 136, 170,

333

60-1, 95, 99-101, 105, 107, 109, 163, 185, 213-4, 218-9, 224, 237-8, 244, 246, 251, 254, 264, 267, 269-71, 276-78, 281, 286, 293, 295, 297, 304, 309, 321, 323, 331
Pagoda, the, 138, 144, 153, 176
Paige, Arthur, 63
Palau Islands, 269
Palmyra Island, 95
Pan American Clipper, 214
Panama, 35-6, 38, 40, 42-4, 78
Panama Canal, 43, 100
Panay incident, 91
Panay, USS, 91
Pánuco river, Mexico, 43
Paris, 83, 86
Parris Island, N.C., 27, 94, 149, 331
Patch, Alexander M., 184, 200-2, 204
Pate, R. McC., 68, 98, 103, 112, 113, 131
Pavuvu Island, 220, 242, 269
PBY aircraft, 134, 136, 144, 176, 223, 226
Pearl Harbor, Hawaii, 18, 98, 105, 107, 185, 214, 225, 227, 244, 245, 264, 267, 278, 285, 287, 309
Peck, DeWitt, 109, 239, 293-4, 297, 311
Peiping, China, 81
Peitaiho, China, 79
Peking, China, 71, 79-86, 88, 217, 294, 298, 301, 310-11, 319
Peking Hotel, 319
Peleliu Island, 269, 274, 276, 278, 332
Pendleton, Joseph H., 42
Peninsular Wars, 25
Penn State University, 64
Pennsylvania railroad, 305
Pentagon, the, 276, 316
Pepper, Robert, 68, 110, 132, 138, 182
Péralte, Charlemagne M., 55-6, 59
Petras, Warrant Officer, 103
Petters, Col., 207
Peyton, Capt., 128, 130
P-400 aircraft, 145, 155, 166
Philadelphia, Pa., 34-5, 45, 47, 51, 65-6
Philippine Insurrection, 32
Philippine Islands, 18, 28, 30, 35, 69, 142, 219, 244, 269, 277,

289
Pickering, Capt., 28
Pickett, Harry, 241
Pickett's Charge, 21, 62
"Pistol Pete," 180, 190, 192, 195
Poha river, Guadalcanal, 192, 196
Point Cruz, Guadalcanal, 135, 166, 172, 192-4
Poland, 91, 93
Pollack, E. A. 139-41
Port Moresby, 107, 117, 206, 209, 219-20, 247
Port Royal, S.C., 27, 29
Port-au-Prince, Haiti, 46-7, 50, 52, 55, 58-9
Port-de-Paix, Haiti, 51
Portsmouth, N.H., 30, 33-5
Portsmouth, Va., 53
Portsmouth Navy Prison, N.H., 30
Portsmouth Navy Yard, N.H., 30, 34, 76
President Adams, USS, 200
President Jackson, USS, 200
Price, Charles, 79, 82, 226
Primrose and Dockstader, 24
Princeton University, 64, 296
prisoners of war, 299
P-38 aircraft, 147
Public Health Service, 75
Puller, Lewis, 58-9, 165-6, 169, 172, 186-7, 194
Punic Wars, 38
Purple Heart medal, 273
Puruata Island, 229
Pu Yi, 81
Quantico, Va., 53, 59-66, 69, 77-81, 87, 90, 93-4, 97, 278, 286, 321-23
Queensland Health Service, 207
Rabaul, 109, 152, 181, 219-20, 230, 246-7
Radford, Arthur, 302
Ragged Mountains, Va., 23
Rainbow Plan, 105
Rameau, General, 47
Randolph, Wilson, 25
Randolph Kindergarten, 22
Red Beach, Guadalcanal, 114, 124, 126
Rekata Bay, 128
Rendova, 220
Rice Anchorage, 220
Richards, Frank, 192
Richardson, J. O., 249
Richardson, Mrs., J. O., 249
Richardson, R. C., 264